Virtual Applications: Applications with Virtual Inhabited 3D Worlds

Springer

London
Berlin
Heidelberg
New York
Hong Kong
Milan
Paris
Tokyo

Peter Andersen and Lars Qvortrup (Eds)

Virtual Applications

Applications with Virtual Inhabited 3D Worlds

 Springer

Peter Andersen
Department of Computer Science, Aalborg University, Denmark
Lars Qvortrup
Department of Literature, Culture and Media, University of Southern
Denmark, Denmark

British Library Cataloguing in Publication Data
A catalogue record for this book is available from the British Library

Library of Congress Cataloging-in-Publication Data
Virtual applications : applications with virtual inhabited 3D worlds / Peter Andersen and
   Lars Qvortrup (eds.)
       p. cm.
   Includes bibliographical references and index.
   ISBN 1-85233-658-7 (alk. paper)
     1. Human-computer interaction. 2. Virtual reality. I. Andersen, Peter Bøgh. II.
   Qvortrup, Lars.
   QA76.9.H85V535 2003
   006.8--dc22   2003061742

ISBN 1-85233-658-7 Springer-Verlag London Berlin Heidelberg
Springer-Verlag is part of Springer Science+Business Media
springeronline.com

Typesetting: Ian Kingston Editorial Services, Nottingham, UK
Printed and bound in the United States of America
34/3830-543210 Printed on acid-free paper SPIN 10880478

Contents

List of Contributors

Peter Bøgh Andersen
Department of Computer Science
Aalborg University
Fr. Bajersvej 7E
DK-9220 Aalborg Ø.
E-mail: pba@cs.auc.dk
Website: http://www.cs.auc.dk/
~pba/

Eigil Boisen
Department of Health Science
and Technology
Aalborg University
Fr. Bajersvej 7D-1
DK-9220 Aalborg Ø.
E-mail: eb@hst.auc.dk
Website: http://www.hst.auc.dk/

Anders Drejer
Aarhus Business School
Department of Organisation and
Management
Haslegaardsvej 10
DK-8210 Aarhus V
Denmark
E-mail: and@asb.dk

Agnar Gudmundsson
Department of Production
Aalborg University
Fibigerstræde 16
DK-9220 Aalborg Ø.
E-mail: agnar@iprod.auc.dk
Website: http://www.iprod.auc.
dk/internet/i9-visitkort/agnar-
gudmundsso.htm

Jens Haase
Department of Health Science
and Technology
Aalborg University
Fr. Bajersvej 7D-1
DK-9220 Aalborg Ø.
E-mail: jph@miba.auc.dk
Website: http://www.smi.auc.dk/
members/jph/

Jesper Kjeldskov
Department of Computer Science
Aalborg University
Fredrik Bajers Vej 7
DK-9220 Aalborg Ø
E-mail: jesper@cs.auc.dk
Website: http://www.cs.auc.dk/
~jesper

Erik Kjems
VR Media Lab
Aalborg University
Niels Jernes Vej 14
DK-9220 Aalborg Ø.
E-mail: kjems@vrmedialab.dk
Website: http://www.vrmedialab.
dk

Bent Bruun Kristensen
Maersk Institute
University of Southern Denmark,
Odense
Campusvej 55
DK-5230 Odense M
E-mail: bbkristensen@
mip.sdu.dk
Website: http://www.mip.sdu.dk/
~bbk

Niels Lehmann
Institute for Aesthetic Studies
Department of Dramaturgy
University of Aarhus
Langelandsgade 139
DK-8000 Aarhus
E-mail: dranl@hum.au.dk

Peter Musaeus
Psykologisk Institut
Asylvej 4
DK-8240 Risskov
E-mail: petermus@psy.au.dk
Website: http://www.psy.au.dk/

Claus B. Madsen
Computer Vision and
MediaTechnology
Aalborg University
Niels Jernes Vej 14
DK-9220 Aalborg Ø.
E-mail: cbm@cvmt.auc.dk
Website: http://www.cvmt.dk/
~cbm/

Daniel May
Maersk Institute
University of Southern Denmark,
Odense
Campusvej 55
DK-5230 Odense M
E-mail: dmay@mip.sdu.dk
Website: http://www.
thedanielmay.com

Michael May
LearningLab DTU
Technical University of Denmark
Building 101 – DTV
Anker Engelundsvej 1
DK-2800 Kgs. Lyngby
E-mail: mma@dtv.dk
Website: http://www.maritime-
hfe.com

Palle Nowack
Maersk Institute
University of Southern Denmark,
Odense
Campusvej 55
DK-5230 Odense M
E-mail: palle@nowack.dk
Website: http://www.nowack.dk

Lars Qvortrup
Department of Interactive Media
University of Southern Denmark,
Odense
Campusvej 55
DK-5230 Odense M
E-mail: larsq@litcul.sdu.dk
Website: http://www.qvortrup.
info/

Janek Szatkowski
Institute for Aesthetic Studies
Department of Dramaturgy
University of Aarhus
Langelandsgade 139
DK-8000 Aarhus
E-mail: drajsz@hum.au.dk

1

Introduction

Peter Bøgh Andersen and Lars Qvortrup

The present volume differs from the earlier volumes in this series about virtual inhabited 3D worlds in two respects: as the title says, it is focused on applications (trains, ships, toys, urban planning, brain surgery, design and production, and educational material); but it also took an unexpected turn, partly because half of the chapters are about augmented reality and partly because the concept of a *habitat*, originally proposed by Daniel May, turned out to be useful in a number of chapters.

In addition to this, the focus on applications raised the issue of evaluation criteria: what is a "good" virtual reality application? Is a "realistic" application (i.e. an application that looks like reality) better than an application that does not look like the real world? Not necessarily. For instance, the animals in the virtual environment for small children analyzed by Madsen don't look like real animals, but the application still works. So what are the criteria for good VR applications?

1.1 Virtual and Augmented Reality

That augmented reality is closely related to virtual reality should come as no surprise: both technologies are based on a mapping between two coordinate systems. In virtual reality, the user's view point is mapped into the coordinate system of a virtual world, so that he sees what he would have seen had he been located at a certain position in the virtual world. In augmented reality, the mapping works the other way around: the user's position and orientation is now the point of departure, and the virtual world is presented in such a way that the user sees what he would have seen had the virtual object been located at a certain position in the real world.

Therefore, augmented versus virtual reality is a matter of balance: is the real world strong enough to make the virtual one adapt, or does the virtual world succeed in forcing the user to see and hear according to its logic?

The chapters in Section 1 of this book are about the world in the computer that users can enter, i.e. about virtual reality applications. In Section 2, the chapters deal with computer applications that are placed in the real world. In both cases, the problem reminds one of Chinese boxes: one box must fit into another box. In some cases, pieces of the real world, including real users, are put into the computer application's virtual world. Here the application provides real-world simulations in which users can act and navigate. In other cases, the computer application's virtual world is put into the real world in order to help users to navigate in the real world. However, in both situations, of course, the final aim is to help people perform better in the real world. For instance, a 3D brain model (cf. Chapter 3) is a virtual reality application that users can enter in order to practice their surgery skills, or simultaneously to navigate better in a real brain. The user goes from the real world into the virtual world in order to perform better in the real world. In the interface designs for mobile augmented reality analyzed by Kjeldskov in Chapter 8, the application "enters" the user's real world. The application's virtual world is being merged into a physical space supporting the real-world users' collaborative behaviour.

1.2 The Habitat Concept

The proliferation of the concept of habitat is at bit more surprising. It was tentatively suggested as a common framework at a meeting in spring 2002, and a number of authors, more or less reluctantly, tried it out in their work. As might be expected, the result was a number of variants, but still sharing the same kernel.

One constant feature is the idea of a *boundary* with an inside and an outside (Brown, 1971). The conditions inside are markedly different from those outside, so what can be said or done inside cannot necessarily be said or done outside, and conversely. For very good reasons this notion is heavily stressed in Chapter 3, which deals with various kinds of surgery: macroscopic surgery in an operating theatre, micro-surgery and endoscopic surgery. It is also a major idea in the Chapter 9, which looks at information needs in railways.

When one is inside the boundary, certain things can be done according to this particular habitat's conditions and rules of behaviour. But when one crosses the boundary (i.e. makes a transition from one habitat to another), new rules apply. It is important for a well-functioning virtual reality or augmented reality computer application to support the user in understanding and managing these changes.

Another recurrent feature is the idea of *simplification*, i.e. reduction of complexity. Once inside a habitat, one can ignore many choices and complications that are dealt with outside. This simplification may be a necessity in order to survive, but can also be counter-productive – even lethal. The former is stressed in Chapter 6, which discusses organizational habitats, characterized by specialized languages and modes of thinking, as an obstacle for developing efficient design and production processes; the latter is important in Chapter 10 on wayfinding on ships during maritime accidents. In such cases, passengers really live in small chunks of space and have difficulty in getting the overview that might help them to escape to the muster stations.

Nevertheless, a useful "overview" is not necessarily a grand model of everything. On the contrary: overviews are often too complex and provide too much information; that is, information that is not relevant in a specific situation. Thus what is needed is support to get from one habitat to another. In the wayfinding example, one set of wayfinding signs should lead the user into a new set of signs, and the "virtual" signs on signboards should not contradict the implicit directional signs of staircases etc.

A third idea is the notion of something moving in and out of a habitat. In this case, the habitat is seen as a *context*. This was probably the original motivation for using it in connection with mobile technology, which is exemplified in Chapters 7 and 8. In both cases, habitats are seen as a context that can cause movable devices to adapt their information to the needs associated to particular places and times.

Finally, there is the notion of *evolution*, stressed in Chapter 7 and hinted at in Chapter 9. Many existing habitats need a historical account in order to be understandable, since they have evolved piecemeal: they are altered to support certain activities, but in their altered shape they give rise to other activities that in their turn motivate the next change, etc.

Whether or not the habitat concept will survive this book is difficult to judge; however, it does stress the importance of *context*, which is indisputably an important feature of the new types of technology.

A discussion that has caused several heated arguments among the editors is the relation of (real) space and time to the other aspects of the habitat concept, which includes the notion of a *social system* – the way people interact – and the notion of a *restricted language* – the way people communicate. If the boundary of the habitat *must* be physical, the Internet is not a habitat; in fact, it is quite the opposite! A dialect can be said to be part of a habitat, whereas a sociolect cannot. If we do not require a physical anchoring, then ideologies are conceptual habitats, since they provide the necessary conceptual infrastructure for some thoughts and convictions while excluding others. If one wants to speak about conceptual habitats in general, the spatial restrictions must be abandoned, but then the concept may tend to become synonymous with the notion of a social system.

1.3 Application Quality Criteria

The of editors also discussed how a virtual reality or augmented reality application qualifies as a good application. How do we measure quality?

In the chapters on urban planning (Chapter 2) and brain surgery (Chapter 3) the VR model must allow the users to navigate and act within a realistic virtual world. When supporting urban planning the users must know what happens if a new house is built within a certain location. When supporting brain surgery it is a matter of life and death for the user to know what will happen if she makes a cut one millimetre to the left of the present position. These models should look like reality.

In the chapters on virtual environments for small children (Chapters 4 and 5) a fictional world is presented that is not realistic in any naturalistic sense. The animals, buildings and landscapes provided for the child users are not aimed at making them believe that they are in a real world. Nevertheless the VR application functions because it supports an understanding of emotional conflicts and dramaturgic choices.

Finally, in Chapter 6 on 3D applications in design and production the aim is at least partly to support social and organizational behaviour in an enterprise. How can a VR application support communication between people from different parts of an organization? How can it support processes such as organizational change and learning? Here, neither physical realism nor dramaturgic conflicts are asked for. Here, in order to function, the VR application should represent a social habitat.

1.4 Kant in Virtual Reality

Among the editors we found a solution to the discussion of application quality criteria by turning to the German philosopher Immanuel Kant. He made a distinction between three forms of reason: pure, practical and aesthetic. In the 20th century the German sociologist Jürgen Habermas elaborated the characteristics of these three forms of reason in a linguistic direction. Inspired by the American language philosopher John Searle he identified three types of speech acts: constatives, regulatives and expressives. Constatives are about the way in which the world is according to truth criteria. Regulatives are about the way in which the social world is or should be according to practical criteria. Expressives are about the way in which the world is or should be according to aesthetic criteria.

It is our suggestion that the quality of 3D applications can be evaluated according to similar criteria. Thus, three classes of applications can be identified. One class of applications works in so far as these applications look like the phenomenon represented by the application. These models are constatives. Another class of applications works in so far as these applications have a practical relevance for the social or organizational world that they represent. These models are regulatives. Finally, a third class of applications works in so far as these applications are beautiful or sublime. The landscape of a computer game should not necessarily be naturalistic, but it should create exciting situations or express particular emotions. These models are expressives. The point is that the evaluation criteria for identifying good or bad applications are different within these three application types.

A further point, however, is that although one form of reason dominates a particular application, all three are present in and relevant for every single application. A computer game should be aesthetically attractive, but of course it should also function. An application aimed at physical planning should also be beautiful.

1.5 Good Theories Are Practical

In our editorial work with virtual and augmented reality applications we have been through lots of different theories: the philosophy of Kant, Spencer Brown's laws of form, Searle's speech acts, biological theories of habitats etc. We do hope that our readers also agree that in such practical realms as VR and AR applications there is nothing as practical as good theories.

Actually, this has been the general ambition of the four volumes on virtual interaction, virtual space, virtual reality methodologies and, finally, virtual reality applications: to bring together theoreticians and practitioners, analytical and construction-oriented approaches, media theory and computer science, dramaturgy and engineering, in order to demonstrate not only that inter-disciplinarity is requested, but that it must be developed into new paradigms with shared basic concepts. One such concept, suggested in the present volume, is the habitat concept, which has a computer scientific, a humanistic and a sociological significance. Another is Spencer Brown's concept of form. These concepts are, in other words, two of many bridge-building concepts that may support the ongoing construction of a common computer science paradigm crossing the gap between those two cultures that were introduced by C. P. Snow in 1956, but which should not be kept apart in multimedia: science and arts. Returning to Kant, any virtual reality application has a pure, a practical and an aesthetic dimension. Any such application must be constructed and analyzed according to constative as well as regulative and expressive criteria. For some years in academia this has been taking place through the meeting of colleagues from different realms. The next step is the building of common paradigms. These four books on virtual reality have aimed at bringing this process one small step forward.

Acknowledgement

This book could not have been written without the support of the Danish Research Councils, which through their Centre for Multimedia research funded major parts of the work on which it is based.

References

Brown, G. S. (1971) *Laws of Form*. London: George Allen & Unwin.
Madsen, K. H. (ed.) (2002) *Production Methods: Behind the Scenes of Virtual Inhabited 3D Worlds*. London: Springer-Verlag.
Qvortrup, L. (ed.) (2001) *Virtual Interaction: Interaction in Virtual Inhabited 3D Worlds*. London: Springer-Verlag.
Qvortrup, L. (ed.) (2002) *Virtual Space: Interaction in Virtual Inhabited 3D Worlds*. London: Springer-Verlag.
Searle, J. R. (1970) *Speech Acts*. Cambridge: Cambridge University Press.
Snow, C. P. (1956) "The Two Cultures". *New Statesman,* 6 October.

The World in the Computer

Introduction

Erik Kjems and Janek Szatkowski

One of the important lessons to be drawn from the Danish National Research Project "The Staging of Inhabited Virtual 3D Spaces" is connected with the fact that we have been producing applications ourselves as well as analyzing other applications. It is important to reflect on this: in some domains of science (engineering for example) the need to produce applications is just a banal part of the daily routine. In other domains (humanities), the work involved in producing an application may be considered unnecessary for the research and the development of theory. Our involvement in the production processes creates new types of question in the theoretical landscape. We have experienced the need to challenge the existing theories and develop new concepts. We have met the need for interdisciplinary studies. It seems obvious that the kind of society we are heading for will promote a kind of knowledge and science that relies on an ability to work in new non-compartmentalized cross-scientific sections where knowledge from different domains within sciences cooperates. Thus, humanities are needed because this new language of science must draw not only on the language of nature and the language of mathematics, but also on the insights in human interaction and production of meaning (cf. Qvortrup, 1998, p. 208). Each participant in these research processes has had to revisit and revise the dogma of his or her original domain only to find that questions had to be reformulated and theories had to be readjusted. This cooperative and inquisitive spirit has been an important element behind the different applications presented.

This section deals with an attempt to represent the world in the computer using advanced 3D techniques of visualization. The "worlds" represented vary greatly in size and complexity: from the macro perspective of urban planning to microsurgery, working with a precision within tenths of a millimetre. There are complex planning procedures for modern plants integrating different sections in the design and production of new, standardized modules, where the use of virtual reality to represent the products seems to facilitate cooperation. Another type of world is represented by the virtual puppet theatre, where a fictional world with a farmer and his cow tries to challenge 6–8 year-old children in other ways than the standard computer game may do.

In three of the examples the construction of the virtual worlds is heavily dependent on fidelity: the representations of the real world in the computer must be... and here we must stop a second to reflect: what words should we use? Realistic? Is that a good word? Will they be as lifelike as possible? Is that the aim? The argument could be that to a certain degree we do look for lifelikeness – "resemblance". We depend on the virtual presentation to be realistic, but this is not sufficient. Kjems (Chapter 2) makes the point that a model should be trustworthy: it is not a landscape model that is manipulated to make a certain development project look good and pleasing in order to secure the owners a profitable sale. The 3D model should be as accurate as possible in order to provide facts. Fidelity may be the word. We trust that the representation has chosen the most important features and provided them with a suitable expression. Haase *et al.* (Chapter 3) state that the decision as to what these features are relies on the analysis of the real-life situation that functions as a model. Thus visual inputs, colour, sound and haptic senses must be involved when a 3D training studio for an operating theatre is designed. In almost phenomenological terms they describe the complication that the microsurgeon is presented with. Here the world to be operated in is already transmitted into another visual medium, the surgeon being unable to see either his own hands or the assisting personnel in the operating theatre. When a 3D environment is constructed for this training it depends on the precise representation of the brain, allowing haptic and other sensual inputs to be generated as well as the merely visual inputs. Drejer and Gudmundsson (Chapter 6) show us the use of a 3D representation of the product to be designed and produced, and point to the fact that this must also be as illustrative as possible of the environment in which the product has to be installed. Using a reliable 3D representation of the product from an early stage of the product life cycle, and developing it and using it through several habitats during the phases of creation and implementation, can reduce costs simply by avoiding errors.

We need to be able to trust these applications. They must have high standards of constatives – they must be truthful. What we discover, of course, is that the principles behind such representations are highly specific to context, to the habitat in which they function. Even the most realistic virtual 3D representation is based on highly abstract principles depending on the actual technology: how many polygons can be calculated per second? How do we integrate and combine the haptic sense machinery into the visual representation? It is in this fertile cross-field that new knowledge seems to be growing.

Drejer and Gudmundsson argue that the use of the virtual 3D representation creates surroundings that stimulate organizational learning – members of the company's various departments sit together with their different orientations and languages and are focused on their common target – the product to be designed, produced, installed and marketed. The entire scenario for training surgeons is based on a notion of learning where interactivity and feedback from the system are of great importance to the development of the skills of the surgeon-to-be. The Virtual Puppet Theatre, as described and discussed by Madsen (Chapter 5) and Lehmann and Szatkowski (Chapter 4) provides an opportunity for the child to navigate in a 3D world inhabited by a Farmer and a Cow who function as playmates for the child, thus stimulating the child in a way that alters the complex mechanisms of the child's ordinary play structure. In this way the virtual world may produce regulatives: ideas as to how the social world is or could be. The applications need to be conscious of how they present themselves and how they invite social learning. This may be evaluated by examining the concrete context – the habitat and the practical relevance of the possible interactions between the user and the virtual worlds.

Finally, the virtual worlds are expressive. They communicate using pictures, sounds and movement. For some of the applications that means being as lifelike as possible, but for other applications realism in the one-to-one sense of photographic representation is not a milestone as such. Lehmann and Szatkowski argue that realism may be seen as an obstacle when programming autonomous agents and their three-dimensional worlds. Here the use of aesthetic criteria seems to be important. Madsen describes the challenges in the virtual puppet theatre seen from the programmer's point of view. The need to shift the position of the user from an active involvement inside the fiction to a distanced observer's position was facilitated by Madsen by inventing a special way to stop the 3D world whenever a sound file was about to be played, and allowing the children to record their own versions of the lines to be spoken. Thus Madsen provided the project with a very important and successful interface that enhanced the learning possibilities and the aesthetic pleasure.

The chapters in this section show us that the constative, regulative and expressive criteria enter the evaluation of the applications with different weight. It seems important to stress the fact that all three criteria are relevant for each application, but of course with different weight. We could say that each application has its own hierarchy of criteria; we might not yet be able to produce convincing typologies to subsume the many different hierarchies, but we have learned a lot from trying.

Reference

Qvortrup, L. (1998) *Det hyperkomplekse samfund*. Copenhagen: Gyldendal.

2

VR for Decision Support in Urban Planning

Erik Kjems

2.1 Introduction

Since the beginning of civilization, drawings or models have been produced to illustrate ideas of buildings and development plans. From small cabins to large urban areas architects and planners have used different tools to present and sell their ideas as convincingly as possible. One of the most widespread methods nowadays is the use of artistic posters and small precisely scaled wooden models with nice miniature trees and light arrangements. As beautiful as they may look, they are still downscaled and modelled representations of an idea that has to be interpreted in each spectator's head. As technology develops and highly specialized visual presentation techniques become affordable, more and more politicians and professionals want to use these techniques for decision support.

Large immersive display systems make it possible to present models in a real-time VR situation so that the impression of the model is as close to reality as possible. The VR facilities at VR Media Lab, Aalborg University, have been used during a more or less normal planning process in a project in Denmark. For the first time an official local plan has been visualized in these environments.

The Danish Planning Act always requires such a local plan for a new housing area. Therefore the municipality of Kjellerup and the private company Cowi (Consulting Engineers and Planners AS) prepared a preliminary local plan for a housing area in the outskirts of Ans. The plan formed the basis for a pilot project concerning the site development. The purpose was to investigate whether it would be a realistic option for a municipality to defray the expenses of the infrastructure or not, so the following questions arise.

Can the area attract new citizens? How will the new buildings influence the neighbouring areas (not only with regard to view and access, but also very much with regard to the value of property)? Will the price of the properties be acceptable? Are

Figure 2.1 The local plan.

the road junctions and the road alignments appropriate or do they perhaps worsen the conditions of the existing neighbouring areas or other parts of the town?

The municipality of Kjellerup wanted to be able to make a better evaluation of its plans – plans that until now had been presented and discussed on the basis of outlines similar to that shown in Figure 2.1. The visualization project originated from that wish, and therefore Cowi offered the municipality of Kjellerup an examination of the possibilities of creating an actual visualization of the existing local plan. Cowi contacted VR Media Lab at Aalborg University to assist them and provide the project with know-how in the field of VR and the right facilities for the visualization part. A model of the existing local plan was made by VR Media Lab. It was intended to support the decision that was going to be made by the municipality; a decision where the municipality had to decide whether the project was to start and what alterations would eventually have to be made.

In order to understand the importance of this particular VR presentation and to understand the influence of the presentation, the external circumstances and the legal context in which the project has become a reality, will be discussed in the following section. Therefore there will be a description of the Danish Planning Act, which regulates the planning of a community local plan, and also a description of the technology used in the project, including display facilities, the quality of the model presented and the presentation circumstances.

2.2 The Danish Planning Act

The Danish Planning Act was revised in 1975, which led to its existing form. Civic involvement was then introduced as a central element in the Act. The planning process through which a local plan will be approved is clearly characterized by the possibilities and deadlines for objections against the project. In general the planning processes are very different, as the project character and size determine how much the municipality is involved in the process. The act is not very detailed in its demands on the content and form of published material, only at what point in the planning process it has to be produced. The municipality therefore provides broad opportunities for interpretation, and it is the job of politicians to demand adequate material to provide the possibility of making the right decisions and informing citizens of the actual consequences of the project.

A normal planning process for the implementation of a local plan looks as follows (Spatial Planning Department, 1999):

1. Previous publication
2. The preparation of a local plan proposal
3. The adoption of a local plan proposal
4. The publication of the proposals
5. Commenting period
6. Objection reading
7. Adoption
8. Publication

This planning process varies a lot in duration, with the exception that the period of "publication of the proposal" – step 4 – must last at least 8 weeks. Thus the local plan preparation might make slow progress, especially if the project is met with a lot of opposition from politicians and citizens. The Ans project was in phase two, i.e. a local plan proposal was being prepared. Depending on what consequences a plan has, greater or less resources are being used. In the case of Ans a lot of resources were used in order to ensure that the right decisions were made, as the municipality needed to develop the site at a price of approximately €1 million.

It turns out that today's local plans are made in almost the same way as when the Danish Planning Act was introduced. Today the population also asks for better documentation. Thus Lars Bodum concludes (Bodum, 1999): "There is a need for a revitalization of the local plan process and an active discussion of the use of different media in order to get further in the efforts of achieving goals concerning public planning as they are described in the Danish Planning Act".

However, this is not without problems and requires much preparation and thought, which is also shown in this project.

2.3 The Modelling

The implemented model is of great importance to what the politicians gain from the presentation and what influence the model has on the decision process. A detailed and very realistic model is expected to have far more influence than a model with very few details, simple constructions and simple textures. Therefore the following section describes the structure of the model as detailed as possible in order to explain the "level of detail" which has been used in the planning process.

In principle the model consists of three parts: a terrain part, covering the entire area (and more) in order to give a natural presentation of the horizon; a road part consisting of a piece of regulated terrain, where the road is cut into the basic model;

and an element part, which contains elements placed on top of the terrain (i.e. all the buildings, trees, street lights etc.).

2.3.1 The Terrain

There are two different elevation models of Denmark. This model is retrieved from the National Survey and Cadastre Agency, as they can provide a 50 metre grid of Denmark with a point accuracy of approximately 2 metres. The model was supplemented with a local terrestrial survey of the central area, where houses and roads were established. The local survey was provided as contour lines and then converted to a grid. The entire grid was converted to a TIN (triangular irregular network), i.e. polygons consisting of triangles. On this polygon net a texture with so-called orthophotos (DDO) is draped (see Figure 2.2). These photos have a resolution of 80 cm. The photos are aero-triangular avionic photos from June 1995 with an accuracy of approximately 2 metres corresponding to the elevation model. These data do not provide a high level of accuracy, but it is adequate for the visualization purpose.

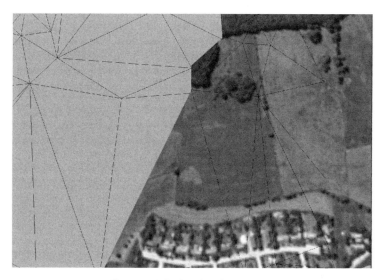

Figure 2.2 Orthophoto draped upon the TIN.

2.3.2 The Road Model

Compared with general models of town and landscape areas this area has undergone an actual engineering project work. Alterations of the terrain have been made, especially in connection with the local roads which are part of the project and which are cut into the terrain (see Figure 2.3). This cut gives a nice alignment of the road in the model. When moving along these modelled surfaces one has a good impression of the road versus the landscape model. Due to its nature the road alignment has very high accuracy in its calculations.

Figure 2.3 The road model cut into the terrain.

2.3.3 The Elements

The model looks like a typical Danish housing area from the late 1990s. Textures were photographed and mounted on simple model boxes. Trees, hedges and bushes were placed casually in the area. Here the billboard technique was used, i.e. their faces always turn towards the viewer while moving around in the model. Trees look like trees, but they are merely a transparent image using the alpha channel of the image, placed on a surface consisting of two polygons (two triangles); see Figure 2.4. Similar techniques were used for street lights and other elements, such as cars.

Thus the model consists of a large modified terrain part and other loose elements placed upon it. This construction is important to bear in mind when considering future use and alternative presentations.

2.4 Handling the Model in a VR Environment

The model is generated while moving through the model in real time, thus enabling the viewer to look at a specific part of the model. It is possible to stop and turn and to look in any direction. It is also possible to go back to the starting point, or to rise above the buildings to view the area from above, or to imagine oneself as a small child sitting on a tricycle at street level. Interactive control of the movement requires that the number of polygons seen simultaneously in the model does not exceed 80 000 polygons for the time being, given the equipment and software available. If this requirement is fulfilled the system is theoretically able to generate a maximum of 120 images per second per projector. This number is equal to 60 images per second per eye if the model is shown in active stereo. The high number of images is required particularly in connection with the panning situation in order to present a flowing model with a high frame rate in the graphics.

Figure 2.4 Trees on two-dimensional billboards.

Theoretically both eyes perceive approximately 40–50 images per second, as they are not able to perceive the single image by themselves but can perceive that an image is missing. The change in image during the panning is seen much more clearly than a forward movement in the image, which is a far larger alteration in the image. To achieve flowing graphics it is necessary to obtain a high image frequency. The television medium cheats by using 50 images per second, showing only every second field per image, thus actually showing only 25 images per second (interlaced) (Watkinson, 1996).

The model has to be divided into several pieces, and different methods, taken especially from the gaming industry, are used to meet these very high requirements for the image frequency. The largest geographic division is made on the terrain itself, as it is divided into a large number of coherent squares. This means that the software used in this model does not have to memorize the entire terrain at all times. The software needs only handle the part of the model which is looked at on the screen. The terrain is the largest single object, making this particular work a very important part of the project. Furthermore, a qualitative selection of the terrain description has been carried out, as the need for an accurate description of the terrain varies a lot. The large open spaces surrounding the area need only very little information in contrast to the model covering the local plan. To a very large extent, a number of polygons are needed along the roads as both kerb and ditch constructions are cut into the terrain model (Figure 2.3). Often the curved road alignment needs a large number of polygons as well. Nevertheless, the number of polygons can easily be reduced using a dedicated software package. In this way even complex models can achieve a considerable reduction in the number of polygons. VR Media

Lab often uses the software "Rational Reducer" which uses algorithms based on the "edge collapse" technique (http://www.sim.no/). Depending on the model, it is possible to decrease the numbers of polygons to 10% of the original number.

When presenting landscape models on large display systems the horizon is very noticeable. At a model presentation on a 21" screen it is relatively easy to ignore the edge of the model, as the whole situation itself is very artificial and the focus area is very narrow in the human field of vision. If one is seated in front of a 160° Panorama screen one also views the model using one's peripheral vision. This causes "cyber-sickness" when moving too fast in the model. If one has to look at the model at a realistic large size using peripheral vision, a number of significant requirements must be fulfilled concerning the area surrounding the fairly accurately defined local plan. Thus the entire view of the neighbouring meadow is of great interest to the modelling work. Various methods have been tested. The best method involved fixed billboards, over which textures from bushes, fringes of the forest or a couple of trees were draped. This created a very lifelike vision of the horizon and gave very fine depth to the model, and at the same time the edge of the model disappeared.

The model looks very much like the real thing, which will be documented later, but one misses some kind of dynamic features in the model, such as small animations to add some life to it. Light and shadow are factors which have not been dealt with in the first phase of the project. However, these functionalities do not work so well on large display systems, where real-time graphics are used. Proper light calculations require lots of processing power and are therefore difficult to implement as dynamic factors. Several sustainable methods exist, in which complicated light calculations are made in a specific light calculation program, such as LightScape. The texture surfaces calculated for a specific light scenario on a PC are then assembled on the model in the presentation program, for example in the Panorama facility. However, the problem is not entirely solved by doing this, as large display systems using this particular technique find it difficult to reproduce colour depth satisfactorily, and at the same time the use of the stereo technique converts a beautiful summer day into a sad grey day. The biggest problem is caused by lack of texture memory, as it is not possible to use the same texture information several times in the same model. Every little surface must have its own texture because of the special lighting conditions. In this project only a few simple lighting conditions were used. No shadows were used because the model became very dark, and on several occasions when walking towards these dark areas it did not look right.

Of course one would prefer that the model represented both light and shadow. Figures 2.5 and 2.6 show the variation in the model with actual light calculations (Figure 2.5), and the way the model is shown during the VR presentation (Figure 2.6). Available software might compensate for the lack of light calculations by using other methods; however, this is typically the only feature that this kind of software has and interactivity within the model is not possible.

VR's strongest point is the interaction itself; the possibility of being able to move around freely in the model and also to make alterations on the way, e.g. moving houses, trees and signs.

Figure 2.5 Smooth texturing with light and shadows.

Figure 2.6 Rough texturing with ambient light.

2.5 The Panorama Facility

To understand the uniqueness of a presentation in the Panorama facility a short description of the physical surroundings is given.

The facility (Figure 2.7) looks like a small cinema. It is almost a crime to call it a cinema, because it is driven by a very expensive "ONYX Infinite Reality 2" computer from SGI, which has 16 CPUs and 6 graphical pipes. Showing a movie in it would not even be very good because of the curved screen and the digital output.

Figure 2.7 The Panorama facility.

A maximum of 28 people in four rows can be seated in the facility. The floor in the Panorama slopes, so that the back row is sitting somewhat higher than the front row.

The screen is approximately 10 metres long and 3.5 metres high with a 160° field of view, which means that if one is seated in the middle of the front row looking straight ahead the screen totally covers one's field of vision. This is the ultimate experience, where the immersiveness of the model is felt in the whole body, especially in the stomach, but the other seats in the facility also allow a reasonable experience.

2.6 Mono Versus Stereo

In the Panorama it is possible to present both mono and active stereo. A presentation in mono is very common, but a presentation in active stereo will be a new experience to most people. Active stereo makes it possible for people to perceive depth in the facility as the left and right eyes each receive an image that is proportionately shifted. By using active stereo two images are generated simultaneously – one image for the left eye and one for the right eye. At the point when the screen presents an image to the left eye the special glasses (shutter glasses) close the right eye and vice versa. As mentioned earlier, this is done at a frequency of 120 images per second. The shutter glasses obscure part of the field of view and are not suitable for all kinds of presentations. In general, when presenting models of large buildings or landscapes a mono presentation is preferred, as the effect of stereo is lost and the advantages are less than the disadvantage of using glasses, which diminishes the field of view and darkens the model (Edelman *et al.*, 1992).

A normal precept often used: models observed from a distance of more than about 10 metres can profitably be watched in mono, as the stereo effect is practically vanishing from that point.

The Panorama facility is very good at a large number of presentations, as the immersiveness in the presentation technique is something between a presentation on a large flat screen and a presentation in the Cave.

The Panorama facility holds a very important element that is practically unattainable in other display systems. When 10, 15 or 20 people are seated in front of the Panorama screen, looking at the same model, something inexplicable happens. VR Media Lab has seen presentations, graduations and PhD defences where the viewers almost forget where they are gathered, and animatedly discuss the model – engineering detail solutions, the form of the design element, or the possibilities of interaction with the virtual media. The reasons for the success of the Panorama facility are the possibility of interacting with the model and having animated discussions when seated in a comfortable chair, reaching essential decisions on the same basis based on visual input within the same frame of understanding. If we compare the presentations of Ans in the Panorama facility with the basis material shown in Figure 2.1, it is obvious why the Panorama facility is preferred. Often it is only experts who are able to perceive a two-dimensional plan as a spatial model. The transformation from two-dimensional to spatial understanding has some elements of uncertainty. It is surprising how many different interpretations of a drawn plan can be perceived by observers and formed into a spatial model. It is just like reading a book. Everybody who reads the same book has different experiences when reading the book using their own imagination. The same aspect exists when describing a plan.

2.7 Presentation of the Ans Local Plan for the Municipality of Kjellerup

The first presentation was held on 23 August 2000. Unfortunately, not every member of the Town Council was able to attend the presentation, but the majority of the political representatives and some municipal officers from the Department of Technical Administration found their way to Aalborg and VR Media Lab.

Prior to the presentation VR Media Lab and council engineer Bendt Bjergaard discussed the presentation in order to explain what was going to take place and to enquire whether it would be possible to hand out a questionnaire to the participants from Kjellerup. It was essential to the questionnaire that it was completed immediately before and after the presentation. VR Media Lab and Bendt Bjergaard agreed to have two presentations of 45 minutes each; one in mono and one in stereo (see above). A 30 minute coffee break was held between the presentations. The presentations each started with a short traditional two-dimensional presentation in a meeting room.

The breaks and the course of the presentation are not without interest to the final result. Whether the presentation was in mono or in stereo was based on internal discussions in VR Media Lab. Experience shows that if the presentations in the Panorama facility last too long the viewer normally feels nausea when navigating in a town and landscape model, for example, where the visual input does not correspond to the physical surroundings of the body. Moving very fast when panning increases the phenomenon. Moving forward in the model does not create any problems, but moving from side to side may cause nausea. If one tends to get car-, flight- or seasick, it is relatively easy to become "cyber-sick" in the Panorama facility. Experiments also show that one does not feel nausea in the same way when working with the head-mounted display (HMD) systems, as there is no peripheral vision to create confusion in the human brain. So the very large immersive images have both positive and negative sides (Hodges, 2001; Howarth, 1994).

By clever navigation in the model and exact planning of the presentation programme the nausea problem should not be an issue. The presentation normally starts with a "guided" tour. This means that a walking path has been predefined before the actual presentation is given. This gives a very smooth kick-off for the first 10 minutes or so, passing all the nice spots and maybe even the bad ones. After that the "VR pilot" strolls very smoothly around in the model waiting for somebody from the audience to ask for a special view or path to take. Thus it is the audience in front of the screen who decides where to go. It would be possible to let the audience navigate by themselves, but this is not easy to handle with 15 or more people. In addition, it takes some time to get used to the pointing device, so it is better for everyone to let a trained VR pilot handle the navigation.

Alterations to the model can be programmed into the presentation. This has been done on several other occasions with minor projects when deciding on different architectural proposals. In this project only one plan was to be discussed and no alternatives were prepared or desired.

The relatively long presentation of 1½ hours, divided into two parts, including breaks, was also used to introduce the participants to the techniques used in the project and not least the facilities of VR Media Lab. One of the big problems when we present our models in our large display facilities, such as the Panorama, is the so-called "wow effect". In this case it would be of great importance whether the decisions are to be made on the basis of an impressive presentation or on the basis of the actual project. Some of the questions in the questionnaire were designed to uncover whether the "wow effect" would influence the effect of the presentation. The basis of the participants was very alike. Nobody had visited VR Media Lab before, although some participants had seen a film on a panoramic screen. After the presentation the participants unanimously estimated VR Media Lab's facilities as being impressive and the presentation very good. Both estimations were the top answers on a scale from 1 to 5. Thus it is impossible to say whether the surroundings influenced the final result.

2.8 Immediate Reactions During the Presentation

When the participants sit in their chairs looking at the presentation they are quiet for some time, usually because it is difficult to breathe evenly. The large screen right in front of the viewer gives some fantastic visual experiences which take some time to get used to. After a few minutes moving through the area of the model the questions start. Initially the questions are about the techniques used in the model, but after a while questions about the project itself and the form of the model are asked: the form of the roads, the size of the lots compared to the size of the whole area, or the architecture of the houses, including number of floors.

While moving through the area, looking at the attractive views from the houses, one of the first quick decisions by the politicians was made concerning the shape of the houses. All houses were to have one floor only. In this way all property owners would have a nice view from both their houses and their gardens. Other conditions, such as considerations of existing houses, were also discussed. The model presented some black buildings which mark where part of the existing houses are placed. During the presentations it was possible to estimate what the view from the existing houses would be like in the future. The general estimation was that it would be possible to place and form the new housing area in a way that it would have only a minor influence on the clear view from the existing houses; it would not totally block their view of the meadow area. Their clear view was highly important for the form of the area. The municipality thought that it would be impossible to sell lots in this area if the clear view was blocked. In this connection the model assisted in solving various problems. An area in the north-western part was given up, as it was plain to see that the requirement of a clear view could not be met. At the same time the lots were enlarged, creating a better view for houses placed further up on the slope. These questions or problems were solved or discussed during the presentation and then decided by the Town Council of Kjellerup.

The road alignments were briefly discussed. Everybody agreed that the curved road alignments were very effective in connection with traffic safety in the housing area, as limited vision would prevent drivers from speeding.

Giving the area an image as a green area was of very high importance to the council. This could be confirmed by using the model. Thus the placing of the green "wedge" in the area was discussed during the presentation. The wedge was viewed from both within the area as well as from the meadow, at eye level in the street, and from the air. It was very well received. The revised local plan contains two green wedges, as illustrated in Figure 2.1.

One of the participants knew the area very well, as he grew up in the town of Ans. He confirmed that the realism of the model was striking and the view of the meadow very similar to that of the real meadow. Along with our own observations this confirmed that the computer made model was of high quality and had a good match with reality.

2.9 The Survey

The main purpose of the survey was to measure the effect of a presentation of a development plan using the newest existing VR techniques, compared with normal material, which in Denmark usually contains two-dimensional plans and written text.

This section is a summary of the most important questions, which are obligatory to illustrate the problems described above. Fourteen questionnaires were handed out and 10 were returned. As a statistical basis this is hardly enough, but because of the homogeneity of the answers, it is clearly an excellent documentation of the use of VR in town planning.

2.9.1 Before Visiting VR Media Lab

Before the town council arrived at VR Media Lab they were asked what their expectations of the presentation were. Some did not know how to answer, probably because they had no idea of what they were going to see or experience. Most had great expectations of the presentation.

Everybody expected that the presentation would be able to contribute more information about the project, even though they knew that the model was based on existing plans and objectively would not offer any new information.

At the same time, most participants thought that the presentation either might or would definitely change their opinions of the project. No one rejected that possibility.

To the question of what was expected regarding the realism of the computer model, the answers were "medium". Perhaps the participants did not have high expectations of the technique.

Most of the participants were enthusiastic about the project in Ans and positive towards the implementation. Either the project's opponents stayed at home or the town council was generally in favour of the project but was simply not convinced that the lots would be easy to sell.

2.9.2 After Visiting VR Media Lab

Different questions were asked regarding the presentation itself, for example whether the presentation had clarified the project. Almost everybody answered "a lot", which was the top answer on a scale from 1 to 5. In general, the presentation was estimated as certainly meeting the expectations of the participants, again at the top of a scale from 1 to 5, which might be difficult to understand, as expectations were already high before the presentation.

A very clear question of how important it is to be able to move perfectly freely in the model was asked. The answer was unambiguous, as everybody answered "great value", again the top answer on a scale from 1 to 5. This unambiguous accept of the VR medium with its powerful ability to manoeuvre freely in the model was unmistakable.

Another important issue was the question of how much this presentation influenced the perception of the project. The answers were that the presentation had only a small effect on this; approximately 50% answered that they had been influenced somewhat in their perception and others not at all. This matches the fact that everybody was positive towards the project. Thus their perceptions of the project were not changed that much.

2.9.3 Finances

The politicians were very clear in their answers that the costs of the presentation and the modelling were worth their money, and that they were likely to use these means in the future, depending on the project character and project size.

The most popular presentation form was the mono presentation. This has been explained in previous sections. Altogether, the presentation was seen as being very realistic, which is a compliment to the VR graphics designers. The most popular way to view the model was from eye level. This is very interesting, as most perspective reproductions today are presented from a bird's eye view, which came in as the least favoured option on a scale of 1 to 5. To nobody's surprise there was a very positive reaction to the fact that the model could be made public on the Internet and used as a kind of sales material. It is possible to implement a panoramic view from each house in order for buyers to check the view. Various complete animations were also a way of presenting the area.

Finally the viewers were asked if the presentation was worth driving one and a half hours for. The answers were unanimously yes.

2.10 Conclusions

This project has clearly shown that persons without any knowledge of VR technology or of three-dimensional computer technology are very ignorant of and insecure in the use and applications of these technologies. The project has shown that by demystifying the technology and by a thorough presentation it is possible to achieve the desired effects with VR applications.

Experts and technicians who have been working with these technologies for years, including recently VR media, have always understood that this was an excellent tool to use in order to improve planning, for example. It is strange that most highly trained architects have not really adopted this technology. The reason is probably found in traditions and cultural barriers rather than in a real resistance towards the technology itself.

By making a survey of how easy it is to use VR in a positive and inspiring way, it is possible to convince everyone that VR is a fantastic technique that develops better projects. This particular project has shown that VR is a basis for and contributes to the making of important decisions. Of course, acts of law will follow, but these acts will be based on the fact that a number of persons have seen and perceived the same thing. No one has been forced to imagine the spatial model, which in general is shown to be more difficult for women (Pease and Pease, 1999).

This project has also shown that interaction is of great value when presenting a model. Being able to move freely in the model provides the presentation with yet another dimension. When the visual aspect is of great importance to a decision-making the opportunity of viewing all details from various positions and angles is of extreme value. Not only the free movement but also the possibility of altering the model, while moving around in real time, opens a completely new paradigm for decision making for larger audiences. It is possible to model a compromise while all parties are gathered. The drawing or in this case the model does not need to go back to technicians for alterations, this can be done while looking at it.

One could go another step forward and add sound to the experience. In this case, for instance, sound from traffic, birds or playing children would add another dimension to the experience and increase the aspect of realism.

On the other hand, one must not be blind to the common enthusiasm for technology. When describing the model it was stated how a presentation might influence the decision of a city council. When examining the planning process for the local plan it is obvious that different levels of model detail should be presented at different phases in the planning process.

Everybody wants increased realism. Models have to be as realistic as possible. But it is important to bear in mind what the presentation actually shows and what its purpose is. A rough idea is a rough idea, and should be understood and read as such. It is not a thought-through product, but only a step in the right direction. It can be dangerous to present a rough idea using a medium which makes everything look and sound real. In the actual project the process was still ongoing; it was even at its very beginning. From a discussion based on more or less "loose lines" we moved into an area where everything was finished. This is definitely dangerous to the planning process, as its natural course is destroyed. No consideration had been given to these new interactive media in the planning process; illustrative material is used to make it easier to understand the spatial form, but to experience the space and to feel that you are part of the model is an entirely new paradigm. The model would have been even more dramatic if light calculations had been carried out. The fidelity of the model is therefore of extreme importance. It matters a lot if buildings are presented as simple grey boxes or if they are presented with high realistic bump-mapped texturing calculated with translucent materials and light coming from several sources.

Decisions should be made on facts not on dreams.

In this particular case, perhaps too many details were shown, as the aim, in principle, was supposed to state whether the project was sound or not. Thus the local plan preparation should have had other kinds of sustainability analyses. Possibly the presentation has influenced the overall argument to carry through the plan. The convincing high-fidelity presentation might have caused the sceptics to be convinced that the project would sell.

A lot more work and experiments must be carried out to get the use of 3D models right. How could and should politicians, technicians, and perhaps first of all the public, use VR media in order to make the right decisions?

2.11   Addendum

An additional meeting within the town council of Kjellerup was held in the Panorama about nine months after the first presentation. A new and improved model with alterations was presented. Most of the alterations were made due to the discussion held at the first presentation. The politicians were quite satisfied with their new plan. The new model supported some of the intentions they had with the alterations, for instance giving the area a luxury park-like appearance. The politicians were much more familiar with the Panorama and the facilities. One of the older politicians was moving in front of the Panorama display in a quite lively manner. The possibility of moving houses in the model, to give for instance a better view for existing housing, gave the politicians the chance to act as landscape architects. This is not necessarily an ideal situation, as the plan was a very rough one and not really suited for alterations such as moving single buildings around. It should be done by the real estate buyer, and eventually by a real landscape architect.

The second presentation underlined some of the conclusions made during the first one, and it definitely showed that the planning act should seek to clear some of the possibilities that large interactive display systems give to the less professional audience: what kind of influence and decisional power it is possible to handle with big display systems and what kind of decisions are not suited for these kinds of mostly visual presentation.

References

Bodum, L. (1999) Nye medier i lokalplanlægningen. *PhD Thesis*, Aalborg University, Aalborg.

Edelman, S. and Buelthoff, H.-H. (1992) Orientation dependence in the recognition of familiar and novel views of three-dimensional objects. *Vision Research*, 32(12): 2385–2400.

Hodges, L. (2001) Using the virtual world to improve quality of life in the real world. Keynote Address, *VR-IEEE Conference 2001*, Yokohama, Japan.

Howarth, P. A. (1994) Virtual reality: an occupational health hazard of the future. Paper presented at RCN Occupational Nurses Forum, Glasgow 1994.

Spatial Planning Department (1999) *The Planning Act in Denmark*. Spatial Planning Department, Ministry of Environment and Energy, Denmark.

Pease, A. and Pease, B. (1999) *Why Men Don't Listen and Women Can't Read Maps*. Pease Training International.

VR-IEEE (2001) *Virtual Reality 2001 Conference*, 13–17 March 2001, Yokohama, Japan. IEEE Computer Society Order Number PR00948.

Watkinson, J. (1996) *Television Fundamentals*. Oxford: Focal Press.

3

Virtual Reality and Habitats for Learning Microsurgical Skills

Jens Haase, Peter Musaeus and Egil Boisen

"Es irrt der Mensch, so lang er strebt."
[Man commits errors as long as he aspires]

Goethe (Faust)

3.1 Introduction

The potential of Virtual Reality (VR) as a training tool in microsurgery has not yet been realized. This is surprising, since VR has been introduced with great success in neighbouring areas, such as laparoscopic surgery (Gallagher, 1999). This is regrettable for anyone, like the first author of this chapter, with a clinical background in microsurgery: how many futile training sessions on animals have been performed, how much faster could the novice doctors learn to master microsurgery, and ultimately how many human lives could have been spared if VR was an integral part of microsurgical training programs? This chapter will discuss attempts carried out at the Virtual Brain Group, Aalborg University, to remedy this crucial lack of proper training tools within microsurgery.

If we want to develop a training device for microsurgery, whether this tool includes VR or not, one is faced with several challenging questions about what good surgery is and how it is learned. Thus, in the first section of this chapter we will draw on various theories to characterize the prerequisites for performing microsurgery: which skills and abilities are necessary to be an expert microsurgeon? We will approach this question by looking at surgical knowledge, skills and abilities. Later, we introduce the concepts of interface and habitat, in order to emphasize the interrelationship between the surgeon's "own" competence and circumstances in the environment. Furthermore, we introduce the concept of orchestration of action in order to stress the importance of training surgical skills in a real-life (or VR) setting, contrary to the predominant cognitive and behaviourist paradigm of learning within surgery. We have derived these concepts from a socio-cultural paradigm (e.g. Kaptelinin, 1996),

Secondly, we shall discuss relevant VR tools for learning surgical skills in different habitats. Thirdly, we will discuss how VR can be used as an effective tool that supports and anchors learning in real and surgical habitats.

3.2 Expert Surgical Performance

In order to support the acquisition of surgical skills, we might want to study what expert surgeons actually do. Obviously it takes more than a medical doctor with a knife in his or her hand to be an expert surgeon. Competence in surgery depends on a plethora of factors and skills (Schueneman *et al.*, 1984; Barnes, 1987; Bardram and Rosenberg, 1999). According to Gilsbach (1999, personal note) a surgeon is:

> A healthy, intelligent, tenacious, dynamic, psychologically intact and sincere candidate with manual dexterity, resistant to psychological and psychiatric stress.

This quote illustrates that it takes more than a handful of tools and simple techniques to carry out surgery. Thus in high-risk surgery, surgeons are facing special demands in terms of physical and emotional stress. Thus, studies have shown that surgeons need a certain psychological profile in order to become experts, very much as is the case with world-class athletes (McDonald, 1993). Furthermore, ethics could play an equally important rôle in the surgeon's performance.

Although we acknowledge the importance of these aspects, and do not rule out that personality, ethics, stress management etc. can be taught through VR, this is not our present focus. Instead, we will analyze the prerequisites in terms of surgical knowledge, skills and abilities.

3.2.1 Knowledge, Skills and Abilities

Microsurgical performance requires a great deal of knowledge of various types. Gilbert Ryle (1949) distinguished between theoretical knowledge, "knowing-that", and embodied knowledge, "knowing-how". On this account, "knowing-how" is characteristic of the expert, who acts without explicitly reflecting on the principles or rules involved, whereas "knowing-that" involves consciously accessible declarative knowledge, a type of prepositional knowledge which can be explained either verbally or symbolically, in a matrix etc. Much surgical inference during an operation depends on declarative knowledge in terms of solid background knowledge of anatomy, physiology, pathology and surgical techniques and procedures. However, surgical *performance* also heavily depends on "knowing-how", i.e. procedural knowledge. In our view, these types of knowledge go hand in hand within surgery. Knowing how to carry out a certain step in a surgical procedure involves, for example, knowing what obstacles to look for, knowing when to do it (if at all) and so forth. Even though these types of knowledge are interrelated, we will not be focusing on declarative knowledge. Instead, we will be focusing on the kind of knowledge that constitutes the "knowing-how", the surgical skills and abilities.

A distinction must be made between skills and abilities. Whereas a person may learn the skill of walking, he or she may later develop a traumatic paraplegia leaving him or her without the ability to employ the skill. Or the person could become paralysed at birth, making it impossible to develop the skill of walking. Thus, in our understanding, abilities are the prerequisites for the training and performance of skills. These prerequisites will be due to circumstances that are either internal or external to the subject. As for the concept of skills, we will follow several other authors (see Adams, 1987) in defining skills strictly as relating to human *motor* skills. When the microsurgeon masters a technique, he or she can perform it almost without committing errors. Thus skills become automatic, with little or no conscious control (Haase, 1999). Automatic skills are necessary for a flexible or adaptive performance by the surgeon (Patrick, 1992). Having made this distinction, we will now look more closely at surgical skills and abilities.

According to Fleishman and Quaintance (1984), the abilities of surgeons can be divided into four areas. First there are the cognitive abilities, such as abstract thinking, spatial orientation and mental imagery. These factors can, for instance, be important when the surgeon has to form a representation of what an organ looks like when it is rotated. Mental imagery is related to perceptual experiences in a given sensory modality. Probably visual imagery is by far the most important mental imagery needed in microsurgery. But tactile imagery or even auditive imagery might have been overlooked aspects, when for instance the microsurgeon imagines what it feels and sounds like when he moves the micro-suction in the operative field. Second, the psychomotor abilities of the microsurgeon are also important. These include, for instance, control precision, reaction time and finger dexterity. Sensorimotor skills depend on hand–eye coordination, thus providing the basis for skilled performances. This is commonly accepted within the fields of piano playing and sport, but also applies to microsurgery (McDonald, 1993; Waterworth, 1997). Third, there are the physical abilities of the surgeon, such as strength, flexibility, coordination and stamina. Micro-operations require a certain degree of physical vigour to sit or stand, perhaps with the neck bent, for hours when looking into a microscope. Finally, sensory and perceptual abilities are important. They include, for example, visual acuity, colour discrimination and depth perception. These abilities are important for the microsurgeon when he is considering, for instance, the amount of tissue to remove from a brain tumour based on a visual impression of brain structure and colouring combined with sensing of the hardness/softness of tumour and brain.

Our analytical distinction between skill and ability is important, but not always easy to draw. This is evident when scrutinizing the above taxonomy by Fleishman and Quaintance. Thus sensorimotor skills may rely on abilities (e.g. hand–eye coordination), and an ability such as forming mental images may be a skill to the extent that it is amenable to training. The point is that according to our use of the term *ability*, there is more to the surgeon's abilities than the factors stated above. We will also speak of abilities in terms of appropriate tools, for the handling of which the surgeon has to develop new skills. In what follows we will look at the concepts of interface and habitat.

3.2.2 Surgical Interface and Habitat

Even the best surgeons are not able to operate without the use of tools! Obviously, having the right tools is necessary for the surgeon to employ his or her surgical skills. Hence, according to our definition of "ability", the tools are among the surgeon's (external) abilities. The main point we would like to make here is that with the advent of new surgical tools and techniques, the surgeon has to develop new skills in order to use them. Although this sounds self-evident, we claim that this everyday experience has not been taken seriously enough in the field of micro-surgery, as it has implications for surgical training that are quite difficult to tackle. Our point will be that a good way of tackling these implications will be through the development of VR-based learning environments.

In order to express the implications of the interrelationship between surgeon and tool we use the terms "habitat" and "interface". We will use the latter term in a way that is slightly different from the traditional sense. In the traditional sense, an instrument carries two interfaces: one between the instrument and the surgeon, the other between the object and the instrument (Kaptelinin, 1996). When the surgeon gets familiar with new tool, the tool will get "internalized", thus forming a "functional organ" together with the surgeon. While the two terms "tool" and "interface" are far from having identical meanings, the tool can thus be thought of as an interface between the surgeon and the object (e.g. the patient that is to be operated). However, in this process the surgeon has to develop specific skills in order to operate with the tool. In our view, the necessary skills for operating with the tool are an integrated part of the interface. Thus, we use the term "interface" in a broader sense than usual to denote not only the border between tool and user (and tool and object), but also the necessary skills for using the tools appropriately. In the following discussion we will give some examples to further clarify our understanding of the term "interface", but before doing so we will introduce the other term, "habitat".

By the term "habitat" we refer to a structured field of activity which acting subjects can inhabit for a shorter or longer time. Among the objects in the habitat are the case to be dealt with, the inhabitants themselves, and their tools, having various affordances (Gibson, 1986) for the inhabitants. The surgical habitat may be "macro", as in the normal world; it may be a microhabitat, made accessible through magnification; or it may be endoscopic, with the surgeon carrying out the operation by means of monocular pipes. Thus for the microsurgical habitat, the case is the patient to be operated on, the inhabitants are the surgical team, and their tools are the microscope and micro-scissors affording magnification and cutting through the interface of these instruments. The affordances hold the functional side of the habitat. But since cognition is situated (Lave and Wenger, 1991), both the case and the affordances will depend on the socio-cultural context of the inhabitants. This context also conditions when and how the process is supposed to unfold within the habitat.

The surgical habitats are very different. In a traditional macroscopic habitat a human body is placed on an operating table in an operating theatre. The surgeon depends upon large volumes of information resembling daily items, e.g. sounds from using suction devices. Furthermore, he manipulates and thus senses organs with fingers and hands and by visually perceiving changes of colour of organ surfaces. This habitat bears close resemblance to daily life. Thus, for instance, palpation of the gut or the liver is similar to handling meat in a butcher's shop. Microsurgery, in contrast, involves the manipulation of small objects, for instance nerves and vessels less than 1 mm in size. With this dramatic change of proportions, the surgeon can no longer automatically rely on skills developed in the macrohabitat. Making a knot in macro-space is like tying your shoestrings – something the surgeon has done successfully for years, but this is not the same as trying to make a knot with micro-instruments and 18-micron thick sutures, which break easily. Therefore, the surgeon needs to make use of visual feedback and not haptic feedback from the suture when tying the knot. Other implications have to do with altered perception. We all know that an aircraft in the sky, though it appears smaller, is in fact much larger than the seagull we see flying above us. The microsurgical habitat lacks definition of sizes, which gives rise to perceptual problems (Drascic and Milgram, 1996). Thus, when the experienced neurosurgeon sees an aneurysm in a microscope, he needs to calculate its true size partly from the MRI demonstrating the aneurysm. This fused visualization is rehearsed as part of the year-long training, with operations performed with the aid of a microscope. The experienced neurosurgeon has learned to function and navigate in this microhabitat.

If the neurosurgeon turns to use endoscopes, for instance in order to visualize an aneurysm, again the situation will be altered completely and new modes of inhabiting (navigating, sensing, judging etc.) must be developed. In doing so, the surgeon makes use of techniques that are very different from perception in daily life (having 3D eyesight) and from techniques employed in the micro-habitat. Endoscopic surgery is performed with a special interface of monocular pipes: so-called endoscopes. Their small size makes it possible to introduce them through small skin incisions/burr holes (the so-called minimal invasive technique). With an endoscope fitted with special surgical tools it is possible to cut and coagulate just as with normal microsurgery. This is making them a fine alternative to traditional surgical tools. However, a consequence is that the surgeon cannot rely on her experiences from her normal habitat when using these instruments. In the endoscopic habitat only monocular vision, and hence 2D perception, is available. In order to determine distances and target sizes the surgeon takes account of the dynamic changes of the sizes of objects in the field while moving around in the habitat. Similarly, in the microhabitat the surgeon is able to exploit the fact that a large magnification, e.g. 16 times, implies that the focal plane has an acuity of less than 1 mm. Hence the blurring of structures outside of the focal plane gives an indication of the relative distances in the field.

Thus, in order to function in new habitats, the surgeon needs to develop a new ways of perception including and a series of hand movements that function as interfaces between the surgeon and the object.

3.2.3 Orchestration of Actions, and Surgical Training

To sum up, microsurgery relies on a large amount of theoretical knowledge concerning pathology, anatomy and surgery techniques. But as we have pointed out, microsurgery also relies heavily on the practical abilities of the surgeon and on the development of certain skills as part of the interface between the surgeon and the object. Surgical performance does not occur independently of the surgical habitat, and we argue that before the necessary skills have been developed for moving around in this habitat, a resident will not have adequate capacities for perceptual judgement in this habitat. The microsurgeon working in spatial habitats uses sophisticated but largely unconscious abilities and sensorimotor skills (Waterworth, 1997). First of all, the microsurgeon ought to have a high degree of dexterity, and ought to have complete sequential control of each of his finger movements, as well as bi-manual coordination. However, there is more to it than this, since all the single acts are carried out in concert within the surgical habitat. Thus, in addition to these abilities, he has to possess the skills of timing the entire sequence of movements with absolute accuracy according to the feedback that he receives in terms of, for example, visual and auditory stimuli in order to orchestrate all the single tasks into a single whole. While simple motor actions may be developed by repetitive performance, the orchestration of more complicated motor skills, including the various coordinated physical or cognitive activities to achieve a goal, has to be trained in the specific habitat.

Thus we argue that the behaviourist and cognitive paradigms of learning have failed to recognize the transaction between an active surgeon and a dynamic habitat. These models have to a large extent conceived of learning in terms of acquiring and storing "fixed quantities" of declarative knowledge and skill units. To illustrate this point: if one wants to learn how to ride a bicycle, it is not sufficient to read a book about it. In medicine these theories and models have focused on motor-skill learning in terms of receiving the necessary information for executing movements (Smith *et al.*, 1998; Grantcharov *et al.*, 2001). Thus within such a paradigm surgical skills are often thought of as being decomposable to their units, such as the single hand movements carried out when punctuating a ventricle in the brain. This understanding has to a certain extent proved beneficial when training specific skills. But it also has its limitations when thinking of surgery as a whole – as an entire activity carried out in an inhabited environment involving a team of specialists.

Figure 3.1 demonstrates the traditional operating microscope and Figure 3.2 depicts a traditional habitat for microsurgery training. The setup for microsurgical training in this example shows a rat positioned under a black box. The micro-suturing is carried out through a hole in this box.

Figure 3.3 shows a microscopic view of an end-to-side anastomosis of the two rat carotid arteries. The vessels are close to 1 mm in diameter. The pulsation of the brain and the brain water (cerebro-spinal fluid) flushing a human brain is not found with this habitat and therefore suturing in the real habitat cannot be perfectly rehearsed with this animal habitat. However, it is evident that the habitats of microsurgery compared to macrosurgery are fundamentally different, thus warranting a different approach to VR development and application.

Effective learning depends on creating the right habitat for learning (e.g. Patrick, 1992; Auer and Auer, 1998; Larsson, 2001a; Shah and Darzi, 2001; Webster *et al.*, 2001; Witzke *et al.*, 2001). Today the surgeons perform in operation theatres, but

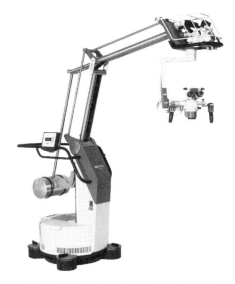

Figure 3.1 Operating microscope (Möller-Wedel).

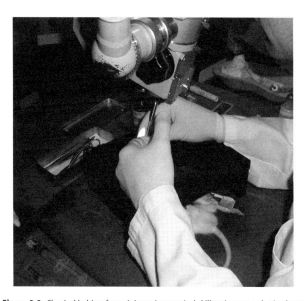

Figure 3.2 Classical habitat for training microsurgical skills using anaesthetized rats.

they train their skills remotely from such a habitat, e.g. in laboratories or at home, reading textbooks. However, the transfer of learning from such contexts to that of the operating theatre may not be as easy as assumed by many medical training programs (Schueneman *et al.*, 1984; Patrick, 1992; McBride, 1998; Shah and Darzi, 2001; Tracey and Lathan, 2001; Moody *et al.*, 2002). We also note that the goal of learning to perform a suture is very seldom clearly defined in surgical programs.

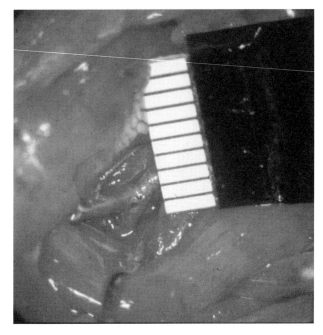

Figure 3.3 End-to-side anastomosis on rat carotid arteries (1 mm diameter).

Nor is the individual potential of the resident to adjust to the new habitat ("abilities" in our terminology) included as input in standard surgical training programs. We do not want to argue that the use of VR as a learning tool is a panacea for all problems relating to the traditional surgical training system, i.e. apprenticeship. However, our basic point is that surgical learning should take place in environments that are as similar to the various surgical habitats as possible. And it is our contention that VR provides the opportunity for the development of such learning environments.

3.3 Developing Microsurgical Skills With VR

VR has been called a tool that allows "broadening our channels of sensation and communication" (Waterworth, 1997). Within microsurgery, VR is to be considered a new medium for the communication of surgical skills. In accordance with our distinction between skills and abilities, VR can be employed to test the essential abilities of a surgical candidate, and (later) to test and train surgical skills in order to orchestrate actions in a new surgical habitat (Kockro *et al.*, 2000; Paisley *et al.*, 2001). Also, rehearsal and testing of human reactions to stress is also possible and supports the medium as a future habitat for learning skills. VR introduces the possibility of creating learning environments that are similar to surgical habitats, but where failures will not lead to human disasters. This is ethically more acceptable in Western society, and it may be cheaper compared with the continued use of animals. And by being an electronic environment, VR makes it possible to track development during training, thus enhancing the opportunities of the trainee to get feedback from supervisors as well as stimulating the self-administered training process. Also, we must not forget that it is fun to play games, and that this might stimulate the learning process.

Laparoscopic surgical learning in a VR scenario has been found to be a simple, effective, valid and relatively cheap alternative to animal models (Reznick *et al.*, 1997; Bardram and Rosenberg, 1999; Rosen *et al.*, 2001; Sue-Lynn *et al.*, 2002). This is supported by the work done on the test bed at the University of San Francisco (Tendick *et al.*, 2000). Validation of VR teaching with the MIST-VR (Minimally Invasive Surgery Training System) laparoscopic simulator showed that experienced surgeons outperformed trainees, and also that using this technique in a course lead to fewer errors (Taffinder *et al.*, 1998; Gallagher 1999). It was found that experienced surgeons performed the tasks significantly faster, with fewer errors and more economy of instrument movement and diathermy, and had greater consistency in their performance. Trainees with higher spatial skills did not respond as positively from training in a simulated environment. In Denmark, Grantcharov *et al.* (2001) also validated MIST-VR by testing skill acquisition and found that there was a positive effect of *in vitro* training with MIST-VR.

The use of VR techniques in the training of microsurgery skills is still experimental (O'Toole *et al.*, 1999; Bruyns *et al.*, 2001; Larsson, 2001a). One of the few VR tools in relation to microsurgery is a system called VIVIAN: "Virtual Intracranial Visualization and Navigation" (Kockro *et al.*, 2000). It is used as a pre-surgical planning device. In this system, data from different imaging techniques (e.g. MRI) are fused and visualized as stereoscopic three-dimensional objects. This enables the user to obtain different views of the tissue on which he or she will subsequently perform an operation. However, to our knowledge there have not been other validated VR tools, and none that have been directly aimed at training microsurgical skills.

The reason for this may be that microsurgery until now has been considered to be macrosurgery in normal 3D space, just with added visual information via microscopic enlargement of structures. This is erroneous since, as indicated earlier, microsurgery is qualitatively different from traditional surgery. Clearly microsurgery has more in common with laparoscopic (endoscopic surgery in the abdominal region) surgery than with, say, orthopaedic surgery. The difference between microsurgery and laparoscopic surgery is largely a matter of interfaces. Thus in the endoscopic habitat there are different tools used, while the tools for microsurgery look like those used for macrosurgery. This similarity is another source of mistake due to the analogy with everyday experience: even though everyone has learned to use scissors as children and these seem similar to the scissors used by the microsurgeon, it takes great practice to use the latter. The scissors used for microsurgery are much smaller than their macrohabitat counterpart, and the microsurgeon visualizes in the microhabitat only the tip of the scissors. The surgeon's hand and the rest of the instrument are obscured from vision and the surgeon must thus learn how the interface here serves as an interface, being an extension of the hand/fingers.

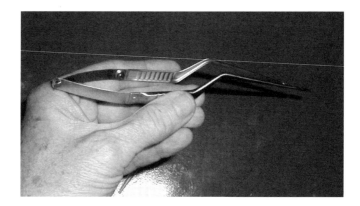

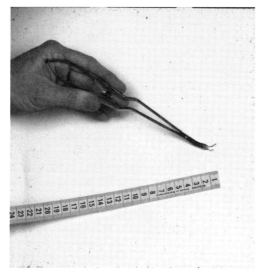

Figure 3.4 Microinstruments and the hand interface. Top: a pair of scissors; bottom: an aneurysm applier.

This is shown in Figure 3.4, where two different instruments are being used for different purposes, cutting and clipping, by the microsurgeon. A significant problem in creating a VR habitat for microsurgery is the importance of the depth of the perceptual field. The position and spatial orientation of an object (e.g. an aneurysm) are important factors in relation to the perception of visual stimuli. When using an operating microscope, the hands and the handles of the instruments leave the stage completely. Peripheral vision is ablated and the microsurgeon has to rely on sounds and position sense to a much larger extent. Communication in the microhabitat is therefore different from that of the macrohabitat.

It is therefore a significant part of the Virtual Brain Project to develop not just the final sophisticated brain model, but to construct, step by step, different habitats in which our individual skills can be developed based on personal abilities. We thus focus not only on the final goal but mainly on the process of reaching this goal in accordance with our Problem-Based Learning paradigm.

3.4 Application – Virtual Brain Project

In this section we will look at the approach and applications developed at Aalborg University concerning microsurgery skill learning in various habitats, including ones supported by VR (`http://www.virtualbrain.auc.dk/`).

The work carried in our research group took its point of origin in the Dextroscope VR system from Virtual Immersion, Singapore (`http://www.volumeinteractions.com/products/product_dextroscope.htm`). This system enables the surgeon to experience the brain visually in 3D and to manipulate it by means of one or two instruments. Thus the system makes it possible to simulate an operation, as with the VIVIAN system mentioned above (Kockro *et al.*, 2000). Our original contention was that using such an instrument would be both economically and technically efficient, i.e. it would result in more skilled neurosurgeons and shorter working hours in the hospital. Another perspective was that the preplanning procedures that are necessary for the use of the device are highly educational and that VR enhances the opportunities for the trainee to be evaluated and controlled by the teacher before an actual operation is carried out. In other words, we aimed at a high degree of interaction. This led to the introduction of haptics in our VR environment in order to create habitats more sophisticated and usable (Haase *et al.*, in press).

3.4.1 Hand–Eye Coordination

The Dextroscope was used for to test the skills of experienced neurosurgeons and student engineers from our university in performing simple tasks in VR such as moving a loop along a wire or hitting balls, either fixed or jumping freely, in a virtual 3D space (Wang, 1999). The first part of the test was the layout of a control puzzle. It was decided to set two difficulty levels because of the potential differences in skills and abilities between the groups of subjects. All participants were right-handed and they performed the task with both hands. This control was followed by a training puzzle involving fixing a static ball to the setup and then placing a moving ball in the puzzle. Finally, the last task was to move the instrument along a string without touching the string with the open instrument, as demonstrated in Figure 3.5.

These studies showed that the performance of a simple Virtual Reality task of hand movement and hand–eye coordination became significantly better after virtual training. Furthermore, it was shown, perhaps not surprisingly given differences in abilities, that neurosurgeons performed significantly better than student engineers.

3.4.2 Haptics

In microsurgery training – whether on animals or VR – haptics has until now been reduced in importance or totally avoided (Bruyns *et al.*, 2001). This is because of the need for high-speed rendering of the visualization and surgical tools (Cotin *et al.*, 2000). However, Moody *et al.* (2002) showed that adding force feedback to vision in

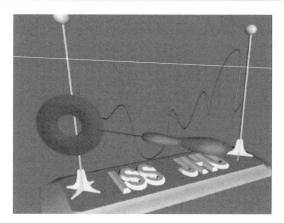

Figure 3.5 The hand–eye coordination experiment.

a standard system, aimed at testing objective surgical performance, reduced the time taken to complete a task of suturing. This study documents the importance of adding haptics as an essential dimension to enhance microsurgical performance.

Haptics feedback has recently been introduced commercially in the ReachIn (Thurfjell, 2001) and LapSim systems (Larsson, 2001b). Small motors determine how much the instrument can be moved in a 3D space volume of $20 \times 18 \times 13$ cm. During the simulation the computer measures how big a force the instrument exercises on the brain surface and estimates how much brain tissue is deformed from the force. Using haptics in a VR system is one of the approaches of the Virtual Brain Project at Aalborg University

The shape and function of the available VR systems that include haptics are not sophisticated enough for our purposes. Our experience tells us that surgeons need to have real instruments in their hands when interacting with virtual items. As part of the Virtual Brain Project (Larsen *et al.*, 2001), a model for an interface for the haptics sensation is being developed called the haptics pen (Figure 3.6(a)).

This tool is changed into the instrument the surgeon needs. But not only is it present in the user's hand for tactile sensation, it is also visualized in space, so that, for example, a brain spatula will both feel and look like such a tool. This is important for the reality of simulation, as surgeons hold instruments in different ways.

Trainees were furthermore tested using haptics to determine the resistance to pushing different boxes, as depicted in Figure 3.6(b). They have to compare and, for example, report which is the harder between two series of boxes. The test results are computerized and kept so that each person can rehearse and monitor progress.

3.4.3 Brain Spatula

In brain surgery it is important to position a brain spatula for the retraction of the brain in order to develop a working space under the brain. This spatula will then transfer pressure to the brain. Lesions of the brain surface, caused by pulling too

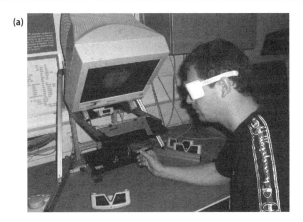

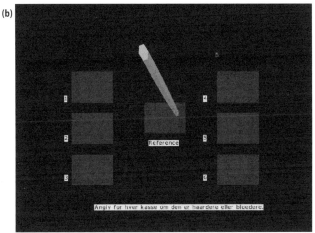

Figure 3.6 (a) Reachln system and test boxes; (b) boxes.

hard, for instance, can easily be detected, but the consequences of a smaller force leading to changes in brain circulation (and later brain death) are not clear. Today the neurosurgeon learns to use a brain spatula by simple observation of the master surgeon. This does not suffice to give a feel for the master's sensing of the spatula as it touches the brain. On the other hand, this can be achieved in virtual space when training for the first time using haptics feedback (as shown in Figure 3.7) (Hansen *et al.*, in press).

3.4.4 Ventricular Puncture

A last example of haptics is virtual ventricular puncturing (Figure 3.8). The puncture of a human ventricle in the brain is a difficult surgical task. It involves visualization of trajectory and sensing of a catheter passing through the brain tissue and reaching the ventricle with great precision. We have developed a VR habitat where both can be learned (Hansen *et al.*, in press).

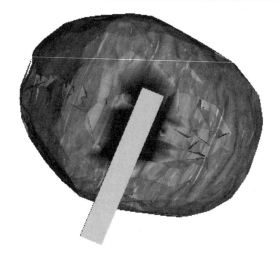

Figure 3.7 A brain spatula in VR.

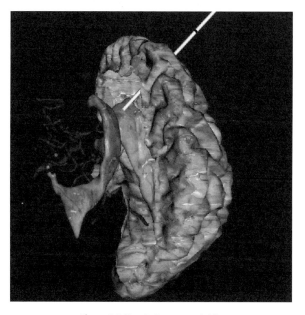

Figure 3.8 Ventricular puncture in VR.

3.5 Discussion

Effective learning depends on creating the right habitat for learning, and it is our contention, based on our work, that this should include the following: the novice microsurgeon must receive verbal instructions and view direct demonstrations through real or virtual habitats, with the opportunity to practise and receive feedback on performance. An example of a real macrohabitat from a normal operating theatre is seen in Figure 3.9, and the habitat for performing a minimal invasive surgical procedure using the operating microscope is shown in Figure 3.10.

VR can serve as a tool for enhancing such a practice, for example when performing in a Cave. Through VR, the trainee can learn to manipulate real instruments with fake virtual objects. This may train hand–eye coordination, for example, but more importantly it may support telelearning, where learning is no longer confined to a single habitat such as the operation room in a hospital. In such a scenario, it is

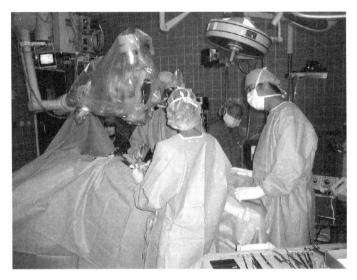

Figure 3.9 A macrohabitat – the normal operating theatre.

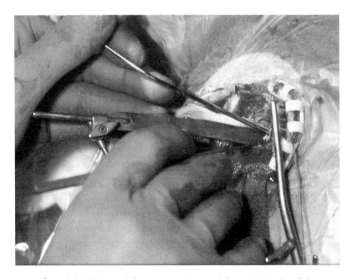

Figure 3.10 Microsurgical setup – operation carried out via a 2 cm burr hole.

possible to import data such as images from operating procedures by experts at any time in order to support the trainees, make decisions etc. The importing of "test operations" performed by senior neurosurgeons also includes the possibility of rehearsal on "mistakes", just like in popular computer games. Thus by means of VR the surgeon can learn new procedures or rehearse already learned ones. However, the ramifications of using VR are not purely pedagogical, but also beneficial for the patient: using imaging data in simulations allows detailed exploration of data and thereby possible surgical interventions with minimal harm to the patient.

There are limitations, however, to using VR in microsurgery (Arnold and Farrel, 2002; Tracey, 2001). Taking the example of performing a microsurgical operation in a virtual habitat, in such a situation the surgeon will of course be aware that she is not operating in a real surgical habitat. Thus if a catastrophic reaction, such as a bleeding, is created in VR, this complication does not transfer to the real world in terms of human consequences (Haase, 2003). This is the whole point of training with VR, but it may mean that a VR habitat can never fully replace real habitats. VR may merely teach the possibility of something happening (e.g. complications) and lead to virtual developed experiences that surgeons today cannot adopt in real life due to lack of operating procedures. While VR is an important tool for developing surgical skills, its effectiveness is based on the operative space as something that emerges from the way in which humans perceive or live in their environment. VR cannot replace the surgical habitat as a learning habitat.

Learning in general is said to be tied to the motivation of the subject (Hedegaard, 1995). Surgical games in VR, focusing on problems and thus creating projects, increase the awareness and enthusiasm for learning. Learning in a VR habitat is therefore interactive and not merely passive transmission of knowledge. Furthermore, learning in a VR habitat lacks the stressed atmosphere found in the operating theatre and is therefore an optimal educational environment for the novice surgeon (O'Toole et al., 2001; Gallagher, 1999). Another feature of VR teaching is that in the normal surgical training programs the surgeon rehearses at random based on a time-based system. Here some trainees devote significant time in their education, whereas others will rely on merely passively receiving the types of tasks and skills that experienced surgeons demonstrate. Here it should be repeated that these tasks and skills are not easily defined, verbalized or institutionalized: there is no strict personal plan for developing surgical skills and absolutely no information within the training on the rôles that different habitats give us. It is fairly easy to describe how to make a strategy for an operation, e.g. how one should be handling a forceps during the procedure, where the difficult parts of the operation are and where the possibilities of errors are high.

The special skills of a brain surgeon overlap only partly with the skills of the laparoscopic surgeon, demonstrating the differences in training perspectives. To learn to use material tools requires what have already been introduced as "technical skills". These skills relate mostly to motor skills, such as tying knots and cutting, but abilities (mentally representing the organ) were also included and discussed in the previous section. Thus it is of great benefit to devise methods for more efficient ways to acquire or refine these specific surgical skills. However, is it necessary to learn the skills in the operating habitat or can part or all these skills be rehearsed in other habitats, including virtual habitats? Can we observe movements as part of hand–eye coordination and rehearse only parts of these movements and still obtain a better function?

3.6 Conclusion

In this chapter an attempt has been made to improve on our present understanding of instructing and training surgical skills by using a timelier paradigm for understanding learning, including VR techniques. By this we do not wish to throw ordinary apprenticeship overboard. No doubt apprenticeship will still be the dominant means of teaching microsurgeons, since it is a habitat with which surgeons are familiar. But simply to learn by mistakes made when operating on patients is not ethical. Within a few years microsurgery will be learned through simulation because it is ethical, safe, scientifically validated and amenable to rehearsal, thus being linked with the surgeon as an object linked to motivation. Training must be moved from the traditional system of feeding information to the trainee towards an interactive IT system where motivating tasks and projects facilitate learning.

The performance of a surgeon is closely linked with socio-cultural variables different from just moving two fingers; performance depends on variables such as the personality of the surgeon and ethics. It is well known that pilots are tested for abilities and psychological behaviour before introduced into a training program. Why not do the same with microsurgeons through VR? Individual differences in surgeons (e.g. in terms of dexterity and mental imagery) should be taken into account, but interpreted with caution in order to be used as heuristics for predicting surgical performance.

There is still a long way to go before VR is standard in teaching, training and testing surgical skills (Apuzzo, 2001; Arnold and Farrel, 2002). This chapter is intended partly to bridge this gap. The focus of the chapter is on VR as a means of teaching and learning surgical skills. The chapter points to the limitations in current conceptualizations of learning, within both VR and traditional surgery. Like Faust in the opening quotation, we may strive towards better tools and better operations, but we cannot actually afford to make mistakes; particularly not since these could be avoided. While a plea is made in this chapter that training with VR of microsurgical skills used in inhabited worlds is possible, many questions remain unanswered:

• How much is gained when using VR compared with real-life simulations?
• Given that individual abilities constitute an important factor for surgical performance, how can this variable be introduced in VR training tools?
• What mechanisms are involved in learning microsurgery through VR?

These questions, however, do not alter our contention that VR is an important training habitat in the future. A test bed for microsurgery should be flexible, i.e. it should be possible to change and thus simulate the macrohabitat of the surgeon. Such a habitat can be adapted to our purposes, whether we intend to plan surgery, rehearse or develop surgical skills, or operate or evaluate operations. With VR we can build up a habitat for training and customizing it to the user: is the user an inexperienced medical student or surgeon or the experienced master? Such considerations may give raise not only to assignments with varying levels of difficulty, but also to qualitatively different tasks. Given such requirements and aspirations, VR, with the almost endless possibility of introducing new sounds, new views etc., seems very promising. But in order to test and develop skills in using micro-instruments, for instance, we are faced with certain basic requirements. Such a VR system should be realistic in comparison to the microsurgical habitat. This poses demands with regard to visualization (e.g. tissue deformation, visual rendering) and manipulation (real-time response and haptics feedback when interacting with tools and tissue/bone structure). The surgeon who thinks he can carry out a microsurgical procedure just by grabbing the microscope and the entire toolkit of micro-instruments has not understood this particular habitat and fatal consequences may follow. Introducing VR as a training tool cannot in itself alleviate this problem, but may act in concert with other means of learning, such as observing in real-world habitats. The training of micro-surgeons is too important an issue not to try to solve by aspiring (like Faust or otherwise) and possibly acting out of a limited knowledge base.

References

Adams, J. A. (1987) Historical review and appraisal of research on the learning, retention, and transfer of human motor skills. *Psychological Bulletin*, 101, 41–74.

Apuzzo, M. L. J. (1996) Schneider Lecture: new dimensions of neurosurgery in the realm of high technology – possibilities, practicalities, realities. *Neurosurgery*, 38, 625–639.

Apuzzo, M. L. J. and Liu, C. Y. (2001) Things to come. *Neurosurgery*, 49, 765–778.

Arnold, P. and Farrel, M. J. (2002) Can Virtual Reality be used to measure and train surgical skills? Ergonomics, 45, 362–79

Auer, L. M. and Auer, D. P. (1998) Virtual endoscopy for planning and control of minimally invasive neurosurgery. *Neurosurgery*, 43, 529–548.

Bardram, L. and Rosenberg, J. (1999) Assessment of surgeons' operative skills. *Ugeskr Læg*, 161, 5518.

Barnes, R. W. (1987) Surgical handicraft, teaching and learning surgical skills. *Am. J. Surg.*, 153, 422–427.

Bruyns, C., Montgomery, K. and Wildermuth, S. (2001) A virtual environment for simulated rat dissection. *Studies in Health Technology and Informatics*, 81, 75–81.

Cotin, S., Delingette, H. and Ayache, N. (2000) A hybrid elastic model allowing real-time cutting, deformations and force-feedback for surgery training and simulation. *The Visual Computer*, 16, 437–452.

Drascic, D. and Milgram, P. (1996) Perceptual issues in augmented reality. *Stereoscopic Displays and Virtual Reality Systems III*, San Jose, February. SPIE Volume 2653: 123–134.

Eyal, R. and Tendick, F. (2001) Spatial ability and learning: the use of an angled laparoscope in a virtual environment. *Studies in Health Technology and Informatics*, 81, 146–152.

Fleishman, E. and Quaintance, M. (1984) *Taxonomies of Human Performance: The Description of Human Tasks*. Orlando, FL: Academic Press.

Gallagher, A. (1999) Virtual reality training. *Endoscopy*, 31, 310–313.

Gibson, J. J. (1986) *The Ecological Approach to Visual Perception*. Hillsdale, NJ: Lawrence Erlbaum Associates.

Grantcharov, T. P., Bardram, L., Funch-Jensen, P. and Rosenberg, J. (2001) Laparoscopic performance after one night on call in a surgical department: prospective study. *BMJ*, 323, 1222–1223.

Granum, E. and Musaeus, P. (2002) Constructing virtual environments for visual explorers. In Qvortrup, L. (ed.) *Virtual Space Spatiality in Virtual Inhabited 3D Worlds*. London: Springer-Verlag.

Haase, J. (1999) Image guided surgery/neuronavigation/SurgiScope – a reflexion on a theme. *Minimal Invasive Neurosurgery*, 42, 53–59.

Haase, J. (in press) Experimental laboratories – organization and importance for microsurgical education. *EANS Congress Proceedings 2003*. Monduzzi Publishers.

Haase, J., Hansen, K. V., Pedersen, C. F. and Brix, L. (in press) Brain spatula training in virtual reality. *Surgical Neurology*.

Hansen, K. V., Brix, L., Pedersen, C. F., Haase, J. P. and Larsen, O.V. (in press) Modeling of interaction between a spatula and a human brain. *Medical Image Analysis*.

Hedegaard, M. (1995) *Tænkning, viden, udvikling. [Thinking, Knowledge, Development]*. Århus: Aarhus Universitetsforlag.

Kaptelinin, V. (1996) Activity theory: implications for human–computer interaction. In Nardi, B. (ed.) *Context and Consciousness: Activity Theory and Human–Computer Interaction*. Cambridge, MA: MIT Press.

Kockro, R. A., Serra, L., Tseng-Tsai, Y., Chan, C., Yih-Yian, S., Gim-Guan, C., Lee, E., Hoe, L. Y., Hern, N. and Nowinski, W. L. (2000) Planning and simulation of neurosurgery in a virtual reality world. *Neurosurgery*, 46, 118-137.

Larsen, O. V., Haase, J., Østergaard, L. R., Hansen, K. V. and Nielsen, H. (2001) The virtual brain project – development of a neurosurgical simulator. *Studies in Health Technology and Informatics*, 81, 256-262.

Larsson, A. (2001a) An open and flexible framework for computer aided surgical training. *Studies in Health Technology and Informatics*, 81, 263-265.

Larsson, A. (2001b) Intracorporal suturing and knot tying in surgical simulation. *Studies in Health Technology and Informatics*, 81, 266-271.

Lave, J. and Wenger, E. (1991) *Situated Learning. Legitimate Peripheral Participation*. New York: Cambridge University Press.

Lazar, H. (1989) Clinical performance versus in-training examinations as measures of surgical competence. *Surgery*, 87, 357-362.

McBride, D. K. (1998) Individual differences in the performance of highly learned skill. *Perceptual Motor Skills*, 86, 985-986.

McDonald, J. M. (1993) Mental Readiness and its Links to Performance Excellence in Surgery. Ottawa: Kinetek.

Moody, L., Arvanis, T. N. and Baber, C. (2002) Objective surgical performance evaluation based on haptic feedback. *Course Syllabus MMVR*, pp. 111-112.

O'Toole, R., Playter, R., Krummel, T., Blank, W., Cornelius, N., Roberts, W., Bell, W. and Raibert, M. (1999) Measuring and developing suturing technique with a virtual reality surgical simulator. *J. Am. Coll. Surg.*, 189, 127-128.

Paisley, A. M., Baldwin, P. J. and Paterson-Brown, S. (2001) Validity of surgical simulation for the assessment of operative skill. *Br. J. Surg.*, 88, 1575-1532.

Pascual-Leone, A., Dang, N., Chohen, L. G., Brasil-Neto, J. P., Cammarota, A. and Hallett, M. (1995) Modulation of muscle responses evoked by trancranial magnetic stimulation during the acquisition of new fine motor skills. *J. Neurophysiology*, 74, 1037-1045.

Patrick, J. (1992) *Training: Research and Practice*. London: Academic Press.

Reznick, R., Regehr, G., MacRae, H., Martin, J. and McCulloch, W. (1997) Testing technical skill via an innovative "bench station" technique. *Am. J. Surg.*, 173, 226-230.

Rosen, J., Solazzo, M., Hannford, B. and Sinanan, M. (2001) Objective laparoscopic skills assessments for surgical residents using hidden Markov models based on haptic information and tool/tissues interactions. *Medicine Meets Virtual Reality. Outer Space, Inner Space, Virtual Spaces*. ISO Press Inc., pp. 417-423.

Ryle, G. (1949) *The Concept of Mind*. London: Hutchinson.

Schueneman, A. L., Pickleman, J., Hesslein, R. and Freeark, R. J. (1984) Neuropsychologic predictors of operative skill among general surgery residents. *Surgery*, 96, 288-295.

Scott, M. W., Johnson, J. A., Ellison, E. C. (1996) Laparoscopic skills enhancement. *Am. J. Surg.*, 172, 377-379.

Seehusen, A., Brett, P. N. and Haarison, A. (2001) Human perception of haptic information in minimal access surgery tools for use in simulation. *Studies in Health Technology and Informatics*, 81, 453-458.

Shah, J. and Darzi, A. (2001) Surgical skills assessment: an ongoing debate. *BJU International*, 88, 655-660.

Smith, C. D., Stubbs, J. and Hananel, D. (1998) Stimulation technology in surgical education: can we assess manipulative skills and what does it mean to the learner? In S. J. Weghorst, J. D. Westwood, D. Stredney and H. M. Hoffman (eds.) *Medicine Meets Virtual Reality*. Amsterdam: IOS Press and Ohmsha, pp. 379-380.

Sue-Lynn, W., Keehner, M., Hwang, J., Wong, D. and Tendick, F. (2002) Spatial ability and laparoscopic pointing movements. *Course Syllabus MMVR* 02/10, pp. 181–182.

Taffinder, N., Sutton, C., Fishwick, R. J., McManus, I. C. and Darzi, A. (1998) Validation of virtual reality to teach and assess psychomotor skills in laparoscopic surgery. In S. J. Weghorst, J. D. Westwood, D. Stredney and H. M. Hoffman (eds.) *Medicine Meets Virtual Reality*. Amsterdam: IOS Press and Ohmsha, pp. 124–130.

Taffinder, J., Russels, R. C. G., McManus, I. C., Jansen, J. and Darzi, A. (1998) An objective assessment of surgeons's psychomotor skills: validation of the MIST-VR laparoscopic simulator. *Br. J. Surg.*, 85(suppl), 75.

Tendick, F., Downes, M., Goktekin, T., Cavusoglu, M. C., Feygin, D., Wu, X., Eyal, R., Hegarty, M. and Way, L. W. (2000) A virtual environment testbed for training laparoscopic surgical skills. *Presence*, 9, 236–255.

Thurfjell, L., Lundin, A. and McLaughlin, J. (2001) A medical platform for simulation of surgical procedures. *Studies in Health Technology and Informatics*, 81, 509–514.

Tracey, M. R. and Lathan, C. E. (2001) The interaction of spatial ability and motor learning in the transfer of training from a simulator to a real task. *Studies in Health Technology and Informatics*, 81, 521–527.

Waldron, E. M. Jr and Anton, B. S. (1995) Effect of exercise on dexterity. *Perceptual and Motor Skills*, 80, 883–889.

Wang, H. (1999) *Dexterity training function of 3D virtual reality workbench*. Project 1072, Spring, Aalborg University, Dept Health Science and Technology.

Waterworth, J. A. (1997) Personal spaces: 3D spatial worlds for information exploration, organization and communication. In *The Internet in 3D*. London: Academic Press, pp. 97–118.

Webster, R. W., Zimmerman, D. I., Mohler, B. J., Melkonian, M. G. and Haluck, R. S. (2001) A prototype haptic suturing simulator. *Medicine Meets Virtual Reality*. In S. J. Weghorst, J. D. Westwood, D. Stredney and H. M. Hoffman (eds.) *Medicine Meets Virtual Reality*. Amsterdam: IOS Press and Ohmsha, pp. 567–569.

Witzke, D. B., Hoskins, J. D., Mastrangelo, M. J., Witzke, W. O., Chu, U. B., Pande, S. and Park, A. E. (2001) Immersive virtual reality used as a platform for perioperative training for surgical residents. In S. J. Weghorst, J. D. Westwood, D. Stredney and H. M. Hoffman (eds.) *Medicine Meets Virtual Reality*. Amsterdam: IOS Press and Ohmsha, pp. 577–558.

Theatrical Virtuality – Virtual Theatricality

Virtual Narrative, Autonomous Agents and Interactivity in a Dramaturgical Perspective

Niels Lehmann and Janek Szatkowski

4.1 Introduction

This article is about a farm – a *virtual* farm, to be precise. Here, a farmer lives together with his cow and a few other animals. He and his cow don't see eye to eye on many things. In fact, they are involved in a continuous domestic drama. The farmer likes order and wants the cow to be in its shed. Unfortunately, the cow likes freedom and tries to escape whenever the farmer has caught it. As the two antago-nists are equally stubborn, the conflict can go on forever. This farm, with its ongoing conflicts, came into being because of a research project sponsored by the EEC. The aim of the project was to investigate what it takes to construct a virtual puppet theatre. As dramaturges our rôle in the project was first and foremost to work out scenarios that would work in a computer-based theatre.

When we started the virtual puppet theatre project, certain decisions concerning the premises of the work had already been made. Firstly, it was decided that the puppet theatre should involve *a virtual 3D space* in which it should be possible to manoeuvre (almost) as freely as we do in the real world. Secondly, autonomous agents should inhabit this space, i.e. there should be characters like beings in a virtual world (such as the farmer and his cow) with whom it should be possible to interact in real time. For the record we should probably mention that it was, in fact, a research interest in the problems involved in the construction of autonomous agents that led to the idea of a virtual puppet theatre. It was hoped that the use of such agents could open the doors to an interesting form of interaction. As opposed to the puppets of a *real* puppet theatre, the puppets in a *virtual* theatre may possess the ability to talk back at their puppeteers. Thirdly, the project should allow for an interaction with the autonomous agents via *an avatar,* i.e. your representation within the virtual world. Added to these three premises regarding the particulars of the technology involved there was also an overall premise concerning the aim of the project. Thus we were faced with the demand to make the virtual puppet theatre worthwhile as a useful tool for *early learning.*

In Chapter 5, Claus Madsen outlines the technical rationale behind the construction of the virtual puppet theatre. Here, we take the opportunity to present some of the dramaturgical thinking that governed our attempt to come up with aesthetically satisfying solutions to the problems inherent in virtual histrionics. In doing so we hope to arouse the interest of a double audience. On the one hand we would like to address drama teachers who may have wondered whether computers could be turned into a useful tool in drama. On the other hand, we have computer engineers and multimedia developers who are engaged in developing inhabited virtual worlds in mind as addressees.

To *drama teachers* we would like to suggest that virtual theatricality is in fact a worthwhile endeavor to be pursued. By displaying our experiences with the creation of a virtual puppet theatre we hope to show how drama in education may be a useful tool for understanding and developing interactive computer programs. We have also seen that this use of theory of drama in education has forced us to reconsider and reconstruct central concepts. Finally, we have had a glimpse of a future where drama in education may also benefit from the use of improvisations within a virtual theatre as yet another creative method. We believe that inhabited virtual worlds have a potential that has yet to be investigated. As far as we can see, this potential may even be harvested without changing much of the mental make-up that informs our regular practice radically.

To *computer engineers* we would like to suggest that a dramaturgical approach to the construction of inhabited virtual worlds might prove beneficial. Not only is it possible to establish a paradigm for thinking about interaction from the rationale of the improvisational branch of theatre in education that we have employed in our project. More generally, we believe that a dramaturgical approach to thinking about autonomous agents, as well as the fragile relationship between emergent activity and causal storytelling, may help us avoid some of the problems that otherwise may seem inevitable. In fact, we shall argue that, in general, the theory of interactive narratives would gain a lot from giving the way of thinking *a dramaturgical turn.*

In the next section we shall argue that a particularly relevant form of theatre to be used as a model when constructing inhabited virtual worlds is *the improvisational form of drama in education.* Furthermore, we shall point out the most important consequences of this choice of model. In Section 4.3 we address the difficulties involved in making the narrative interesting enough when it has to allow for interaction with autonomous agents whose actions are supposed to be emergent. We shall argue that, seen from a dramaturgical perspective, some *cheating* may prove the best way to obtain the desired effects. In Section 4.4 we offer a dramaturgical approach to thinking about autonomous agents. Here, our main objective is to overcome what might be called the *mimetic fallacy* inherent in making agents too much in the image of man. To argue our case we have found it beneficial to discuss the view of autonomous agents presented by Christopher Kline and Bruce Blumberg. Section 4.5 contains an outline of the attempt to create a rationale of interaction based on improvisational drama in education. For this purpose we have elaborated on the idea of *a dialectic between I and me* originally suggested by the British drama theoretician Gavin Bolton. Finally, Section 4.6 presents a summary.

4.2 The Virtual Puppet Theatre as Computerized Drama in Education

To a dramaturge the aforementioned premises suggest that a certain type of theatre is called for. To be specific, we have in mind a particular improvisational branch of the thing called *drama in education*. This form of theatre is best described by evoking a certain distinction. In contrast with "ordinary" theatre, which is produced by professionals *for* a (rather passive) audience, educational drama is in its essence theatre *with* an (inevitably active) audience, or perhaps we should rather say with a group of *participants*. When everybody participates in the production of the theatrical illusion, there are no spectators any more. Thus, inherent in the distinction between *with* and *for* is also a distinction between *active participants* and *passive spectators*. To be sure, the history of theatre has seen many different attempts at participatory theatre. It is, however, important to acknowledge a crucial difference between two diametrically opposed versions of the attempt to involve the audience directly in the action.

4.2.1 Participatory Theatre

Many of the theatre people working with participatory theatre have not merely opted for a breakdown of the separation of the actors on the stage from the audience in the auditorium. Often they have also pressed for a transgression of the distinction between fiction and reality. Augusto Boal is probably the most evident example of this tendency. He invented a form of theatre which he called the *invisible theatre* (Boal, 1980). In this theatre only the actors know that there is in fact an element of fiction at work. As he was aiming for political results, he believed that theatre should provoke people to start taking politics seriously in a very concrete way. Consequently, he suggested that actors should rehearse simple conflicts that might be performed as if they were for real, and then perform these small scenarios in public spaces. Imagine, for instance, that you would like people to get seriously involved in the issue of how we treat handicapped people. A furious conflict between an allegedly handicapped man in a wheelchair and an allegedly busy businessman should probably do the trick. If, say, the man in the wheelchair maximizes the difficulties with which he tries to enter a bus, and the businessman who is already inside the bus scorns him while demanding that the timetables be kept, the situation is bound to provoke a fierce response from some of the regular bus travellers. In an event like this the "spectators" do not know that the actors are in fact acting. Because they are given no clues that suggest otherwise, they can only believe that they are witnessing an authentic event from real life. This absence of knowledge of what is really going on is actually the *sine qua non* of the invisible theatre. Only in so far as the "spectators" do not suspect that there are any histrionics involved in the event will they respond with the proper moral indignation.

An early performance by *The Living Theatre* provides another example of participatory theatre aimed at overcoming the distinction between reality and fiction. In *Paradise Now* the theatre group invited the audience to participate in making love on stage with the actors and other spectators (things were different in those days...). As opposed to the invisible theatre of Boal, there is no element of manipulation at work in this strategy, which was developed in order to actualize paradise here and now. There is definitely an element of mass suggestion, but in so far as the individual spectator decides consciously whether or not he or she wants to accept the "invitation", there is no manipulation. Nevertheless, the strategy of *The Living Theatre* results in merging fiction and reality no less than the invisible theatre of Boal. After all, an active participation in a performance like *Paradise Now* demands a rather real activity: copulating in public. If Boal wants to bring the stage to the public space, *The Living Theatre* aims at bringing the public onto the stage while at the same time transforming the acting from fictitious to real actions (*The Living Theatre*, 1971).

We imagine that both of these strategies are applicable to virtual worlds. A lot of invisible theatre is probably already going on in "places" like chat rooms. It seems reasonable to believe, for instance, that a fair share of acting that is only recognized as such by the "actor" is involved in Net-based dating. Who can resist the possibility of appearing "larger than life", which is offered by the bodiless presence on the Net? To us the parallel to the invisible theatre of Boal is striking, even if the purpose of the covert acting here is of an erotic rather than a political nature. For the very same reason that virtuality seems to favour the ends of Boal, the strategy of *The Living Theatre* seems harder to transform to a virtual setting. As much as the absence of the body proves an excellent means for disguising yourself, it makes it hard to obtain a reality that can match that of a public sex orgy. Work by the performance artist Stellarc suggests, however, that a strategy in line with the performances of *The Living Theatre* may be dreamed up. The point in a piece like *Ping Body*, in which Stellarc is hooked up to the Net, thus allowing hits on various homepages to make his body move involuntarily, seems to be that the movements on the net can be made to have real consequences for Stellarc's body. (cf. `http://www.stelarc.va.com.au/pingbody/`).

4.2.2 Drama in Education

Now, the form of participatory theatre that seemed best suited for our purposes is equally opposed to the strategies followed by Boal and *The Living Theatre*. In drama in education it is paramount to maintain the distinction between illusion and reality. Whereas the wish to overcome the illusion is founded on the feeling that art should wake us up and make us *face* reality, drama in education is founded on a belief in the prosperous effect of dreaming. Here, the creation of fictive situations is precisely used in order to *suspend* the pressures of reality. The element of fiction is believed to allow for certain experimental investigations that the participants would probably never dare to undertake in real life. Thus, drama in education may be a prime example of what Ziehe and Stubenrauch once called "unusual learning processes" (Stubenrauch and Ziehe, 1982).

With all due respect to this common denominator, it should be noted that there are many forms of drama in education. As a matter of fact, a distinction very similar to the distinction between a theatre *for* an audience and a theatre *with* a group of participants tends to surface in much debate about aims and means in this form of theatre. The unspoken truism is almost always that it is all about participation. In spite of this common understanding, much heated debate arises when teachers start discussing whether the participation should be seen in the light of the *director's* work or rather in the light of the *actor's* work. In one camp, the interlocutors argue that the aim of drama in education should be the making of theatre productions that come as close to "real" performances as possible. In other words, they want the participators to construct theatre of the kind that we have called theatre for an audience. This view often leads to a rather *cool* kind of participation. As everything is oriented towards the creation of an aesthetically satisfying montage, participation means finding a proper order in the material at hand. If any theatre is to come of the efforts, some of the participants will have to work as actors, of course, but their experience of being somebody else is subordinated to the process of finding an adequate expression. On the other hand, interlocutors from the other camp think in terms of experience. Consequently, they focus on letting the participants play different rôles, i.e. behave like actors. For them, drama in education is not about creating neat wannabe performances. On the contrary, the real aim is to facilitate what has become known as *a living-through-experience*. The reason for this choice of a purely experiential form of drama is to be found in the belief that profound insight is best obtained if you go beyond the purely theoretical level of understanding and advance to the bodily level of (gut) feeling (cf. a telling title from the seventies, *The Intelligence of Feeling*: Witkin, 1974). Thus, teachers in this camp go for a more *heated* kind of participation than the detached form called for by the other camp.

This opposition is often summarized with the help of the distinction between one kind of drama in education, oriented towards the product, and another oriented towards the process. However, we find this description of the opposed camps rather misleading. On the one hand no good performances will appear if you do not take an interest in optimizing the process. On the other hand, it is no less necessary to create aesthetically satisfying illusions in order to establish a worthwhile living-through-experience than it is to consider the formal aspect when you want to produce a full-scale performance. This is why we find it more adequate to describe the opposition as a split between a form that favours the detached participation of the director dealing with the illusion from the outside and a form that favours the direct involvement of the actor experiencing and creating the material from the inside of a fictive framework.

We take pains to unravel the two basic forms of drama in education because we have experienced the need to draw the distinction adequately when we were to make use of concepts from this field for the purpose of constructing a virtual puppet theatre. It is easy to realize that constructors of computer games are facing a choice that is quite similar to the choice of the drama teacher. As the latter needs to consider the rôle of the participant, the former must decide whether the user of a particular computer program should be placed in the position of a director or as a fellow actor. As in drama in education, it is a matter of how far the limits of the illusion should be stretched. If you limit it to the surface of the screen, the user is excluded from the direct action. If, on the other hand, the illusion includes the user (for instance via an avatar), he or she is forced to partake directly. The producers of applications like, for instance, *3D Movie Maker* (Microsoft, 1996) have bet on the first possibility. As a director you watch what is going on from a distance and intervene by altering the prerequisites for the action. This leads basically to an *offline* form of interaction, as the user (working as a director) has to address the actors when they are *out of play* while refraining from doing so when they are *in play*. In contrast to this, creators of any game of the *shoot 'em up* type have chosen the latter option. The fascination of these games undoubtedly stems from the fact that you participate as a fellow actor at the same level as the constructed agents. In other words, the user interacts directly in an *online* mode.

We find no reason to valorize one of these forms over the other. It may be equally interesting to pose as a director as it is to become involved as an actor. We are only trying to underline the fact that one of the two options has to be chosen. This is important because the choice is ripe with consequences. In so far as we were to create a virtual puppet theatre with a potential for early learning, we could have chosen to go in both directions. Considering the premises concerning the technical issues of our project, however, we found that we had to opt for the improvisational form of educational drama. For starters, navigating in a 3D space implies that the user should partake directly in a fictional universe. As opposed to a 2D image, a virtual 3D landscape which can be investigated as if you were walking in a forest produces a feeling of *being-there* that seems to match the experience of being on stage. With the decision to add an avatar this feeling is enforced significantly. As it gives the user an *alter ego,* it immediately places him or her in the position of an actor.

All things being equal, the knockdown argument for choosing the improvisational form of drama in education as the matrix for our work came from the decision to fill the virtual world with autonomous agents. A director has no use for autonomous agents capable of acting on their own behalf. Like a puppeteer, she needs controllable characters that do what the script tells them to do. For her, dealing with autonomous agents would be like trying to control Pinocchio *after* he has come alive. Having established a scene with the help of, say, *3D Movie Maker*, you don't want the characters to rush out in any direction that they find interesting themselves. On the contrary, you want them to act according to your guidelines. If participating in an improvisation as a fellow performer, on the other hand, you want the autonomous agents to do surprising things that beg a reaction from you. Without impulses from the other participants an improvisation is no fun at all. As far as direct improvisation is concerned, raising the level of the agent's autonomy from the simple level of "I wanna get you" known from *shoot 'em up* games would only seem to enhance the fun.

In principle, anything can be used as material for an improvisation in drama in education. In practice, however, there will almost always be a drama for the participants and another drama for the teacher. Basically, the interest of the participants (especially if they happen to be children) is to have as much fun as possible, but normally the teacher will have other objectives in sight. Concerned with optimizing the learning potential of an improvisational session, he or she will tend to produce some sort of resistance to the absolutely free flow of the improvisation. From the teacher's point of view the speed at which an improvisation unfolds will often have to be slowed down if the participants are to investigate the situation more thoroughly. In other words, the teacher finds him- or herself trying to find ways of framing the improvisation, i.e. setting up limits for what can take place in the improvisation. Of course, this control over the improvisation may be performed *from the outside* by deciding the premises in advance or by altering these along the way. However, control can also be established *from the inside* with the help of a device that has become known as *teacher in rôle*.

4.2.3 Teacher in Rôle

Consider the ordinary situation of a teacher in a classroom (or for that matter an auditorium at a university). This situation relies on a very distinct distribution of rôles. The teacher is supposed to be the active part in control of what is going on, whereas the pupils (or students) are cast in the rôle of passive listeners. The teacher may use different pedagogical tools (like a blackboard or an overhead projector) and to a certain degree the pupils may become actively involved in a discussion with the teacher, but this does not alter the distribution of rôles significantly. The pupils are only supposed to get involved in the issues raised by the teacher. Talking about, say, soccer in the middle of a class on physics would most certainly be considered inappropriate. It goes without saying that this frame is heavily supported by the traditional scenography of schools: the blackboard situated at one end of the space behind the teacher's desk and the many chairs behind desks facing the teacher for the pupils and so forth.

This frame is easily transformed, however. Imagine that as a teacher you ask the class to take part in a small experiment and then you leave the room. On re-entering the room in slightly different clothing (another jacket, a pair of glasses etc.), you may say something like: "I'm happy that you are all here. As you have probably all guessed by now, I have asked you to hold a meeting this morning because of the tragic events that took place yesterday evening at the prom. I must inform you that the police are on their way. As the principal of this school I need to know exactly what took place yesterday evening. Who, for instance, had the keys to the sports area?". Because the teacher has taken on a rôle, the situation has been changed completely. Note, however, that because of the choice of a character with a higher rank than the rest of the group, the teacher is still in control of the situation. With a group of people with substantial experience with this kind of theatre this trick might not be needed. With an inexperienced group it probably is.

No matter which rôle is chosen, the point is that "the audience" has now been asked to partake more actively in the creation of a fictional universe. From now on the teacher will have to take any suggestion from "the auditorium" seriously as a contribution to the development of the narrative. If dealing with an inexperienced group of people, you will often see people showing small signs of discomfort, such as looking down or giggling. A good way of dealing with these types of reaction is to make them relate to the illusion. If somebody giggles, you may say, for instance: "You might find this funny, Miss Thompson, but I am sure that you will stop giggling when you have to face the police.... By the way, where were you yesterday evening?". Nobody can tell precisely how the drama will develop, but at the same time the opening contains enough clues to create a fragile framework. We know already that this improvisation takes place in a school. From the opening remark we also know that something terrible has happened; as the police are involved, we may even be faced with a crime. Finally, we can take it for granted that the school principal is a key figure in the action. As prescribed, for instance, by Viola Spolin (1983), the teacher has established the *where*, *what* and *who* of the improvisation.

4.2.4 Improvisation as Open-Endedness Within a Frame

Improvisation means "not foreseen". Thus, in an improvisation the actions of the participators are not supposed to be pre-scripted and rehearsed. To improvise is like walking backwards. You can see where you have been walking, but you don't know exactly where you are going. To improvise is to play. Like children's play, improvisation is based on a suspension of the need to have a single rationally determined aim and a suspension of disbelief as well (Buytendijk, 1933). An improvisation will only be kept alive in so far as the participators feed in interesting and surprising impulses. Thus it depends on each participant's ability to take initiatives and accept the impulses from the fellow improvisers. Only if everybody accepts the give-and-take situation, will the significance of the improvisation build accumulatively.

It follows from this that theatrical improvisation is open-ended. It would be wrong to infer from this, however, that an improvisation is beyond any control. On the contrary, an improvisation (like a rôle-play of children for that matter) needs to be framed very carefully. There is always a set of rules that limits the potential actions. Not everything is possible in an improvisation. If no rules were set up, the participants would spend all their creative powers on negotiations concerning the rules. Paradoxically, framing is the very factor that liberates the improvisers from the pressure of being inventive from scratch and lets them become creative.

This is why it is important to establish the where, who and what of an improvisation clearly. Determining where an improvisation is to take place and who the characters playing the scene are means deciding which universe should be evoked and, to a certain extent, which aesthetic code should be used. If you set a scene in a bakery in which two bakers are baking bread, you have most certainly invited a realistic play. If, on the contrary you ask the improvisers to become two aliens looking for gasoline for their space vehicle in the bakery, you will probably end up with a somewhat more absurd improvisation. Deciding on what should take place helps the improvisers to direct their actions, especially if you formulate the content of the improvisation in terms of objectives to be gained. Just asking two actors to become bakers and play a scene in a bakery does not help them much. If you add that they are going to become competitors in a cake contest that they both badly want to win, they are much better off. Now they know what to do. One performer may begin to cheat by stealing the flour of the other, while the other may secretly slip a huge amount of pepper into the other baker's dough and so forth. In fact, setting a definite task for the performers to pursue is often the most liberating factor of the framing. The ideal setup is open enough for the participants to become creative, yet closed enough for the universe to be suggestive.

Our example is meant to display this very dialectic. Even if the teacher decides the frame of the improvisation, he leaves blank spots for the participants to fill in. As yet, nothing has been said about the exact nature of the alleged crime. Furthermore, the rôles for the participants have not been completely decided. The improvisers can still choose whether they want to partake as a board of teachers, as a particular class, or perhaps as the sports team of the school. It is even possible for an individual participant to take on a specific character, such as the caretaker, the vice principal or even the villain of the story. If there is no immediate reaction and the teacher feels the need to establish a clearer framework, he may try to heighten the tension by suggesting that, say, Peter from the sixth grade has drowned under mysterious conditions. Hopefully, something like this will prompt an interrogation into the whereabouts of everybody yesterday evening.

For the virtual puppet theatre we were looking for a way to construct a similar dialectic between framing and openness. We saw the autonomous agents as stand-ins for the teacher in rôle. Like the teacher who plays a rôle, autonomous agents in character create a frame that invites a certain improvisation to take place. When the farmer and the cow appear in the farm scenario, the child is immediately introduced to the *where* and (some of) the *whos* of the improvisation. When the cow tries to escape from the shed and the farmer struggles to prevent it from doing so, the child has also fathomed the *what*. At the same time this setup is open enough for the user to play along creatively. When allowed to enter the improvisation as an avatar (whether in the rôle of a magical haystack or a sheep, to mention only the two rôles that we decided to create), the child may choose to help either the cow or the farmer.

4.2.5 Setting Simple Tasks and Establishing a Contract of Fiction

A strategy of framing that is much used in drama in education is breaking down the improvisation into smaller units (cf. for instance Lambert and O'Neill (1982) and Bolton (1979)). For the teacher the job is to find definite tasks to be solved for each small unit. Imagine that a group of children were to investigate the competition between the two bakers more carefully. Just letting the children perform the scene would probably lead to a lot of fun, but no real investigation would take place. Consequently, the teacher may decide to divide the children into two groups and ask them to begin by considering which strategy should be employed by their combatant. Then, the teacher may ask the two groups to improvise a scene with the purpose of investigating how they can help build up the self-confidence of their representative in the competition. By slowing down the pace like this with these two steps (which may, of course, be multiplied if need be), the teacher attempts to transform a scene that the children simply want to perform for fun into a potential investigation of sports psychology.

Using this strategy in the development of the virtual puppet theatre we ended up dividing the run through into six distinct phases:

1. Allowing the child to navigate in the virtual space until the autonomous agents come alive.
2. Giving the child the opportunity to investigate the agent's actions from different angles as a cameraman.
3. Letting the child become a haystack avatar, thus allowing him or her to experience that the agents actually respond to the actions performed by the avatar, i.e. illustrating that what is happening on the screen is not just pre-scripted animation.
4. Letting the child play along as a sheep avatar with more functionalities than the haystack.
5. Allowing the child to give lines to the agents in an offline type of interaction.
6. Giving the child the opportunity to re-record the utterances recorded in a previous session.

We acknowledge the fact that the two first phases are not very improvisational. There is, however, a reason for beginning with two phases in which the child can only partake as a cameraman: the need to establish what may be called *the contract of fiction*. This notion has been developed (by Szatkowski, 1989) as an analytical tool to help describe the set of rules concerning the way in which a theatre production establishes its communication with the audience. The point is that a performance (or a written drama for that matter) creates the rules by which it hopes to be measured.

In good productions these rules are set up from the very beginning, or even, as it were, before the show begins. For instance, the PR strategy is important. Whether a piece is advertised as a theatre production or a performance, as a farce or a melodrama, or as great entertainment or food for thought, will considerably influence the expectations with which the spectators enter the theatre building. A poster may also send significant signals as to what is to be expected, and if the events on stage do not match these signals, many spectators will very likely feel cheated. Apart from the importance of how these external aspects of the contract of fiction are framed, the production itself needs to be very precise in every detail of the signs it uses for communication. When the curtain goes up, the set design must immediately give us a clue as to which type of theatre the audience may expect. Is the scenography, for instance, a naturalistic environment or an abstract space in the tradition of minimalism? The same goes for the first appearance of the actors. What kind of acting are we dealing with? Psychological realism or abstract symbolism? And so on and so forth.

To us, the need to be clear about the contract of fiction seemed even more urgent in relation to the construction of a *virtual* theatre production. Not only does virtuality seem to radicalize the *aesthetical* problem, it also raises certain *technical* issues. Let us first address the technical aspects.

In this day and age any child can operate an avatar within a virtual world. Computer games have taught them that. Nevertheless the child needs to get acquainted with how the interface works in a particular application. As we used a mouse, the child needs to find out what the buttons are used for. The child also needs to investigate the speed at which the mouse allows him or her to navigate in the virtual world. Furthermore, it is important to allow the child to discover the constitution of the virtual world, in which ordinary rules do not necessarily apply. For instance, is the world restricted by gravity? (In our world it was; thus we refrained from making it possible for the child, for instance, to teleport the avatar from one place to another.) Do the things in it have the density of the objects in the real world, or may I, perhaps, pass through them? (We experimented with a few fences without density, mostly because we knew that children love to pass through things, but it was not in tune with our foundational concept to make comprehensive use of this.) Is the world infinite, or does it have distinct borderlines? If it does, where are they, and what are they like? (In our world the borderlines consisted of mountains, which were insurmountable.) Is it possible to experience time? (As we did not have any particular need for time, we chose not to use this possibility.)

Aesthetically it is important for the child to get acquainted with the formal make-up of the location in which the action is going to take place. This implies the issues from a regular theatre production, i.e. the style of the design and so forth, but there is an important difference between a virtual world and a theatrical space. In a regular theatre, you can orient yourself very quickly. Here, the space is very limited. The scenography can be seen *in toto* from the very beginning. When investigating a 3D virtual environment this is not the case. Here, we are dealing with a world rather than a scenography, a space rather than a place. Consequently it takes longer time to get an overview of it. Is there for instance more than one place in the space? In computer games this typically seems to be the case. Knowing that, we chose to include caves and canyons in the far backyard of the farm, but as we were concerned with focusing the narrative interest on the farm, we did not want to make these places too attractive.

Thus, phase one, in which the child is only allowed to navigate in the virtual world as a virtual camera was meant as a way to secure a solid introduction of the improvisational *where*. For the contract of fiction to be fully developed, however, we also needed to make sure that the questions of *who* and *what* were properly answered. For this purpose we introduced phase two. Here, the child is allowed to witness the struggle between the farmer and his cow (or, on the metaphorical level, between a force pressing for order and a counterforce of chaos). Not until the child has realized the nature of the conflict between the two antagonists will he or she be capable of deciding how to enter the improvisation as an avatar.

4.3 Interactive Narration with a Dramaturgical Turn

Much has been said about the difficulties involved in the construction of narrativity in interactive fiction. We believe that there are very good reasons for this. Allowing the recipient to interfere with the narrative progression is asking for trouble. To start with, you are forced to transform the rôle of the author if you open the door to direct interaction. He can no longer be a demiurge in absolute control of the universe that he has created. Instead he must start seeing himself as a sort of facilitator who creates a field of possible experiences. However, this transformation of the author's rôle is the easy part. It is fairly unproblematic to pass on the creative rôle to the recipient. You just have to provide him with bits and pieces of a narrative structure and let him decide how they should be turned into a whole. The real difficulty is to be found in the opposite direction. Even though the author has to think in terms of being a facilitator, the artistic job is still to construct *interesting* fictional universes. Interaction isn't interesting in itself. A coherent framework, a set of rules, or a distinct universe is needed if the recipient is going to find it worthwhile to become interactive at all. Compared with "ordinary" pieces of art, interactive pieces even radicalize the need to make distinct selections. Without a clear-cut premise an interactive work can hardly inspire the recipient to interact for a sustained period of time.

Changing from a theatre performing *for* an audience to a theatre working *with* an audience implies that the artist should lose some control over the work of art. This might be one of the reasons why some (traditional) artists furiously resist the idea of interactive works as works of art. In interactive art there is no longer one artistic genius responsible for the form. If we accept the notion of an open work of art as defined for example by Umberto Eco (1989), however, we might be relieved of this anxiety. According to Eco, an open work of art is conceived in order to allow the recipient to mingle with it. Thus, taking Eco's reflections as a point of departure would mean that you would tend to look at the change positively. While upgrading the open work you would see it as a chance for the spectator to experience the work from the inside and to change some of the structures actively. "I am making something happen to the work and to me" seems to be a central dialectic for the interactive work (as we shall argue later on). This change raises questions like: How much freedom can the participant in the interactive narrative cope with? How much should the participant be allowed to do? Is the sky the limit? To us, it seems fair to look for an adequate response to questions like this in an attitude that balances the views of those who decline interactive works as such and those who claim interaction to be the promised land of new hypertextual landscapes of unrepressed communication and an unforeseen "empowering" of the reader (as argued by Landau (1997)).

If the question of narrativity has come to play such an important rôle in discussions about interactive fiction, it is probably because suspense is the most common strategy of seduction in linear narrative. Suspense is what makes the reader keep reading. Bereft of the absolute control of the narrative, the author of interactive fiction is incapable of using this very device. She seems to be left with a choice between two options. She must either work much harder to construe the causal form of temporality that is needed for suspense to appear or she must give up causal time and go for other points of interests, like investigating a universe. There are, after all, other forms of narrative than the causal form. At this point, we found that our knowledge of the many different dramaturgies used by theatre *for* an audience came in handy. Related to the first choice is the difficulty of keeping the causal development in place when the recipient begins to interact. Conversely, if you opt for the second possibility, you are faced with the strenuous problem of making the universe interesting enough for sustained exploration. As the dramaturges in a project aiming at investigating what it takes to construct a virtual puppet theatre, we have tried to think through both options.

In this section we would like to present some of the conclusions that we have reached concerning the issues involved in the framing of an interactive fiction. For us it makes sense to regard interactive narratives as ways of framing that may be positioned in a continuum ranging from (almost complete) openness to a firm structure. At the open end of the spectrum you may simply choose to present the users with a toolbox that will allow them to create a piece of art from scratch. Earlier, we have mentioned *3D Movie Maker* as an inspiring example of the type of application that is based on an open-ended framework. At the other end of the continuum we find the majority of common computer games, where, driven by ongoing suspense, the user is asked to solve specific tasks and make the right choices in order to save the princess. The really tricky challenge is to create an application in the middle of this continuum. In order to do so you will need an interactive narrative that presents recipients with a consciously shaped and chosen material within a given structure, but at the same time allows them to experience the work from within, make choices in the process of experiencing, and also add material that will actually affect the application. The following is an attempt to present some of the conclusions that we reached when we tried to meet this challenge. We would like to begin by outlining our dramaturgical rationale.

4.3.1 Interactivity and Narrativity

The dramaturgy of interactivity has much in common with the dramaturgy of flirtation (cf. Kjølner and Szatkowski, 2002). Flirtation is a process that can only be kept alive if two partners participate on equal terms in the activity and if they are able to suspend the need for a particular ending. If one (or both) want(s) to end the flirtation with a definite result, the activity changes and turns into something else, i.e. seduction. We found flirtation interesting because it seems to be *paradigmatic for interaction*. A flirt needs another flirt, which means that flirtation is by necessity a *subject-to-subject relationship*. Like children's play, flirtation is *without a specific purpose* and it is this very *purposelessness* that allows you to improvise. Flirtation only really works when there is *no anticipation* on the part of the participants and when the *rules are constantly negotiated*. These features make us consider flirtation to be a pleasure, as opposed to a need. To be able to flirt, you must want to get involved in the game and you must take pleasure in the constant reconsideration and adjustment. Flirtation is about taking risks. It implies taking chances and it is based on a willingness to suspend disbelief. Losing in a flirtatious situation is not the same as really losing. Flirtation may be said to be working on the edge of reality in a quasi-fictitious dimension. Flirtation creates an uncertain repertoire of possible relationships and possible modes of relationships. It playfully questions what is possible and what is not.

In the project we have thought of flirtation as a good metaphor for the dramaturgical puzzle we had to solve. In the openendedness of flirtation we found the ideal of the fluid dramaturgy that we seemed to be looking for, especially because it challenges our sense of a beginning, middle and, in particular, an end. To study flirtation means to study unstable relationships in which everybody and everything has to be treated as uncertain: values, ethics, words, behaviours, circumstances and so forth. A dramaturgy of flirtation slows down real-time interaction in other words, and finds ways of extending time limits. In doing so, it practises a control over time and space from the inside, i.e. as part of the interactivity.

Transformed to the context of virtual narrativity this way of thinking seems to be in line with the fact that interactive narration is based on nodes and links. As in flirtation, the interaction with an interactive narrative makes you study the way in which the nodes are provided: can they be explored only, or can they be changed? Can nodes be deleted or can new nodes be applied? How are the links between them established? Are all the links given and are they one-way streets (i.e. irreversible) or reversible? Are they chronological or do they follow some other kind of logic? Will the links provide a pre-planned way through the system, or will users be free to create an order of their own? These are the questions with which (on a meta-level of consciousness) you approach an application, just like you always try to detect the rules by which another flirt is playing.

In order to pursue these questions we have found some of the theoretical framework suggested by Brenda Laurel (1991) useful if considered as a questionnaire for practical use, especially because it broadens the scope somewhat. If you ask how often you are allowed to interact with the system, you may measure the *frequency* of the interaction. Asking what *kind* of choices you are given (are they, for instance, limited to an either/or structure, or do they present a wider range of diverse possibilities?) allows you to measure the *range* of interaction. Furthermore, Laurel suggests that you may ask questions like: what kind of feedback does your interaction with the system provide you with? Is it related to the action, to time or space? And how fast is the feedback: is it instantaneous or accumulated over time? Answering these questions provides you with a way of estimating the *complexity* of the feedback mechanisms and describing the *distribution of the feedback over time.*

By thinking in terms of this broad definition of interaction, it becomes possible to make a nuanced distinction between applications with a high and low levels of interaction. This distinction also makes it possible to think about narrativity with respect to important nuances. Like interactivity, narrativity has become a rather broad concept with many different meanings – dangerously many meanings, you might add. In our eyes the difficulty is that, whenever interaction is involved, we want a broad definition, but at the same time we don't want it to become all-inclusive. As an attempt to solve this problem of definition we would like to suggest that we conceive narrative as a consciously formed sequence of events taking place in space and time. This definition has the advantage of being broad enough to avoid unnecessary exclusion, yet narrow enough to impose a certain delimitation. On the one hand it allows you to avoid seeing a linear (causal, as it were) form of coherence to be distinctive for storytelling. On the other hand it is based on an insistence that a narrative is a form of order. Without order, no narrative can evolve. If this definition is used as a compass for the practical work with the creation of narratives, you will have to distinguish between different types of dramaturgical order. Here, we can only hint at what this means

Classical dramaturgy, of course, depends on a form of order that is based on causality. We are presented with a story with a beginning, a middle and an end that is driven by suspense and is inevitably led towards a climax. This climax is the point of convergence that everything is directed at. Here, we find the core action that is supposed to express the idea of the work. Thus the author is supposed to argue for the logical and causal necessity of this idea. There are, however, many other kinds of stories that are driven by other forms of dramaturgy. Many new playwrights offer the spectator something quite different: for instance a non-linear order that creates a much more contemplative and floating experience. In these works focus is typically on the situation as such, rather than the action. We are supposed to dive into a particular atmosphere or feeling. Often these works are oriented towards phenomenology, i.e. towards an experience of "being" as opposed to the "doing" of the characters in classical dramaturgy. Indeed, we also find other kinds of narrative order that force the recipient to oscillate between the causal and the phenomenological type of order. This form may be called a meta-complex dramaturgy, and by causing a destabilization of our normalized codes of interpretation it forces us to accept observations of a second order. Here, the recipient will not be seduced by the tensions of a well-made plot, nor will he or she be dragged into contemplative investigations of the situation. Instead the recipient will be allowed to partake in a flirtation that promises new and unique connections between the work of art and his or her own references.

4.3.2 Interactivity and Narration from a Dramaturgical Point of View

We evoke the differences between these dramaturgies in order to highlight the importance of becoming aware of which kinds of stories are suited for interactions and which are not. Eventually we have been asked whether we were capable of coming up with a good dramaturgical solution to the problem of achieving a high level of interaction while maintaining the well-made story that is artistically as well as psychologically satisfying. Having tried to solve the riddle, today we would probably give an answer of the following kind: "No, so sorry, but we do not believe that this can be done. We can do many other things, but not this". From a dramaturgical point of view we find it paramount to begin with a reflection on the relationship between the demand for interaction and different dramaturgical frameworks, such as the causal and story-based, the phenomenological and situation-based, and the perspective-based dramaturgy. All these types of narrative create meaning, but they do it differently and they are not equally suited to coping with interaction (Figure 4.1). In particular, the causal form will get into trouble because the meaning of it is disclosed as the narrative unfolds, whereas the latter forms let meaning emerge gradually as the user fills in the many "blanks" in the structure, and for that very reason seem more ready for interaction.

Thus, thinking about the problem of interactive narration from a dramaturgical point of view begins by making a choice of an adequate dramaturgy for the specific purpose. There are many equally valid dramaturgies that may be taken as models, but they are not equally feasible for the purpose of allowing for interaction. In our experience three considerations in particular are helpful for making the choice.

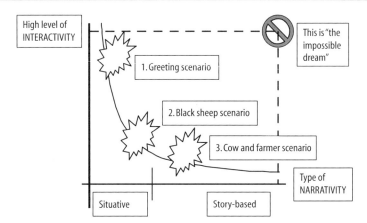

Figure 4.1 According to our hypothesis it is not possible to create an interactive dramaturgy that simultaneously provides the user with a high degree of interaction and a well-made story. We suggest that we abandon this impossible dream, and instead investigate other areas and possibilities.

Firstly, it seems beneficial to draw a clear demarcation line between narratives based on causal time and other forms of narrative. The moment we introduce a substantial element of causality into a story, we have entered a realm of narrative that only seems to allow for a low level of interactivity. The freedom for the user simply has to be rather restricted. Let us add that we do not mean to disqualify the linear form of narrative. In fact, we used many hours trying to explore the area on both sides of the demarcation line (type 2 and 3 interactions). We just want to emphasize that for a virtual theatre based on the use of autonomous agents and interaction via an avatar, a strict linearity seemed unsuitable. As we have already pointed out, the improvisational form of narrative is more appropriate because it is based upon the idea that you can frame a situation without determining the entire outcome of the action.

Secondly, the sheer choice of improvisation as our model does not solve the difficulty involved in constructing a plot of some kind in itself. If the aim is to establish some kind of narrative order, absolute contingency has to be ruled out no less than absolute control of the action. However, between the extremes of everyday life and a thoroughly constructed performance there is a field of possibilities. At one end of the spectrum you have the possibility of determining some specific phases through which the action must develop. This approach comes rather close to a fixed performance, but in so far as it is not predetermined how the actors are supposed to come from one phase to the next, we are still dealing with improvisation. At the other end we have a form of improvisation in which you have only specified the space, the characters and the tasks that each character must pursue. Here, you are much closer to the contingency of everyday life. As opposed to contingency, however, there is a clear definition of the particular tasks that must be related to each other in a very specific manner. Both of these forms of improvisation are based on a dramaturgical setup in so far as they specify a very particular set of rules. Thus, even if we are dealing with very different types of narrative, they are both forms of narrative.

Thirdly, it seems that the different setups that will result from framing more and framing less require very different lines of thinking as far as implementation is concerned. The frame that does not involve causal time allows for an approach based on "truly" autonomous agents. If the framework is reduced to a definition of particular characters with particular tasks, then there is no need for a narrative machine (a god's eye or an implicit narrator if you like) to keep track of the global development of the action. The agents may be allowed to pursue their aims somewhat more freely. As the causally oriented setup determines several points in time that must come after each other, it needs some kind of controlling device in order to make sure that all the characters will always "know" to which point of the narration the story has come. In order to cope with this problem we suggested that an encounter counter was implemented as a way to secure what may be called "the objective time".

When we now turn to a description of three scenarios (two of which were actually implemented), we try to outline the consequences of this line of reasoning in practice.

4.3.3 The Greeting Scenario

We started with a dream. We hoped that over the course of three years it would be possible to construct a program based on two different types of structure. As a matter of fact, we wanted to implement a narrative based on a meta-complex dramaturgy. Thus, we invented a scenario called *Fluffy Firehart*. Fluffy was a rabbit that had lost its voice, which was an appropriate setup for an improvisation where you could not rely on spoken words to be recognized by the system. In order to recover its voice Fluffy was forced to pass through three different worlds. Furthermore, the child should be able to choose between two different ways of experiencing the worlds. One way (constructed with the use of a classical dramaturgy of conflict) was supposed to go through conflicts and battles, while the other way (based on a phenomenologically oriented dramaturgy) was supposed to go through riddles and sensory experiences. Finally, the choices and actions were supposed to influence the way in which the child could go through the next world. We believed that giving a precise task like recovering the voice of Fluffy was paramount and we hoped that the child would find pleasure in exploring the different ways through the system as well as becoming keen on the investigation of the different strategies of interaction. We had to accept the fact, however, that this was not an idea to be implemented by a team with very limited manpower and a tight EU research schedule with deliverables and reviews. Thus we took our first serious step towards a simplification of the scenario and the interactive dramaturgy.

The first scenario that we actually implemented was situated on the farm that would also happen to serve as the place for the creation of all later scenarios. In order to investigate the potentials of our autonomous agents, we designed a Greeting Scenario. Six different agents wandered about on the farm, and when they met, they greeted each other. We believed that studying the greeting behaviours of the agents would give us some clues as to how we could make scripts for agents to come. When analyzing dramatic texts or performances, it is paramount to investigate the actions and reactions of the characters. In fact, the combination of an action and a reaction may be considered the smallest unit of a dramatic text. Knowing this, we wanted to study the interrelation between the agents at the very core of their interaction. To do so we decided that each greeting should be an encounter with a sequence of actions and reactions that had a beginning, a middle and an end.

In order to establish some (hopefully) readable differences between the characters, we invented a taxonomy of possible relations. For instance, one cow would act positively towards the other cow, but negatively towards the dog and the Farmer. In this way, each character was given its own preferences by scripts that expressed an exact attitude. We actually believe that this might have been enough for an interesting story to emerge. If we had given the child the possibility to choose any of the characters as an avatar, it would have been possible to investigate "the mental landscape" of the farm. From this investigation the child might have inferred a story that even had a causal ring to it. At the time, however, we not only lacked the means to make the expressivity of the agents poignant enough for differences to be perceived, but also the means to make scripts that would allow for a more complex improvisational development. Neither had we found a feasible way to allow for an avatar. Consequently, we had to move on from this scenario to another.

4.3.4 The Black Sheep

The really tricky part of bringing an avatar into the fictional framework is, of course, that the child controlling it may choose to let it do something totally unexpected. If the improvisation is to be rescued from going completely astray, it is necessary to have a device at hand. As an attempt to solve this very problem we developed a scenario that would work like a perpetual motion machine. Thus we developed a dramatic situation in which an agent was always ready to do the job of the avatar if the child controlling it would decide not to do it. We called this scenario The Black Sheep.

We imagined a scenario in which a farmer tries to keep his farm nice and tidy and a black sheep tries to disrupt the order created by the farmer. Whenever the farmer had succeeded in bringing his cows, pigs and hens back to their proper places, the black sheep would immediately try to make them leave again, whether by force or seduction. This simple scenario was meant to be cyclical. As long as no avatar has entered the scene, it would keep reiterating itself. This is a case of a non-linear framework for an improvisation. Nothing has been decided about the proper direction of the action; for instance, that the farmer should eventually win after having lost the battle three times. There is only a well-defined situation with a potential for a transitory closure if one of the combatants should succeed in fulfilling his task completely before the opponent starts messing everything up again. But note that each reiteration of the battle will be different from the previous one because it depends on the contingent whereabouts of the agents. If, for instance, the farmer happens to be three steps further away from the shed than the black sheep, it will have an impact on the power balance. We point this out in order to show that the "lack" of causality in the strict sense does not make it uninteresting. It just displaces the point of interest. In an emergent situation like this the emphasis seems not so much to be on *what* happens, but rather on *how* it happens.

Now, what about the avatar? How can it be ensured that the perpetual motion machine would keep working if one of the two combatants did not sustain the conflict? Say, for instance, that the child partaking as the black sheep decides that the sheep is in fact a good sheep that prefers to help the farmer with herding the animals back into their sheds. This choice would rather quickly bring the entire situation to a stand still. We tried to solve this problem with a little help from a moderated actantial model.

The actantial model was developed by A. J. Greimas (1986) as an attempt to find the very logics that governed the fairytale. According to him there is always a subject who pursues a certain goal, for instance a prince who wants to marry the princess. In order to dramatize this model we created another model with two subjects pursuing opposite goals. We have already shown how that works in the scenario with the farmer and the sheep. Greimas adds, however, that in the fairytale there are also always helpers and opponents of the subject (Figure 4.2). A prince has to fight the dragon, but is helped by, say, three magical animals. This very component seemed extremely helpful to us. In a dramatized version of the actantial model the helper of one of the opponents would always be the opponent of the other and vice versa. In this structure we found a way to solve the problem with the intervention of the avatar. We gave the farmer a dog as a helper and the black sheep a grey sheep as a helper. With this device we had found a way of solving the problem of letting the avatar into the game without losing control over the situation.

We decided that the position of the child should be allowed to become the black sheep. If the child decides that it is a lot of fun to disrupt the order at the farm, everything would turn out just fine. If, on the other hand, the child decides to follow the farmer, we would need another agent to keep pursuing the aim of the black sheep. This is the part we intended for the helper: the grey sheep. We implemented this with a script telling it to get much more active in the disruptive project if it realized that the black sheep had abandoned the project. As we had created a symmetrical structure, the same logic would apply if we had allowed the child to become the

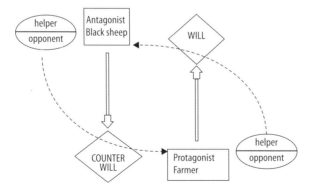

Figure 4.2 Expanding on Greimas's model of forces in an epic narrative we suggested a dramatized actant model with a symmetrical conflict axis where a protagonist (the Farmer with a will to order) is met by an antagonist (the Black Sheep), providing a counter-will. The Farmer's helper (the Dog) would be the opponent of the Black Sheep.

farmer. If the farmer were to give up his project of creating order because the child would prefer to turn him into an anarchist, the dog could take over the project.

We realized that an "if so" script like this was dependent on some kind of "objective" measurement of the development of the battle. If the sheep were to increase its engagement in the conflict when needed, it would have to know exactly how successful the black sheep was at a particular moment. In order to solve this problem we developed what we called *an achievement machine*. This machine was meant to constantly keep track of how the conflict was developing in terms of how many animals were in their sheds. For the farmer, many animals in their proper places would imply a high rate of success, while for the black sheep it would mean a low rate of success. For the grey sheep the question would be whether the level of the achievement machine would be beyond the level that would cause it to intervene more actively in the conflict.

Unfortunately, we never got to see whether this achievement machine would actually work, as the scenario was never implemented. At this time, we, the dramaturges, felt that we had come at least one step further on the road towards understanding what it takes to make interactive narration function. It was argued by other partners in the project that the dramaturgy of situation that we had developed would not be interesting enough to play with. Furthermore, we became aware of the fact that there were other and even more elementary questions to be addressed. Among other things we were faced with the question of how to make the agents expressive enough for the intentions to be readable (for the other agents no less than the avatar and the child controlling it). In order to get at these problems we found that we had to reduce the complexity even further, and we did so by focusing solely on the conflict between the protagonist and the antagonist. At the same time, however, we seemed to be faced with the task of getting closer to the causal form of narration in order to meet the demand for more interesting action. More simplicity, more expressivity and more causal narration with respect to variation: that was the three-fold task with which we had to struggle at this point.

4.4.5 The Naughty Cow

Once more we took our point of departure in the nucleus of classical dramaturgy. We kept the farmer and invented a naughty cow to take the place of the black sheep as the antagonist. Compared with the former scenario, the conflict was no longer related to other animals. Now, the naughty cow simply wanted to escape from its pen in order to practise its anthropomorphic interests (like reading books and dancing to music). As the farmer in this scenario was also of the order-loving kind, this project would clash directly with the farmer's will to get the cow back into its pen. The dismissal of the two helpers was ripe with consequences as far as the position of the avatar is concerned. Without these two characters we no longer had a perpetual motion machine. If the child was allowed to partake as one of the antagonists and decided to disregard the particular projects of these characters, everything would fall apart. Consequently, we decided that the child should only be allowed to partake as a third party who could freely choose to side either with the farmer or with the cow. Hence the invention of the magical haystack and the sheep to be used in phases three and four in the final implementation.

This simplification was meant as an aid to make us focus on creating a little story with respect to the communicability of the agents. With the slight change of focus we decided that we needed to investigate the potential of another set of concepts from improvisational theatre, in particular those related to *status* and *attitude*.

Basically, status is used in improvisational theatre as a very efficient way to communicate shifts and attract an audience's attention. As a matter of fact, changes of status from high to low and vice versa may very well be one of the most economical ways of communicating important developments in a character (cf. Johnstone, 1981). Say, for instance, that you act as if you own the world and give the impression that you are completely undisturbed by the other characters. You will inevitably obtain a high status. If you then start making excuses for being present and act as if you would prefer to melt into thin air, your status will rapidly change from a high to a very low status. The point is that a shift like this begs an interpretation, as the audience is inspired to ask questions like: what happened? Why did he change his status? And so on and so forth.

For an actor it is fairly easy to communicate status (even if it is also possible for the highly skilled performer to present very subtle shifts that a non-actor is unable to get at). For an autonomous agent it is another matter, however, as any position of status needs to be expressed by a distinct signal that will have to be animated. An actor can distinguish between an entire range of positions between high and low status, but in order to reduce complexity we suggested that we restrained ourselves to two different positions of status for each character, i.e. a position of high status and a position of low status. As we read body postures easily (if they are well done of course) and immediately assign meaning to them, we suggested, furthermore, that we should focus on the difference of posture. When a character changes status from high to low (or vice versa), we will read this as a significant shift, and we will try to interpret the reasons for the change. Signals like these are efficient because they are very condensed. Given the right framing, they will most certainly convey a story. On the other hand, if a character remains in the same status and no variations are offered, we tend to get bored very quickly because we see no development.

But even if a reduction of complexity is asked for, this duplicity would probably have been too reductive. Acknowledging this, we suggested that we also worked with shifts of *attitude*.

Thinking in terms of attitude implies the danger of becoming overly involved in aspects of psychology that will inevitably make things extremely complicated. In improvisational theatre, however, attitude is simply used as a practical device. Here it becomes a means of reducing complexity. For a participant in an improvisation, it helps a lot to know with which attitude he or she should pursue a particular aim. If it is possible to translate a certain attitude into a particular action, so much the better. Along these lines we suggested that we should also work with the difference between a positive and a negative attitude and began searching for ways in which we could translate these attitudes into actions relevant for this particular scenario, i.e. actions that would be connected to the overall projects of the characters (Figure 4.3). For the farmer the solution was to be found in a distinction between *luring* and *herding*. The incarnation of the positive attitude (luring) implied inviting the cow back to its pen with the help of a carrot, whereas the negatively connoted herding

(a)    (b)

Figure 4.3 As an inspiration for our animator we asked actors to improvise using a melodramatic acting style with exaggerated movements and huge gestures. While looking at the finished animations the same actors recorded the audio files using gibberish. We argued that this functions better when the same audio files are played repeatedly and in different situations.

was performed aggressively with the help of a big rod. As for the cow, we believed that a distinction between *bursting out* and *sneaking out* would do the trick, at least if the negative attitude of bursting out was performed as a violent action and the positive attitude of sneaking out was performed with a twinkle.

Thus, we had given the antagonists of the improvisation four different sets of expression. With the duplicity of status and attitude they were allowed to perform high status with a positive attitude (H+), low status with a positive attitude (L+), low status with a negative attitude (L–), and finally high status with a negative attitude (H–) (Figure 4.4).

This taxonomy helped us focus the work that had to be done regarding the expressivity of the agents. It seemed to contain enough expressivity for the action. (As a matter of fact, we invited a couple of actors to improvise the scenario in order to seek inspiration for the actual animation of the four expressions of the two antagonists and for the recording of the sound files that needed to go with these animations.) But even more interesting for the discussion of interactive narrativity, the taxonomy also seemed to promise a way to solve the problem of making a more causally based narrative.

For an improvisation to work well, it is important that the performers are capable of creating believable transitions from one status to another and one attitude to another. Thus, we had to ensure that the transitions performed by the cow and the farmer would also be consistent and believable. In order to solve this problem we determined that the transitions should always follow two distinct cycles. The cow had to go from H+, via H– and L– to L+, whereas the farmer should move from L+ through L– and H– to H+. This way the agents would not just go from feeling on top

Figure 4.4 High status/low status and positive/negative attitudes. Each agent had four different positions at their disposal. Using these animations we achieved a dynamic expressivity.

of the world to exploding in rage with no transition. The importance of taking this step is, however, that an element of causation has been introduced in so far as one state of mind has to lead to another state of mind that had been determined in advance. This fact made us wonder whether we could go one step further along this road towards the creation of a causal form of narrative.

In itself, the invention of a cyclical development for each of the characters does not result in much linear narrativity. For a dramatic storyline to develop, the transitions of the character's actions have to look like the result of *an interrelation*. If, for instance, the cow gets angry and tries to bypass the farmer violently, it should look as if it has been provoked by the farmer to do so. Likewise, if the farmer ends up in high spirits, it should be clear that it is because he has defeated the cow. As a consequence of this line of reasoning, we returned to the idea of an achievement machine and asked whether, in this scenario, something like that might be used in relation to the taxonomy concerning the states of mind. The problem seemed to be how we could relate the cycle of the farmer to the cycle of the cow in such a way that a run through of the two sets of transmission would tell a coherent story. Furthermore, we had to consider how we could allow for variation if the cycles had been decided completely in advance. In order to handle these problems we suggested three things: (1) that we transformed the achievement machine into *a success and failure counter*, (2) that we enhanced this with *an encounter counter*, and finally (3) that we related these two "machines" to the taxonomy of status and attitude.

We asked ourselves which kind of stories we could tell with the help of this particular farmer and this specific cow. The answer seemed to be that we could either tell a tragedy with a sad ending or a comedy with a happy ending. As it is the cow's intention to leave the shed that initiates the story, the cow must be seen as the main character in the story. Thus, if the farmer defeats the cow, the child would probably read the story as a tragedy. On the other hand, if the cow succeeds and escapes to the places where it may enjoy its anthropomorphic leisure activities, the child would read the story as a comedy in which the stupid farmer is ridiculed by the successful cow. We decided to implement a version that would allow for both of these potential stories, but if they were to happen we had to make sure that the struggle between the two would actually come to one of the two closures. If the struggle would only keep on going (in the no man's land between the shed and the favourite places of the cow so to speak), we would get neither a comedy nor a tragedy, but just conflict.

Consequently, we had to determine when the cow and the farmer should keep pursuing their respective projects and when they should give in. If they were allowed to insist on their projects all the time, it would be impossible for anybody to win and there would be no transitory closure. If the cow did not have the capacity to give in, it would never return to its proper place, and if the farmer would never accept defeat, he would never let the cow reach its favourite spots. As we wanted to allow for both endings, we had to avoid the scenario turning into a game of hand-ball played in front of the two goals only. We needed, in other words, a device to tell the cow when to be persistent and when to give in (Figure 4.5). This device was the success and failure counter. Its job was to constantly count to four failures (defined as being herded back home) and three successes (defined as a successful arrival at one of the spots). Each time the counter had counted four failures, it would tell the cow to become persistent, and each time it had counted three successes, it would tell the cow to give in. Using this counting (F-F-F-F-S-S-S) would allow us to tell both the comedy and the tragedy.

Imagine that by default the counter is set to have already counted one failure. The cow would still be outside its shed and try to reach its destination. When intercepted by the farmer, it will accept defeat three times, but then it will become persistent and insist on reaching one of its destinations. Here, no further action would

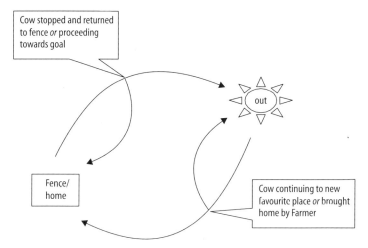

Figure 4.5 Illustrates the simple home–out–home cyclical structure behind the farmer/cow scenario. We planned the agent scripts to provide variations in the run-through of this cycle. The Cow should know when to give in to the Farmer and follow him home to the fence, and when it could continue to the bookshelf or gramophone.

take place if the cow was allowed to stay at its destination. If we were to make the tragedy possible as well, we needed to kick start the action again. This is why we decided to have more than one place for the cow in play. Letting the cow enjoy its victory for a short period of time, we send it out to look for another of its preferred places. Here, the farmer who would be looking for the missing cow would intercept it and we would have the reverse situation of the comedy. The first two times the cow resists the farmer because the counter must count to three before it tells the cow to give in and follow the farmer.

With the success and failure counter in place we seemed to have solved the riddle of the overall structure of the causal narrative. But still we had no guarantee that the battles leading to failures and successes for the cow would vary enough to make them appear interesting. If they were too similar, the entire scenario would probably become rather tedious. As a remedy for this potential disease, we suggested the encounter counter. This machine was supposed to count how many encounters (defined in the same way as in the greeting scenario, i.e. as a meeting with a beginning, a middle and an end) between the cow and the farmer there had been at any given moment in time. This counting would allow us to distinguish between long and short battles if we decided to have four encounters between, say, two failures and, say, two encounters between the last of these two failures and the following success. With this way of distinguishing between short and long battles, we hoped to create small narratives at the micro-level, so to speak.

Now only one thing seemed to be left for the dramaturges to do (that is if, for a minute, we disregard the thousands of other questions that seem to pop up in work like this and which it seems completely necessary to disregard if anything is going to be implemented at all). We needed to make sure that the overall development of the escape and the homecoming would progress "naturally". It was for this purpose that we tried to connect the cycles of the mental states of the antagonists with the two counter machines by making the changes in status and attitudes depend on encounters, successes and failures.

We are painfully aware that this way of trying to "square the circle" (as the attempt to develop a causal form of narrative based on the emergent activity of autonomous agents may often be experienced) may be seen as a form of *cheating*. If straightforwardness means accepting total autonomy for each character, we have indeed been cheating. In this respect we went astray already when we invented the achievement machine for The Black Sheep and our sin has only been aggravated with the invention of the two new counting machines for The Naughty Cow. All of these machines function as devices to control the agents from above (or from behind if you prefer). It goes without saying that the use of this type of device implies disregarding the absolute autonomy of the particular agents.

If, however, the use of such machines should be called cheating, then perhaps we should simply indulge in cheating. With the current state of technology we do not see any way to succeed without an element of cheating, in particular if we want to construe interactive narratives based on causality. If we could avoid cheating in the greeting scenario and restrict ourselves to a minimum of cheating in the black sheep scenario, it was only because there was no causal time in the first and only the need for a single moment of causality in the second (i.e. the need for the grey sheep to take over *if* the avatar did not pursue the project of the antagonist). The naughty cow scenario is an entirely different ball game. Here, everything relies on causality (even if theatre people would probably find it hard to discover a linear dramaturgy in a scenario that only tells the tale of the potential escape of a cow!).

The lesson to be learned seems to be that if you want linear causality, you cannot have it without cheating. For research on autonomous agents this may seem to be a sad conclusion. For a dramaturge, however, cheating has always been a respectable way of achieving the effects that are needed for a particular production. In fact, we believe that we may very well benefit from bringing some of this dramaturgical insouciance towards cheating with us when we think about autonomous agents.

4.4 A Dramaturgical Perspective on Autonomous Agents

How should we think of autonomous agents if they are to become efficient characters in a virtual theatre production? This is the question we should like to consider in this section. As dramaturges we are, of course, incapable of forming an opinion about the concrete implementation of the agents. (Madsen and Granum (2001) have presented the agent architecture design used in the project and in Chapter 5 Madsen summarizes the basic structure.) We believe, however, that we may have something (hopefully relevant) to say about the conceptual framework with which the construction of autonomous agents is approached.

A central notion for almost everybody in this field seems to be *believability*. Autonomous agents (or synthetic characters as they are also sometimes called) should be readable in the sense that we will immediately perceive what they want to communicate. If they want something, we should see right away what they want and preferably also why they want it. If they get hurt emotionally by another synthetic character or by an avatar, they should display their feelings clearly. And so on and so forth.

The question is, however, whether believability (or verisimilitude as it has been called by theatre people since approximately 1650) can only be obtained if the synthetic character looks *exactly* like a real individual, if it reaches a level of complexity that matches the complexity of real life, and if, like animals and human beings, it is capable of decision making via a complicated interrelation between considerations, emotions and desires. We tend to think that this is not the case. In fact, we should like to challenge the paradigm of representation, which in our experience informs much thinking about autonomous agents. In spite of the many differences concerning the design of "the interior" of the agents, we have found that verisimilitude is almost always seen from the perspective of representation. If we suggest that we give up the idea of getting as close to reality as possible, it is because we find that it leads to *a mimetic fallacy*.

4.4.1 On the Need to Reduce Complexity

Taking your point of departure in the paradigm of representation when dealing with synthetic characters forces you to pose and answer a question that is as old as

Western philosophy, i.e. what constitutes a subject? The difficulty in trying to answer this question is that it raises a myriad of other questions. For starters, you are forced to consider which dimensions a subject is made of. This consideration will probably take you through a whole range of reflections concerning perception, personality, desires, needs, psychology and consciousness, let alone faculties like memory, imagination and ethical reasoning. As if this was not enough to create confusion, each dimension evokes further inquiries.

When dealing with *perception,* you have to consider which senses are the most important, and perhaps also how they work together in forming the notion of the world on which we rely. This means, of course, that you will have to develop an entire theory about the relationship between the five (or six?) senses.

The issue of *personality* raises the question of whether it is possible to reduce mankind to a certain set of types, or whether we should rather regard personality as the very stuff that an individual character is made of. If we opt for the first alternative, we are forced to formulate a theory of human types. How many types are there actually out there and how is every one of them composed? If we choose the second alternative, we are forced to ask which dimensions work together in the construction of a particular personality. Are they, perhaps, the dimensions that we have just mentioned? Let us pretend that we may answer this question in the affirmative. Then we are faced with the task that we are trying to undertake here, i.e. breaking each dimension down into its different components. Without this analysis we shall never be capable of making an adequate blend in order to create a synthetic character with a particular personality.

Thinking about the rôle played by *desires* and *needs* throws you into considerations about what basically drives people through life. Is it sex, hunger, lust for power or, perhaps, love, laziness and religious beliefs? Here, an age-old problem arises: is it possible to distinguish between natural and cultural needs and, if so, are the former more important for the endeavours we undertake than the latter? You will also be dragged into the field of psychology and become involved in, among other things, investigations of feelings. Which feelings do in fact exist? Are some feelings more fundamental (for instance anger) than others (for instance frustration)? Does it make sense to divide between pure and mixed feelings? If so, can you establish a matrix of primary feelings? If so, is it then possible to figure out which primary feelings work together in the creation of the complex secondary feelings? If so, can you decide whether any primary feeling may mix with any other? Of course, we could go on like this....

Finally (that is, if we decide to follow the division of dimensions suggested here which is hardly fulfilling), the notion of *consciousness* gives rise to so many different ideas about what it means to think that we hardly know where to start questioning. What is cognition after all? Does it make sense to talk about free reasoning or should we rather consider reasoning a product of various chemical processes in the brain? Are thoughts value-free or are they just a disguise for a will to power, as Nietzsche would have it? If we decide that it does make sense to believe in free reasoning, then we seem to be forced into the arms of Kant. Thus we are faced with the task of forming a theory of the faculties of the mind: are there for instance a cognitive, a practical and an aesthetic use of rationality? If so, how do these faculties differ from each other? Did Kant give the ultimate answer with his investigations or should we rather look for the answer in newer attempts by cognitive scientists?

We do not indulge in these speculations about the ultimate truth of the subject because we want to propose a way to solve the riddle. We do not have a theory that can tell us what the subject really is. On the contrary, we try to make good the claim that we would be better off if we stopped hoping for a definition of the subject that could be used as *the* model for the production of synthetic characters. Thus we have tried to illustrate that this road will inevitably take us to a level of complexity that is counterproductive. If an attempt to solve the riddle of the subject ends in an extreme complexity, it may very well be because the subject is too complex for theory, let alone the creation of a synthetic character. Instead of searching for ways to mime the complexity of reality, it seems that the task is rather to find ways of reducing complexity. Pursuing this endeavour, the task seems to be to find a way to reduce complexity without losing sight of believability.

4.4.2 Two Complementary Perspectives

Even if we have found the desire to get as close to true complexity rather pervasive, reasoning about autonomous agents seems to be divided between two approaches that are, in fact, different attempts at a reduction of complexity. Thus we have encountered one approach to agent architecture that is based primarily on behaviourism and another that takes its point of departure in the philosophy of consciousness. This experience of a significant division between two fundamentally different attitudes seems to be confirmed by Blumberg and Kline (1999) (all references are to this article). They argue that within the last two decades there has been a shift in the area of agent research from cognitivist "planning" approaches to models "in which behaviour is characterized by the dynamics of the agent environment interaction".

Taking the point of departure in behaviourism results in agents who are driven by their desires, reacting mainly to inputs from the environment, as opposed to agents built on the philosophy of consciousness, who are driven by intentions founded on reason and who are, consequently, proactive. They basically want to satisfy their needs, whereas the reasoning type of agent tries to pursue specific tasks. Saying that behaviourism leads you to see the synthetic character as an animal whereas the philosophy of consciousness makes you construe them in the image of a human being could also be a way of stating the difference. Or you could refer to the distinction between body and mind and say that the two approaches focus mainly on one side of the distinction. In practice, the distinction may be observed very easily. One approach tends to result in the creation of animal-like beings (often inhabiting a 3D environment), while the other approach results in the construction of humanoids (who are often referred to a 2D environment).

But if it is simply a matter of emphasis on the mind and the body respectively, why not combine the two approaches and work out a promising synthesis? According to Blumberg and Kline this is exactly what many creators of autonomous agents have tried to do: "to leverage the advantages of both approaches some hybrid systems have used a planner to make high-level behavioural decisions while using reactive systems for low-level control during behaviour execution". As a matter of fact, this is an exact description of the overall architecture of the autonomous agents inhabiting our virtual puppet theatre. As described by Madsen in Chapter 5, these agents were divided into a high-level agent concerned with planning and a more reactive low-level agent.

We realize that this double approach appears to be extremely captivating. Yet, in our experience, it leads directly to the problem of having to cope with much too high a degree of complexity. The example that Blumberg and Kline use to illustrate the hybrid approach seems to be a case in point. Even if they have reduced the number of motivational drives (reasoning) and the emotional make-up to six main feelings (reactivity), they end up with 84 (!) distinct behaviours. They are, indeed, aware of the problem and conclude not only that it is "currently very tedious to construct complex characters", but also that "it is very difficult for human observers to visually perceive more than one emotion at a time". We even tend to aggravate the point made by Blumberg and Kline. To us, it seems that even a non-hybrid approach will inevitably result in too much complexity. Behaviourism will make you want to imitate the complex inner nature of a real individual no less than the philosophy of consciousness, even if you want to look for other sources of this nature.

Here we touch on the main flaw of the mimetic fallacy. Thinking in terms of representation forces us to believe that whatever action a synthetic character displays, it should be a result of its inner life, i.e. its thinking, feelings, personality and so forth. Any gesture, any utterance and any movement should be a direct consequence of something that a character has actually thought or felt or wanted. Because we are so used to believing that the physical appearance of a real individual is a product of a hidden psychology (if by this word we may refer to any invisible process going on in the body (sensations), the mind (planning or scheming), or the soul (considerations)), we come to believe that work on synthetic characters should focus on the *inner* life of the agent. Blumberg and Kline seem to be up this alley when they say that the construction of believable synthetic characters "is fundamentally the art of revealing a character's inner thoughts – its beliefs and desires – through motion, sound, form, colour, and staging". Here, if anything, believability becomes a question of representing the subtle inner life of a character as correctly as possible. The problem with this is, of course, that we will use a lot of effort on constructing characters that (like human beings) perform complicated inner negotiations that will never be discernible to anybody, not even the programmer.

To us the real issue is *efficiency*. If the agents become too concerned with complex interior calculations, they lose in expressive poignancy, which is what we really want – especially if we are to construct characters for a virtual theatre. Therefore we opt for *a dramaturgical turn* that might make us capable of breaking with the paradigm of representation.

4.4.3 The Dramaturgical Perspective

It is probably immediately clear why a dramaturgical turn may be of relevance for a project dealing with the construction of a virtual puppet *theatre*. If we are not mistaken, however, taking a dramaturgical turn may also prove beneficial for the construction of synthetic characters in general. Believability should still be the central aim to be obtained, but giving up the paradigm of representation would make us look a little differently on this very notion. This change is a consequence of three displacements of our ordinary way of thinking.

Firstly, our interpretation of what "lifelike" means would be distinctively different from the interpretation inherent in ordinary language. In the mimetic tradition it means being as true to life as possible. To be like life means to reproduce life as accurately as possible. From a dramaturgical point of view, however, you would tend to stress the difference between the representation and what is being represented. The fact that something is *like* something else means that it cannot be exactly the same as what it imitates. This approach would emphasize the element of pretence, the "as if" involved in any representation.

An economical way to underscore the importance of this point is to evoke the distinction between a "cold" and a "warm" actor introduced by Diderot in his reflections on the paradox of the actor. A famous anecdote can illustrate this distinction. Once Sir Lawrence Olivier and Dustin Hoffman were cast in the same production. One day Hoffman was late for the rehearsal. When he finally arrived, he excused himself by explaining that he had been on research. He felt that he had to seek out the milieu to which his character belongs. As a matter of fact he would have liked to live like his character for a prolonged period of time in order to experience the very feelings of his character. Sir Olivier, who was from a classical tradition and did not care much about the ways of method acting, just looked at Hoffman with no apprehension and asked: "Ever tried acting?".

The anecdote illustrates that a "warm" actor believes that he must actually live through what a particular fictitious character would have felt (had he been real) in order to play the part. He must, in other words, recreate the inner life of the character. In contrast to this, the "cold" actor believes in *faking*. Instead of trying to turn himself into a certain character, he tries to find an adequate means of expression for making us believe that he has transformed into another character. He is, in other words, a rhetorician who selects his expressive tools with care. Whether what he does is true (in the sense of relying on an inner life that is really there) is not an issue. What concerns him, solely, is the creation of the desired effect on the audience.

It is probably obvious that we side with Olivier and his acceptance of sheer appearances. This puts us at odds with Blumberg and Kline who (among others) seem to think about synthetic characters from the point of view of "warm" acting. The two theoreticians use the scene from Little Red Riding Hood in which the wolf looks longingly at the girl. As we are dealing with an animal, they interpret the scene in behaviourist terms. The desire of the wolf is to have something to eat, they say, and as it believes that eating Little Red Riding Hood would satisfy its needs, it has to take actions to catch her. In other words, desires make the character scan its environment and reflect on the perceptions it gets. The combination of desires and perceptual knowledge produces beliefs, which are, in turn, turned into action. Had Blumberg and Kline used Little Red Riding Hood as the example, they would probably have had to add a capacity for feelings (as she may feel, for instance, fright) and personality (is she, for instance, clever or stupid) to their matrix. This is, however, a digression from the main point we are trying to make. For now, we simply want to point out the "warm" logic at work in this interpretation. Blumberg and Kline start from the inner operations of the character and work their way causally to the physical expression. A "cold" actor would do the reverse. Starting from the objective of his character, i.e. eating Little Red Riding Hood, he would fake "the inside". By sneering he would make us read "hungry wolf". We think that starting from "cold" acting like this would reduce complexity tremendously without losing sight of believability.

Secondly, a dramaturgical turn would make us start thinking about the actions of the synthetic character in terms of *a specific situation*. The characters of a play are always restricted by the dramatic situation in which the playwright has placed them. Thus it is the situation that determines which actions are adequate and which actions are inadequate. We believe that seeing synthetic characters in this light would mean giving up the idea that any character should always be capable of any action whatsoever. Put another way: we would no longer look for humanoid agents who, at any time and at least in principle, can do what a human being can do. In fiction a lot of possible actions have already been dismissed.

As a matter of fact, it is a little misleading to talk about synthetic characters as actors, even if we add that they should be "cold" actors. Through the use of this notion we have only wanted to stress the "as if" character at work in the liveliness of the agents. Thinking about agents in terms of real actors may, however, be of little help. In fact, it may complicate things even more. Thinking about agents in terms of real actors would mean that we would not only have to find adequate representations for all the dimensions that constitute a human subject (the actor); we would also have to equip the agent with the actor's ability to take on different rôles. As the dramaturgical turn is supposed to reduce complexity, this is hardly what we are after. Consequently, we would rather suggest that we start thinking of an agent in terms of a particular character within a particular framework.

Another way to explain our point would be to introduce the notion of *typecasting*. In ordinary language this word has a negative ring to it, but in this context we may benefit a lot from rehabilitating it. Typecasting means choosing an actor for a particular rôle who is already in tune with the character. Consequently, he can basically stick to "playing himself". He is, so to speak, always already in character as a particular type. Thus typecasting is a very pragmatic approach to the production of a play. What a director looks for are a number of particular types (the good-looking hero who can only look good and act heroically as opposed to the ugly villain who is incapable of looking not guilty) who will suit a particular play. The point is, of course, that typecasting reduces complexity significantly with no loss of believability. What is needed is simply a clear analysis of what kind of characters a particular situation demands, followed by casting of the appropriate types.

Transposed to the construction of synthetic characters, typecasting means beginning with the situation in order to construct agents with the relevant features for this situation only. We are aware that this suggestion results in giving up hope of finding the formalism of a super-agent who can cope with any situation whatsoever. We tend to believe, however, that not even reality lives up to such formalism.

Only a very few people are capable of being manifold, and only a very few highly trained actors are able to play the entire spectrum of rôles. For various reasons most actors are only capable of playing certain parts. If reality is not as malleable as we would like to believe, and if we are faced with the task of reducing the complexity that marks this reality anyway, we imagine that we would benefit from accepting formalisms of a less universal character. We may be in need of different formalisms and different sets of agent scripts for the various agents in a definite scenario. Thus taking the dramaturgical approach would imply asking for agents who can act generically, but only in quite specific and local situations. In order to further the studies of how this may work, we would have to experiment with many different improvisational scenarios.

Perhaps this retreat from the intention of creating an overall formalism for agents will seem to some like a defeat. We do not think, however, that it is. On the contrary, we see it as accepting a public secret shared by many artists in the theatre: to make a well-made piece of theatre is not about having everything there. Rather, it takes the capacity to single out certain material, to condense a situation in order to focus on something specific. Thus, the third consequence of the dramaturgical turn would be to pursue an *ideal of condensation*. Believability does not necessarily demand realism. In fact, it does not originate in feeding in the complexity of everyday life into the production. In order to make an audience believe in a make-believe situation, you do not need to reproduce any movement that a real person would make. On the contrary, this will most certainly blur the communication. Instead you need to reduce the number of signals to a minimum according to the principle of *pars pro toto*.

A return to the example of Little Red Riding Hood may help us illustrate this point. If the wolf simply licks his lips, the entire situation will probably become clear in a second. No matter what goes on in the wolf's interior, the gesture will make us infer that the wolf is hungry and wants to eat the little girl. We get the message, so to speak. If – on top of that – our other character wears a little red riding hood, we have sent a powerful signal that evokes the entire story about Little Red Riding Hood. In itself the hood is enough to send an adequate signal. Even if a man played the girl, Little Red Riding Hood would materialize before our very eyes. In real life there would be a whole range of signals at work, but adding them to the situation would only confuse the recipient and hinder believability. Thus efficiency in communication may be a better leading star for the construction of synthetic characters than verisimilitude.

4.5 Interactivity in Virtual Improvisation

Having discussed the difficulties of making a narrative that allows for interaction and the typical approaches to the construction of autonomous agents, we should like to offer, finally, a particular dramaturgical way of looking at interaction as such. For this purpose we shall return to the theoretical framework of drama in education.

4.5.1 A Double Consciousness

It has been argued by Bolton that there is always a double consciousness at work in improvisational drama. The point is that participants not only perform their actions as characters in a drama session, they also observe themselves at the very same time as characters in an illusion. This means that at one level of consciousness participants accept the illusion, the "as if", as some kind of other "reality", while at another level they keep track of the fact that this "reality" is only an illusion. This could also be formulated with the help of a distinction between acting and spectating: even when performing their parts as actors, the participants do not dismiss their spectator-part altogether. Bolton tries to capture this duplicity with the help of a famous formula: "I am making it happen to me" (Bolton, 1984).

Both of us have worked as drama teachers and we find no reason to disagree with Bolton. Indeed, there seems to be a double consciousness at work in improvisational drama. Only on very rare occasions have we met people who got so engaged in the illusion that they mistook it for reality. In so far as there is an element of fiction in play in an improvisation, participants seem to sustain the double existence as ego (outside the fiction) and alter ego (inside the fiction) fairly easily. But even if we tend to agree with the general drift of the argument launched by Bolton, we believe that his formula needs to be somewhat sophisticated.

It should be noted that there is a polemical backdrop for this theory about the participant's double consciousness. Teachers (like Bolton) who favour the form of drama in education that is based on "living through experience" are often criticized rather severely by teachers from the other camp. These teachers find the improvisational approach much too heated because it seems to condemn the participants to stay on the inside of the established fiction. Allegedly they are forced to give up any reflexive (let alone critical) distance from what is going on and let themselves be driven by the fiction. From this crucial flaw it follows that there can be no learning about form. If you are only *in form,* you cannot learn *about form,* or so it seems to the critics. As the participants are so thoroughly involved in the *what* of the improvisation, they don't seem to have any mental powers left for the *how.* In the eyes of the critics, however, this is only a minor problem. With the bracketing of reflexive rationality the participants are believed to be deprived of their shield against manipulation performed by the teacher. Even if (as opposed to the spectators of the invisible theatre) they consciously enter the illusion of the fictional world, they seem to be completely in the teacher's power. (For a particularly vicious attack along these lines, cf. Hornbrook (1989)).

Bolton's theory about the double consciousness is in fact an attempt to defend the improvisational form of drama in education against this attack. To us, it seems fairly obvious that the criticism misfires. It is true that the participants need to be persuaded to suspend their disbelief in the fictitious world if any drama is to take place. If somebody decides not to sustain the illusion, it breaks down immediately. It is also true that participants in an improvisation may experience moments of sheer pathos beyond the control of rationality. This means, indeed, that a participant in this form of drama must lose some of the self-control on which we rely so heavily in everyday life. But improvisational drama neither needs an absolute suspension of disbelief, nor does it call for an excess of immediate feelings beyond the scope of rationality. What is needed is simply an acceptance from every participant to play along with the frame that is being set up and a willingness to confine his or her acting to this framework.

The fact that the criticism misfires does not necessarily imply, however, that Bolton has stated the ultimate truth of the matter. In fact, he seems to be too engaged in the polemics raised against him to hit the spot. Because he needs to counter the claim that his form of drama annihilates the reflexive distance of the participants, he feels obliged to show that it actually also allows for an element of distance. When, for strategic purposes, he sums up his position with the help of a dialectic between I and me, however, he seems to simplify the image of what is happening in an improvisation too much. As far as we can see, he too readily accepts the distinction set up by his opponents between an active ego *outside* the fiction and a passive alter ego (i.e. the character) *inside* the fiction. This distinction seems to result in an image suggesting that when the participants work as actors within the fiction they are totally immersed, whereas they become active (and reflexive for that matter) only in so far as they relate to the fiction from a position outside it. But this is hardly a description of what happens. On the one hand it mistakenly conflates the position of the director with the position of the spectator. Indeed, the two positions are characterized by being outside the fiction, but this common denominator should not overshadow a crucial difference: in contrast to the director, the spectator is hardly active in the sense that he or she influences the fictional events directly. On the other hand, it is far from true that you are only passive when partaking in a "living through" experience. Indeed, you will have to react on what is offered by the teacher and the other participants, but you may also choose to initiate a certain development of the action yourself.

4.5.2 I/Me and "I"/"Me"

Instead of a dialectic between an active *I* outside the fiction and a passive *me* inside the fiction, we seem to be faced with an intricate interrelation between *four positions*. If the ego is always divided between a real *I* and a real *me*, so is the alter ego always divided between a fictitious "I" and a fictitious "me". If we are not mistaken, participants either oscillate between these four positions or handle them simultaneously. It is this complexity of the situation that made us call for a sophistication of the formula suggested by Bolton. As an attempt to capture the complexity we opt for a reformulation of it: "I, as a character, am making it happen to my character and me" (Figure 4.6).

We happily admit that these reflections are rather abstract and in need of some elaboration. In order to clarify our rationale we would like to illustrate it with the help of an example. Please imagine the following situation in a drama class. A teacher in rôle invites a group of participants to a baptism. The participants are told that the scene to be played is set in the 1950s. In the evening there is a party that is taking place in the large mansion owned by the parents of the young mother, or, to be accurate, by the father, the *paterfamilias*. The drama will begin when the party has already begun. For a while the party is going well, but suddenly the daughter

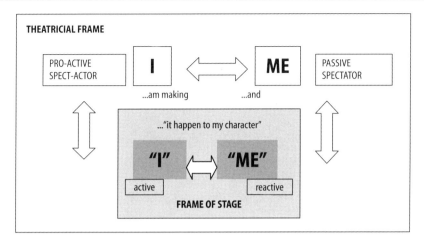

Figure 4.6 Here we try to illustrate the four interlinked positions that can be occupied by the user of an interactive narrative: I am, as the proactive participant who can be both spectator and actor: a *spectactor*, making "it", the events of the narrative, happen to my representative inside the fiction: the character. The character can be acting either as an "I" that is an active and planning character or as an observing and reactive character. The enacted events are displayed to me: the passive spectator.

throws her baby into her husband's arms and leaves the party in a furious rage. At this point the teacher (who has played the *paterfamilias* until now) stops the improvisation in order to investigate this moment a little more carefully. He facilitates this investigation by setting up a new type of improvisation. It is going to take place two hours after the daughter's dramatic exit from the party. All the participants are now gathered in the living room, but the teacher has established a corner in the space with a lonely chair lit by a single spotlight. He introduces the rule that any character can sit in the chair. When someone sits down, the light is changed, the improvisation freezes and everybody listens to an inner soliloquy spoken by the character in the chair. The rest of the group is simply supposed to watch and listen. When the soliloquy ends, the participants re-enter the improvisation as if nothing has happened. At one level (as actors) everybody shares the information, but at another level (as fictional characters) nobody has heard the soliloquy.

Bearing this example in mind, some readers might find it a bit far-fetched to distinguish between the activities performed by the participant's real I and that performed by the "I" of the alter ego. After all, the decisions made by the character will ultimately have to be made by the participant. Of course, we have no quarrel with this point of view. Nevertheless, there seems to be a crucial difference at work. When considering how to act in a specific situation from the point of view of an outsider, you will tend to ask the question of the director: "what should I do in order to have a desired effect on the entire narration?". When, on the other hand, you are trying to decide what to do as a character, you would ask the question of an involved subject instead. Here the question would rather be: "what shall 'I' do in this particular situation?" The situation with the participant who declares the innermost thoughts of the character and shares it with the other participants, but not with the characters, is a poignant illustration of how the two options coexist, even if they are still discernible as two distinct ways of relating to the action.

Perhaps it will seem equally misleading to draw a distinction between a me and a "me" for whom it happens. All things considered, there is only one real me that may experience things. The character's experience is but the actor's experience. We happily admit that, but even if this is true, there is also here a crucial distinction to be drawn. As a character in an improvisation you cannot be totally passive. You constantly have to react to the contributions of the teacher and the other participants. Within the confines of a fictional framework even a non-reaction is a form of reaction. In contrast to this, you may be completely passive as a spectator precisely because you are positioned outside the illusion. It was not until we made a small error in the setup of the soliloquy scene that we became painfully aware of the need to draw this distinction. On one occasion we were not specific enough regarding the status of the pieces of information produced in this scene. Some of the participants regarded them as hard facts that all the characters would share. In contrast, other participants conceived of them (as they were intended) as pieces of information that would have come to the attention of the actors, but not the characters. In other words, some of the participants had related to the scene as spectators outside the fiction (in the position of the me) and others as characters within the fiction (in the position of the "me'). There is no need to spell out the mess that appeared when somebody began playing the scene with the return of the young mother with a privileged insight into her inner life while others played the scene without it.

Now, if all of this is correct, the four positions seem to be distinguished by the degree in which they involve activity. The positions of the real I and the real me seem to mark the two logical extremes of a continuum. In so far as the real I have the capacity, not only to act in a given situation, but also to even (co-) create the conditions of a situation, it may be called proactive. As the real me only watches what is going on, on the other hand, it may be said to be completely passive. Likewise, the difference between the fictitious "I" and the fictitious "me" is also related to a distinction between active and passive, but in this case the distance between the two poles seems to be lesser. As the "I" acts on its own behalf, it is active, but in so far as the actions will always have to be subordinated to a given situation, we may think of the "I" as (only) active (as opposed to proactive). In comparison to the "I", the "me" is less active, but in so far as it will always have to act according to a situation, it is not exactly passive. To capture this particular position the term *reactive* seems more suitable. Thus, while the real participants oscillate between the active director and the passive spectator mode, their characters thus shuttle between setting something in motion and reacting to actions. Similarly, while the real me watches, the fictitious "me" experiences, and while the fictitious "I" acts, the real I (co-) creates the circumstances for the acting.

It is this refined version of Bolton's formula based on four positions of the participant instead of two that we offer as a possible model for thinking about interaction with autonomous agents in virtual worlds. Perhaps it will seem obvious that it seems applicable to the construction of a virtual puppet theatre. As much as any course of drama in education this application is consciously based on the element of fiction and therefore on the distinction between ego and alter ego. It may be worthwhile to consider, nevertheless, whether we can generalize the suggested model beyond this limit. Not every virtual world is an illusion (if by illusion we mean a universe of make-believe in which agents and avatars pretend to be somebody whom they are not). Still there is one central feature which entering a virtual world as an avatar shares with participating in an improvisation as a character, and that is precisely the division of the I into an ego and an alter ego. To us, it is this common denominator that may turn the model based on drama in education into a useful matrix for the interaction with autonomous agents via an avatar in general. If changed to this context, the formula simply ought to be transformed into: "I, as an avatar, am making it happen to my avatar and me".

For the sake of honesty, we had better admit that this offer is based on a normative kernel. We do have a car to sell. Because Bolton was faced with the need to counter the attack launched against his alleged destruction of the reflexive distance towards the improvisational events, he stressed the "I am making it happen" part of the equation. During the three years of our project we have found ourselves stressing, by contrast, the "to me" part of the formula. In a world in which interaction is a buzzword and good interaction is believed to be synonymous with giving the user as many options as possible for being active, it seems necessary to opt for a view of interaction that rehabilitates the passive side of reception (Landau (1997) displays an example of the reasoning that we find, at best, infertile). However, we should try to avoid missing the central point of the paradigm for the sake of polemics. We do in fact believe that multimedia products that involve improvisation with synthetic characters should be made with respect to the intricate interrelation of the I, me, "I" and "me". For us, good interaction with computer-generated universes is like good improvisation. It only works really well, as we put it earlier, if it is open enough for the participants to become creative, yet closed enough for the universe to be suggestive. If, ideally, on the one hand, the user should become an active part, she must also, on the other hand, be driven towards particular actions by the system.

4.5.3 Interaction in the Virtual Puppet Theatre

It is important to add that the ideal of involving all four positions of the participants does not imply that they should all be in play at any time of the interaction. Some phases may very well emphasize one or two positions and disregard the other positions. Thus, when breaking down the improvisational drama of the farmer and the cow into six phases, we considered which dimension of the interaction should be supported by a particular phase.

Analyzed in terms of the suggested four positions, phase one (in which the child was allowed simply to navigate in the virtual space) and phase two (in which the child was given the opportunity to investigate the agent's actions from different angles as a cameraman) put the emphasis on the me. However, even if these two phases are the least interactive phases, they do not leave the child totally passive. In fact, it seems fair to say that phase one establishes a relation between the me and the "I". Yet the child is not allowed to become a fictitious "I" in the form of an avatar, but in so far as he or she is invited into a fictional virtual world, he or she is supported with a quasi alter ego in the form of a subjective camera. The distinction between ego and alter ego has not been established completely, but it is in the making. Likewise, the second phase allows the child to get an impression of what it means to go from the passive reception of the me to the proactivity of the real I. As a cameraman who is "filming" the action, the child is more on the outside of the illusion than he or she is when acting as an explorer in phase one. Consequently, there is no fictitious "I" at work, but instead there seems to be a real I. The possibility of working as a cameraman does not vouch for actual proactivity in the sense of being capable of controlling the framework of the situation, of course. Nevertheless, it seems feasible to say that the opportunity to work with camera angles may let the child experience the feeling of becoming a film director who controls the aesthetics of the output.

Phases three and four (in which the child is allowed to intervene in the action as a magical haystack and later as a sheep) are the two truly improvisational phases. Here, the child is forced to enter the fiction and participate from the inside. Entering the improvisation as a haystack will inevitably make the child give up the position as a pure receptive me, but in so far as a haystack is a poor character as far as identification is concerned, the child will probably first and foremost experience him- or herself as a "me". In so far as it becomes obvious along the way that even as a haystack you may influence the action, the child will probably be more and more inclined to see his alter ego as an "I". When the possibility of becoming a sheep is introduced in phase three, the child may actually be so involved in the conflict that he or she will have almost forgotten that it is important also to sustain the reactive dimension of the "me". With the rising familiarity with the structure of the conflict, the capacity for becoming a really proactive I will most likely grow. Now the child may choose to consider the entire situation and make decisions on behalf of the sheep with respect to the entire improvisational framework as opposed to just making choices from the sheep's perspective. This possibility to see what is going on a little from the outside is enforced by the specific interface that was developed to this phase. When the child is allowed to choose between different attitudes of the avatar sheep with the help of a keyboard with icons, he or she is asked to give input to the avatar from the outside. In the theory of improvisation this is known as *side coaching,* i.e. instructions from a leader of an improvisation to one or more participants concerning how they should perform.

In phases five and six the emphasis is once more on positions on the outside of the fiction, but now the point of departure is the real I. Allowing the child to dream up lines for the agents when they meet is like letting him or her become a directing playwright who, as a real I, can decide from the outside what should be said in the improvisation. In this respect, the reiteration involved in phase six is important. If the child changes from the position of the I to the position of the me when the task is fulfilled and he or she is allowed to watch the scene which has been directed, then it is important for the possibility of becoming really proactive that the child is allowed to change the first shot at directing significantly. You will probably not feel in charge of things until you have experienced that you can even make changes in what you have created yourself.

4.6 In Conclusion

We hope that our reflections on the problems that arise from wanting to produce a virtual puppet theatre have succeeded in arousing an interest among computer engineers to pursue the dramaturgical turn as a way of thinking about the problems. On the other hand we hope that we have made good the claim that virtual reality systems may be a gain for drama teachers who would like to investigate the new media without having to discard old paradigms of drama in education altogether.

For the record, however, we ought to add that in our experience it is far from easy to make a scenario that implies autonomous agents and allows for interaction that actually works. With the current state of technology you cannot help getting a sense of entering an extremely restricted area with surprisingly many limitations. Let us just point out one of the more obvious restrictions. As a teacher you can jump in and out of different rôles when the improvisation seems to need a particular twist. In contrast, an autonomous agent seems to be stuck with its rôle because it takes quite an effort to define, develop and fine-tune the inner life of an agent. In this project, to be honest, we never really solved the problem of reducing complexity to a feasible level while creating something that is truly aesthetically satisfying.

Yet, while addressing the problems we began to fathom what potential the technology actually holds. At a somewhat more sophisticated technological state this piece of equipment may become of great importance to drama teachers. Not only will it become possible to pass on the job as a teacher in rôle to an autonomous agent, but in a virtual setting you will also be able to work with many agents in rôle at the same time. In the real world this only happens on the rare occasions where the budget permits you to work closely together with several colleagues. With the help of autonomous agents you may introduce, for instance, an extra villain in the improvisation if need be. At any rate, that is the vision of which we have caught a glimpse.

Acknowledgments

The work described in this chapter is the result of a fruitful collaboration between many people from many different fields. The authors whish to thank Torunn Kjølner and Anne Line Svelle for their collaboration in the development of the numerous scenarios. Special thanks go to our partners in the project in Aalborg, Denmark (Erik Granum, Claus B. Madsen and Ivan Pedersen (animations)), in Sussex, England (Mike Scaife, Yvonne Rogers and Paul Marshall), and in Saarbrücken, Germany (Martin Klesen, Thomas Rist and Elisabeth André). Mike Scaife died suddenly in the final months of the project. This is a great loss to research in this field; Mike Scaife will be greatly missed. The support of the European research project, PUPPET, ESPRIT Long Term Research EP 29335 under the i3 Early School Environments programme, and the Danish Research Council research project STAGING is gratefully acknowledged.

References

Blumberg, B. and Kline, C. (1999) The art and science of synthetic character design. In *Proceedings of AISB 1999 Symposium on AI and Creativity in Entertainment and Visual Art*, Edinburgh, Scotland.

Boal, A. (1980) *Stop! C'est magique*. Paris: Hachette.

Bolton, G. (1979) *Towards a Theory of Drama in Education*. Burnt Mill: Longman.

Bolton, G. (1984) *Drama in Education. An Argument for Placing Drama at the Centre of the Curriculum*. London: Longman.

Buytendijk, J. F. (1933) *Wesen und Sinn des Spiels*. Berlin: Kurt Wolf.

Eco, U. (1989) *The Open Work*. Cambridge: Harvard University Press.

Greimas, A. J. (1986) *Sémantique structurale*. Paris: PUF.

Hornbrook, D. (1989) *Education and Dramatic Art*. Oxford: Blackwell Education.

Johnstone, K. (1981) *Impro. Improvisation and the Theatre*. London: Methuen.

Kjølner, T. and Szatkowski, J. (2002) Dramaturgy in building multimedia performances: devising and analyzing. In Halskov Madsen, K. (ed.) *Virtual Staging: Staging of Virtual Inhabited 3D Worlds*. London: Springer.

Lambert, A. and O'Neill, C. (1982) *Drama Structures*. London: Hutchinson.

Landau, G.P. (1997) *Hypertext 2.0. The Convergence of Contemporary Critical Theory and Technology*. Baltimore: The Johns Hopkins University Press.

Laurel, B. (1991) *Computers as Theatre*. New York: Addison-Wesley.

Madsen, C. and Granum, E. (2001) Aspects of Interactive Autonomy and Perception. In Qvortrup, L. (ed.) *Virtual Interaction: Interaction in Virtual Inhabited 3D Worlds* London: Springer.

Microsoft (1996) *The 3D Movie Maker*. Redmond, WA: Microsoft Corp.

Spolin, V. (1983) *Improvisation for the Theatre. A Handbook of Teaching and Directing Techniques*. Evanston, IL: Northwestern University Press.

Stubenrauch, H. and Ziehe, T. (1982) *Plädoyer für ein ungewöhnliches Lernen*. Hamburg: Rohwohlt Taschenbuch Verlag.

Szatkowski, J. (1989) Dramaturgiske modeller. Om dramaturgisk tekstanalyse. In Christoffersen, E., Kjølner, T. and Szatkowski, J. (eds.), *Dramaturgisk analyse. En antologi*. Aarhus: Aktuelle Teaterproblemer.

The Living Theatre (1971) *Paradise Now*. New York: Random House.

Witkin, R. W. (1974) *The Intelligence of Feeling*. London: Heinemann Educational Books.

Supporting Interactive Dramaturgy in a Virtual Environment for Small Children

Claus B. Madsen

5.1 Introduction

What does it look like "behind the scenes" of an interactive virtual environment? What technical functionalities are required to support the simulation of a virtual world, populated by computer-controlled characters which interact with each other, and even interact with user-controlled characters? How can we design a system that gives the user the feeling that he or she is influencing a virtual world, has some control over what happens, and has possibilities for creating his or her own experiences?

These are complicated issues to which there are by no means final answers or design guidelines. The present chapter addresses these issues with a starting point in a specific application context: the interactive virtual experience developed by the PUPPET project.[1]

The PUPPET project was a focal point for research into the development of interactive virtual environments populated with computer-controlled characters (autonomous agents, or simply agents) aimed at children in the age group of 4 to 8 years. A concrete result from the PUPPET project is an interactive farm scenario with two agents, a Farmer and a Cow, and an avatar, a Sheep. The avatar is the child user's embodiment in the scenario and the character through which the child interacts with the scenario.

---

1 The PUPPET project (The Educational Puppet Theater of Virtual Worlds) was funded by the European Commission as an ESPRIT Long Term Research Project under the i3 Early School Environments Programme, project number EP 29335. The project ran from October 1998 to January 2001.

By using the PUPPET scenario as the application context, or case as it were, this chapter is closely related to Chapter 4, by Szatkowski and Lehmann. They develop and explore a dramaturgical framework to structure the balance between interactivity and story development for the PUPPET scenario. The two chapters can easily be read independently; they simply provide completely different perspectives on several of the same issues.

In this chapter we present a *technical* viewpoint on the problem area. We will look at some specific functionalities of the developed system and discuss them in relation to the application context. In other cases we describe particular requirements posed by the dramaturgical design of the PUPPET scenario, and discuss various technical solutions. As such, the chapter is quite factual. It is a design description of a concrete software platform. Nevertheless, it is believed that the topics chosen will be of general interest to researchers and designers in the field of interactive 3D virtual environments. The chapter attempts to focus on general aspects, and on discussing them in a manner accessible to a wide audience.

But first, in order to provide the necessary background and insight, we give an overview of the technical platform developed to support the interactive scenario, i.e. a platform for real-time 3D virtual environments with focus on interaction with computer-controlled characters (autonomous agents).

The last decade's drastic increase in home computer performance has caused a revolution in interactive virtual environments. From being the dream of the few such environments are now a standard household entertainment medium: incredibly immersive, believable real-time 3D computer games are abundant, all available for run-of-the-mill desktop computers.

In a famous speech in 1965, "The Ultimate Display", Ivan Sutherland (Brooks, 1999) put forward a vision for what would later become virtual reality, or virtual environments:

> Don't think of it as a *screen*, but think of it as a *window*, a window through which one looks into a *virtual world*.

Although impressive advances have been made, this almost 40-year-old view of "virtual reality" is still ahead of the present day state of the art in many respects. In addition to the above quote Sutherland's vision can be summarized as:

- Displays as a window into a virtual world
- Image generation which makes the picture look real
- Computer maintains a dynamic world model in real time
- User directly manipulates virtual objects
- Manipulated objects move realistically
- Immersion in virtual world via head-mounted display
- Virtual world also sounds real, feels real

Many items from the above list can be considered as having been achieved. Some items have functional solutions, though further improvements are needed, and others have only been rudimentarily addressed. The most noticeable of the latter category is the issue of getting the virtual world to *feel* real. Similarly, *direct* manipulation of virtual objects is not as natural and intuitive as we experience it in the real world. The remaining items have solutions that are sufficiently well-developed to actually suspend user disbelief and make the user feel immersed in a dynamic, virtual but seemingly real interactive world.

Three development areas have simultaneously and cooperatively driven the development of virtual reality (VR): vehicle simulators (flight, ship and automobile), entertainment (games and movies), and "serious" application-specific VR. The latter category does not have a proper heading, but covers applications that do not fall into the first two; it is often referred to merely as "VR" (Brooks, 1999; Astheimer and Rosenblum, 1999). The category covers, for example, surgery simulators, VR systems for rapid visual prototyping in industrial design, and visual data mining (Granum and Musaeus (2002) provide an interesting description of the latter subject). In 1999 VR was estimated to be a US$3 billion industry (Astheimer and Rosenblum, 1999), and the computer games industry was estimated to be a US$7 billion industry (Olsen, 2002).

As mentioned, 3D computer games are good examples of the current state of interactive virtual reality. Better than anything else, they demonstrate to a wide audience that it is possible to create illusions of entire fantasy worlds in which one can explore the world at will and where one can cause things to happen, making them truly interactive. This chapter will attempt to present a "look behind the scenes" of such interactive VR systems. The chapter will give an overview of the main general functionalities required to create such interactive worlds, where one can move around and explore a virtual world, populated with computer-controlled characters (autonomous agents). As such, this chapter is a sequel (or perhaps more precisely a prequel) to Madsen and Granum (2000), which provided an overview of the autonomous agent concepts, and the main issues involved in designing these.

Figure 5.1 shows two screenshots produced by an interactive VR platform developed jointly for the STAGING project sponsored by the Danish Research Council and for the PUPPET project. The specific scenario shown is a farmyard inhabited by

Figure 5.1 Two screenshots from a virtual world providing an interactive farm world designed for children. The Cow and the Farmer are computer-controlled characters (autonomous agents), and the Sheep is the user's avatar. Thus the screenshots illustrate the concept of an inhabited, dynamic virtual world into which the computer display acts like a window.

various animals, but the same VR platform can readily be used to run any other scenario provided 3D models of environment and characters are available. In other words, there is an important distinction between a VR *platform* and a *scenario*, a platform being a general software system designed to execute scenarios, which in turn provide the description of the look and feel of particular virtual worlds.

In the community of computer games the VR platform is called a *game engine*, and scenarios are often called *gameplay* or *content*. The chapter is devoted to giving an introduction to the overall design and key internal functionalities of such a VR platform or game engine. The reason for this is that there is "more to it than meets the eye": there are many complicated issues to address in order to design and implement a VR platform capable of facilitating virtual worlds such as the one depicted in Figure 5.1.

The structure of the chapter is as follows. Section 5.2 gives an overview of the overall design of the technical platform with particular emphasis on the difference between the *visualization* and the *world server* functionalities, and issues such as getting objects to move around are addressed. In Section 5.3 we then pick a set of generic functional requirements from the aforementioned PUPPET scenario. These requirements are discussed from a technical point of view and related to the platform design, and the developed solutions are outlined. For example, we describe some functionalities developed to enable the system, in particular the autonomous agents, to *interpret* the actions of the user in relation to the rôles of the agent's characters. Finally, Section 5.4 summarizes and concludes.

5.2 Technical Overview of Platform

Naturally, there are many different ways to design the architecture of an interactive virtual reality platform for use in a game type situation. Vince (1995) and Watt and Policarpo (2001) present some views similar to those which will be outlined below. It is important to distinguish between (1) the *visualization* of the virtual world involving real-time computer graphics, and (2) the virtual environment server, which maintains the dynamics of the virtual world, provides support for various communication and interaction within the virtual world, and also handles the interface to the user, converting user actions into effects.

In the subsequent sections a platform design will be presented at a block diagram abstraction level. The chapter as a whole will focus mainly on aspects relating to single-user systems, since the idea of the chapter is to give the reader an understanding of the processes going on to facilitate an interactive virtual environment. Readers interested in the particularities of multi-user systems are referred to works such as Greenhalgh and Benford (1995), DeLoura (2001), Carlsson and Hagsand (1993) and Benford and Fahlèn (1993).

Figure 5.2 shows a block diagram of an interactive virtual reality platform, where computer-controlled autonomous agents act and interact in real-time, and where the virtual world is visually and auditorily rendered to a user. Figure 5.1 showed screenshots from such a world.

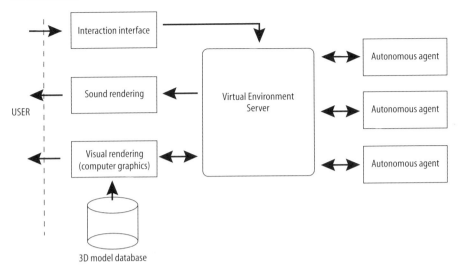

Figure 5.2 Platform architecture overview. The dotted vertical line demarcates the interface to the user. Everything to the right of the dotted line constitutes the platform. In our case the platform includes computer-controlled characters (autonomous agents). The central element, the virtual environment server, handles all dynamic and kinematic simulations, as well as all interaction between characters (and the user).

Referring to Figure 5.2, there are four groups of elements.

1. To the left is the user.
2. Immediately to the right of the dotted line, which demarcates the boundary between the real and virtual worlds, there are a number of interface-mediating modules enabling the user to see (visual rendering) and hear (auditory rendering) the virtual world, and the user can interact with the virtual world using various devices (in our platform these include computer mouse, standard game console interfaces such as a "wingman", and a microphone).
3. The central virtual environment server is in charge of the real-time maintenance of the dynamic virtual world.
4. To the far right three autonomous agent instances are shown, although there can be any number.

In a previous paper (Madsen and Granum, 2000), we gave a detailed description of the concept of autonomous agents and their possibilities for emulating life in virtual worlds. The present chapter will not discuss this in detail, but Section 5.2.3 gives a brief summary of the autonomous agent concept and the particular agent architecture that has been developed for this platform. This summary is important for Section 5.3, which discusses functionalities developed in support of the dramaturgical framework of the PUPPET scenario.

5.2.1 Visualization of the Virtual World

An important feature of any platform for interactive 3D virtual environments is the visualization of the virtual world. It is beyond the scope of this chapter to give an

Figure 5.3 Top row: computer graphics based rendering of three different virtual world scenarios with coloured and textured polygons. Bottom row: the polygonal object structures underlying the images in the top row.

introduction to the fundamentals of real-time 3D computer graphics, as there are so many other excellent works on this topic, e.g. Watt and Policarpo (2001), Watt and Watt (1992), Foley *et al.* (1994), Watt (1998) and Angel (2000), but we briefly describe the primary elements in the visualization module developed for this project.

Figure 5.1 shows screen dumps from a caricatured, cartoonish farm scenario. Every single element/object in this virtual world is comprised of a collection of 3D triangles, and every triangle has a texture, or an image, mapped to it. This is shown clearly in Figure 5.3.

Virtual worlds include static objects, such as terrain, buildings and fixed structures, and dynamic objects, such as characters, vehicles and machines. Most often static, as well as dynamic, objects are modelled using special software for 3D modelling such as Maya or 3DStudio, but is should be mentioned that as an alternative 3D models can be constructed by scanning real objects using one of many 3D scanning techniques. An overview of such techniques is given in Bjørnstrup (2002). Figure 5.4 shows an example of 3D computer models created from using a stereo vision reconstruction technique to scan a real building and a plastic model building.

Using 3D modelling tools or scanning to create 3D computer models of artificial structures is normal practice and gives good results, but it is somewhat more diffi-cult to get reasonably realistically looking results when it comes to modelling natural shapes, such as terrain and vegetation. Interestingly, in recent years it has become popular to use 2D images for modelling terrain. The approach is to "paint" a 2D greyscale image, using the underlying assumption that it will later on be

Figure 5.4 The shed on the left is a 3D model created from stereo vision reconstruction based on images of a real physical shed. The yellow old-fashioned dairy in the middle was created by scanning a plastic model building. Both scanned 3D models have been imported into a 3D virtual world.

interpreted as a height map, where the brightness of an image region is mapped to height. Recent articles by Martin (1999) and Peasley (2001) present excellent descriptions of how to make complicated terrain in this manner. As an example, Figure 5.5 shows how an image of a human face can be converted into a height map for use in virtual environments as a mountainous terrain.

Regardless af whether the 3D geometry of an object or some world element is modelled manually, scanned or otherwise built automatically, it is important to add textures to the geometry in order to achieve visually appealing results. Geometry (shape) alone is not enough. Textures can be real images, or they can be drawn in 2D drawing/image manipulation programs. Figure 5.6 illustrates how a very simple 3D model of a cartoonish, caricaturized Farmer achieves its distinctive visual appearance from 3D shape as well as from the textures mapped to the shape.

Even if recent developments in computer graphics hardware have made it possible to make real-time visualizations of rather complicated 3D models, there is still a limit to how many polygons (triangles) can be shown on the screen. In order for the visualization to appear smooth it is generally accepted that a computer game must

 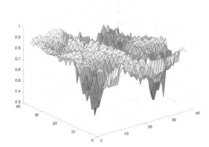

Figure 5.5 Left: greyscale image of a human face. Right: the face image when interpreted as a height map, where the image brightness is mapped to terrain height.

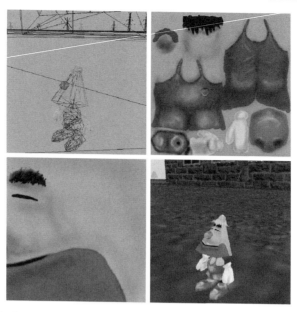

Figure 5.6 Example of how to create a cartoonish character for an autonomous agent. Top left: wireframe character geometry. Top right: textures for body. Bottom left: texture for half the face. Bottom right: final textured farmer model in scenario.

render the visualization with at least 30 images per second, but 50 frames per second is more typical for good virtual environments. The limiting factor on how many frames per second can be visualized is the number of polygons in the scene. Because of this it is common to use cleverly designed textures instead of geometry (polygons). For example, instead of "wasting" polygons on buttons and on the Farmer's eyebrows, these visual elements only appear in the texture. Conversely, the nose of the Farmer is important for his visual appearance in profile, and thus the nose needs to be modelled as a 3D shape, not merely drawn as a texture. Another typical use of textures is for shadows. It is still not generally possible to compute the shadows cast by objects in real time, so in many computer games, as well as in the PUPPET system, shadows cast by characters are implemented as a partially transparent, dark 2D surface below the character, and this surfaces follows the character around as it moves about in the virtual world.

Textures can be switched at run-time while visualizing objects, and we use this functionality to enable our characters to change facial expression. For example the face texture in Figure 5.6 can be replaced by one with a reddish, angry appearance. This causes the facial expression to change from one frame to another. One advantage is that the sudden change makes the mood transition more apparent and more dramatic, but given enough textures a smooth transition from one expression to another can easily be created.

Before the terrain, the objects and the characters can be visualized using modern computer graphics, everything must be organized in a so-called scene graph (Figure 5.7). The purpose of the hierarchical nature of the scene graph is that *transformations*

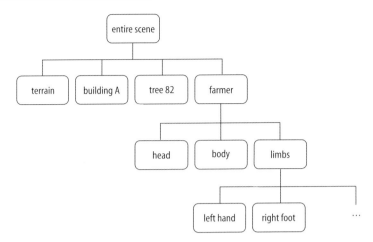

Figure 5.7 All objects in the virtual world are organized in a hierarchical structure called a scene graph, where the entire scene containing all objects is denoted the root (top node in graph), and for every level one goes down in the scene graph the representation is more detailed. At that very bottom of the scene graph (not shown) there are two further levels: the polygonal level containing every polygon in the entire scene, and the vertex level, containing the coordinates of every point in every polygon.

can be applied to every node in the graph individually, but applying a transformation to a node implies that all children of the node are subjected to the same transformation, all the way down to the lowest vertex level. A transformation can be a scaling, a translation or a rotation. Thus it is quite simple to get the entire Farmer character to move around in the scene; it only requires translations and rotations to be specified for the Farmer node, and automatically all geometry subordinate to the Farmer node will be translated or rotated in the same manner. If we only want to rotate the head, the appropriate rotation transformation is specified for the head node. Subjecting the *root* node (the "entire scene" node) to transformations causes a change of viewpoint of the entire scene; that is, when the user "moves around" in the virtual world, exploring it freely, the user's computer mouse movements are converted into translations and rotations applied to the scene graph root node.

The hierarchical nature of the scene graph has implications for how to *animate* objects. For example, if we want it to appear as if the Farmer is actually moving his legs and feet while walking, we have to translate and rotate the legs/feet appropriately, in addition to subjecting the Farmer node to a translation transformation. If we need even more detailed realism in movements, e.g. if we want the feet to bend as they are lifted from the ground, then transformations need to be applied to the polygonal and vertex levels below the foot node in Figure 5.7. If movements are performed at this level it is called vertex animation. Needless to say, the lower the scene graph level the more complicated it is to design/compute the appropriate animation transformation. For this reason we chose the "rigid object" paradigm for animations in the PUPPET system, so that animations are only performed at the limb level, i.e. the lowest level is hands and feet, which in turn are treated as rigid objects and do not change shape over time.

Figure 5.8 The simplistic Farmer wielding a huge club in the air. This is something our PUPPET Farmer will occasionally do when he gets sufficiently frustrated with the Cow's blatant lack of interest in following the Farmer back into the cow pen.

Whether to use vertex animation or rigid object animation is also linked to the visual design of characters. As is seen from the screenshots from the PUPPET system, we have chosen a very simple visual design for characters where the limbs are separated from the body (Figure 5.8). This visual design lends itself well to the somewhat simpler rigid object animation. If we had chosen a more realistic design concept we would have been forced to apply animation at the vertex level, in order for animations to have the same realistic feel as the overall design of the character.

The Farmer in the PUPPET scenario occasionally uses tools. For example, at times he threatens the Cow with a big club. When not in use this club is scaled to a very small item and hidden inside the Farmer's hand. When the Farmer needs to use the club it is simply scaled to normal size and wielded in the air, after which it is again scaled down to miniature and hidden inside the hand. This kind of artistic freedom, or reckless treatment of realism if you will, is accepted by users given the charicaturized visual design, but would be unacceptable for a more realistic looking Farmer.

The transformations used for changing the viewpoint of the user (transformation of scene graph root node), as well as all other transformations used for moving characters about in the virtual world, rigid object animation or vertex animation, are set up or changed between every frame of the visualization. For example, if the user moves the computer mouse slightly to the right, in order to pan the viewing direction to the right, a little rotation is performed on the root node for every frame, for as long as the user is moving the mouse. This movement of the entire scene is combined with any movement of individual objects. If the Farmer character is supposed to move forward at a speed of s [distance units per second] in the direction of some vector $\vec{D}$, where $\vec{D}$ is of unit length, the change in position, ΔP of the Farmer node is computed as:

$$\Delta P = \Delta T \cdot s \cdot \vec{D}$$

where ΔT is the time that has passed since the last frame was visualized, i.e. of the order of 20 ms for a rendering running at 50 frames per second. The time elapsed between frames is never a constant number since the geometrical complexity of the scene changes, causing rendering times to go up and down. However, by using the above expression the movement of the Farmer will appear to have constant velocity, even if ΔT changes somewhat over time. That is, in interactive virtual environments the concepts of time and velocities are dealt with in the visualization, and therefore the visualization module must have access to a quite accurate real-time clock on the computer. In the above expression $s \cdot \vec{D}$ is the velocity vector giving the object velocity in each of the three spatial directions, x, y and z. Similarly, each object can be subjected to rotations with three angular velocities, one for rotation around each of the three axes.

It is important to notice that there are two different ways in which an agent, for example, can move in the virtual world. It can walk by asking to be translated with some speed in some direction (as described above), *and* it can ask for an animation to be run. Our system thus distinguishes between movements that are performed on the entire object (the entire body of an agent) and on movements performed on individual elements of the object (body). The latter are performed as animations which are designed and computed offline by the designer of the object. Thus animations are fixed and are stored along with the 3D model of an object, and the wielding of a club is an example animation for the farmer.

As stated above, there is a limit to how many polygons can be within the field of view and still maintain a reasonable frame rate. This can cause problems for very large scenarios with complicated terrains and many objects, especially in an outdoor scenario, where the user can potentially see very far. In order to limit the number of polygons in outdoor scenarios it is necessary to set a distance-based limit on which polygons are rendered. If a polygon is more than some distance threshold away from the viewpoint it is skipped. This functionality is called distance clipping. It has the negative side effect that, as the user moves into the scene, objects suddenly pop up because they come closer than the clipping plane. To avoid this, the clipping plane is hidden by a simulated fog, which becomes denser and denser with distance, so that at the clipping plane, nothing is visible. This makes objects appear slowly as they gradually become more clearly discernible when moving towards them. The fog has the added benefit that it makes exploring the virtual world more interesting, as you have to move around to discover the entire scenario. In Figure 5.8 there are actually mountains in the background, but they are partially hidden in the fog and partially discarded by the distance clipping plane.

A final element in reducing the number of polygons to be rendered is Level Of Detail, or LOD. LOD involves having multiple versions of each object, ranging from a version with only a handful of polygons, through intermediate polygonal resolution, to full resolution. In the PUPPET system every object is associated with two or

```
Static.Ground:   xyz = (0, 0, 0) ;
                 hpr = (0, 0, 0) ;
                 Geometry="island.flt";

Complex.well:    xyz = (150, 900, 0) ;
                 hpr = (-90, 0, 0) ;
                 Properties="IslandWell.complex";
                 Type="Water";
```

Figure 5.9 Typical content in scene description files. See the text for an explanation.

three different model versions, so that as the object comes closer to the user's viewpoint it will also become more and more detailed in its shape.

The PUPPET system reads a scene description file which is loaded at system startup. The scene description file describes what objects to place in the scenario and where to place them, as well as providing some associated information concerning each object. This makes the system completely independent of the geometry of the scenario, i.e. the same system can be used for any scenario provided the required 3D models for the scenario are available and a scene description file is written. An typical excerpt from a scene description file is shown in Figure 5.9.

Figure 5.9 lists two entries. `Static.Ground` refers to a static object called `Ground`; this is the terrain in the PUPPET scenario. It should be positioned at world coordinate `xyz = (0, 0, 0)`, and the statement `hpr = (0, 0, 0)` means that no rotation should be applied to the object (`hpr` means heading, pitch, and roll respectively). The next line (`Geometry = "island.flt"`) means that the 3D model for the `Ground` object should be taken from the file `island.flt`, which is an OpenFlight file (hence the extension `flt`). OpenFlight is one of many possible file formats for 3D objects models.

The next entry in the scene file in the table concerns an object named `well`, of the so-called `Complex` category. The `Ground` object was of the `Static` category, which is the simplest possible in the PUPPET system. `Static` objects cannot move, cannot be selected by users, and do not have different Levels of Detail. Objects in the `Complex` category cannot move, but they can be selected and have multiple LODs. The `well` object will, as specified, end up in the scene model at coordinates (150, 900, 0), and will be rotated 90° degrees around the vertical axis before being placed. The `well` appears in the background in Figure 5.8. The actual detailed specification for the `well` object is imported from the file `IslandWell.complex`. Excerpts from the content of this file can be seen in Figure 5.10.

Figure 5.10 describes to the system that the object in question has two levels af detail, high resolution and low resolution, and that the high resolution version will be exchanged with the low resolution version when viewed from more than 3800 units away. When viewed from more than 10000 units away the `well` is not visible

```
Create LOD {
        Geometry          = 'well_highres.flt'
        Range             = 3800
}

Create LOD {
        Geometry          = 'well_lowres.flt'
        Range             = 10000
}

Selectable ON
```

Figure 5.10 Typical content in a file describing an object in the so-called `Complex` category.

at all. Finally, the system is told that the `well` can be selected, i.e., the user can click on the `well` and something happens. We shall return to this functionality later.

We have now presented an overview of several key issues in the visual rendering of a virtual scenario. We will not go into any detail of how the sounds of the virtual scenario are rendered to the user. Suffice it to say that sounds are stored as files in a database in the same manner as the objects of the world. Each sound can be played at any point in time, and multiple sounds can be played simultaneously. But every sound has to have a "source", i.e. in the PUPPET system only objects can make sounds, sounds cannot appear out of the blue. The reason for this is that the sound when played in the computer's speakers is attenuated with the distance from the user's current viewpoint to the sound source. Thus the yelling of the Farmer is heard with varying volume depending on how far away he is from where the user is watching the scenario.

5.2.2 The World Server

Having thus presented an overview of how the visualization of the virtual scenario is performed, we now move on to describing the main functionalities of the Virtual Environment Server (or simply Server). The Server is the main controlling element in the entire system, as illustrated in Figure 5.2. Apart from being responsible for all communication between the various modules the Server is charged with everything related to the simulation of cause/effect relationships of the virtual world. An example of this is *terrain following*.

Terrain following is a term used for the functionality that objects moving about in the virtual world follow the terrain (unless they request permission to do otherwise). As such it can be viewed as a simulation of gravity. The benefit of having terrain following implemented in the Server is that dynamic objects do not need to know about how the terrain goes up and down in height. A dynamic object utilizing the terrain-following functionality need only treat navigation as a 2D problem, similar to following a plotted course on a map. The server will automatically ensure that the moving object is at all times following the surface of the terrain. Terrain following is implemented by imposing a notion of a direction of gravity, i.e. a notion of which direction is "upwards", e.g. the z-axis. Given the xy position of a moving object, the height (z-value) of the terrain at that position is calculated and the moving object is then translated along the z-direction so as to ensure that the lowest point on the moving object is at terrain height. Naturally, dynamic objects are free not to utilize the terrain-following functionality, for example if the object is a bird that wishes to take to the sky.

Another related functionality in the Server is collision detection, which, as the name suggests, is the task of detecting when objects in the virtual world collide. From a visualization point of view collisions make no difference. Any two 3D objects can be positioned so as to collide and intersect each other and still be visualized with no problems; the visualization module does not care if 3D objects intersect. But from the point of view of creating a believable virtual environment, collisions cannot always be tolerated: for example, the Farmer should not be allowed to arbitrarily walk straight through the well. There are two aspects to collision detection: (1) How should the detection be performed?, and (2) What should happen if a collision is detected?

In principle, collision detection is a matter of checking, for every infinitesimal movement of dynamic objects, whether any moving object intersects some other object. This could be done by simply taking every polygon in the geometry of the dynamic object and testing it against every other polygon in the rest of the virtual world, but this approach is computationally too expensive, as a walking Farmer may have 1000 polygons, and the rest of the scenario may have 800 000 polygons. Testing every polygon against all other polygons is simply not viable. In reality, collision detection in the PUPPET system is performed on bounding boxes, which are geometric abstractions over all objects. Figure 5.11 illustrates the concept of bounding boxes in the case of the PUPPET system.

The bounding box concept is used in the Server as the 3D representation for all virtual objects. Terrain features such as mountains may be modelled from multiple bounding boxes, but otherwise there is one bounding box per object. The bounding

Figure 5.11 Two examples of an axially aligned bounding box for a cow. Axially aligned bounding boxes can potentially be larger than necessary for objects that are not very compact. When elongated objects rotate, the sides of the bounding box remain aligned with the axes, causing the box to take up more 3D space than the actual 3D object.

box for each object is computed by the visualization module, since that module is in fact the only one with direct access to the exact geometry of the objects. This is also illustrated in Figure 5.2, where it is shown that it is the visualization module that has access to the database of 3D object models.

By letting the Server use bounding boxes as volumetric primitives for all objects it becomes computationally feasible to do collision detection, since it is much simpler to test for intersections on a pair of boxes than on the detailed polygonal geometry of each object. The collision detection is made even simpler by the fact that the PUPPET system uses so-called axially aligned bounding boxes, where each side in the bounding box is parallel to the three main coordinate axes of the virtual world. Axially aligned bounding boxes are computationally simpler to implement collision detection on, but they have the drawback that an axially aligned bounding box can be very large for an elongated object if that object is rotated relative to the main axes. This is illustrated in Figure 5.11. In the concrete example, the cow is more prone to bump into things when walking diagonally in the world, simply because the width of the bounding box is somewhat wider than the actual cow itself. If this negative side effect is unacceptable it is possible to use oriented bounding boxes, which are rotated along with the object, but oriented bounding boxes are computationally more complex to use for collision detection. Thus using bounding volumes will always be a trade-off between how efficiently the bounding volume approximates the actual 3D shape of the object, and how complex the bounding volume is in terms of performing collision computations.

As described in Section 5.2.1, it important to visually render the virtual world with as high a frame rate as possible, preferably more than 30 frames per second. However, it is not always necessary to perform Server functionalities at that speed. In the PUPPET system the Server and the Visualization run in parallel as two separate processes (two threads, in programming terminology), with the internal Server update rate being of the order of 10 Hz. That is, for approximately every two to three frames the Server requests the current position and bounding box of all objects and performs things such as terrain following and collision detection. Furthermore, if, for example, a walking agent wishes to change movement direction or speed, the agent must send a request to the Server, which in turn notifies the Visualization. Thus agents can only perform such changes at the rate of the Server, i.e. about 10 times a second. Similar rules apply for requests for animations or changes of texture etc.

A very important functionality of the PUPPET system is that of generating the so-called percepts for agents. According to *Webster's Dictionary* a percept is "an impression of an object obtained by the use of the senses". Madsen and Granum (2000) address the various aspects of the percept issue in much greater detail. In this context it is introduced as a task performed by the Server. The concept of percepts is relevant for discussion later in this chapter. Simply put, percepts in the PUPPET system are small information packages sent to agents at every Server loop. Each agent will receive a percept for every object the agent senses, i.e. objects that are within the agent's sensing ranges. We currently operate with five senses: vision, audio, tactile, sixth sense and proprio sense (Figure 5.12).

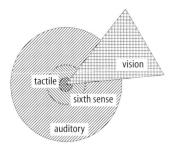

Figure 5.12 Schematic illustration of how sensing is simulated for each agent. The ranges of the four senses can be altered by the agent itself, e.g. to simulate that some agent may have very good vision but poor hearing.

The proprio sense allows the agent to perceive itself, primarily to give the agent access to information about its current position. The sixth sense allows the agent to sense all object in the immediate vicinity of the agent, so if an object is within say 1 or 2 metres of the agent, the agent will sense it, even if the agent is looking the other way, and even if the object is not making any noise.

The Server performs percept generation by taking an agent, looking up its position and orientation, and then checking all other objects' bounding boxes to see whether they are inside one or more of the agent's sensing ranges. Naturally a silent object inside the auditory range will not generate a percept.

5.2.3 Autonomous Agents

The concept of percepts naturally leads to the topic of *autonomous agents*, or simply agents, which are one of the key features of the PUPPET system. The design of the agent architecture is not central to this chapter, and thus we shall only give a brief summary of it here. As was the case with the percept concept, the agent architecture design is dealt with in much higher detail in Madsen and Granum (2000).

A central design element in our agents is that they have two layers: a low level and a high level. These will be referred to as the Low Level Agent (LLA) and High Level Agent, respectively. Each agent or character in the scenario has an LLA and an HLA layer. The difference between the LLA and the HLA is that the LLA provides generic functionalities such as spatial memory (remembering objects that have been sensed and where they are) and abilities to plan and execute movements around the scenario, whereas the HLA layer is in charge of making decisions concerning what to do, and when. That is, the LLA deals with how to do things, and the HLA deals with what and when, and one might say it deals with the why as well, because the HLA layer does reasoning according to the specific rôle of the character/agent in the scenario.

The HLA layer is scripted specifically for a particular character. Thus the Farmer in the PUPPET scenario has a completely different script than the Cow. Scripts are written in a high-level scripting language, and every behaviour of the agent is scripted as plans that each have a set of goals to achieve, some preconditions that must be met for the plan to be executed, and a plan body which contains a sequence of sub-actions to be performed in order to achieve the goal. Sub-actions typically involve requesting the LLA layer to perform various tasks. The LLA layer is capable of executing a range of actions that can be grouped into four categories:

- **Gross body movements.** Actions that involve moving the entire body of the agent, such as following another agent, moving to a named object, turning etc.
- **Animations.** Actions that involve moving the individual parts of the agent body; as described previously, each agent can choose animations from a set of animations designed and modelled in advance for the particular character. Animations can be played at various speeds (fast or slow) and can be repeated a number of times.
- **Sounds.** As with animations, the agent cannot produce sounds that are not in a library of sound files.
- **Textures.** Actions concerning the use or changing of one or more textures of the agent model, for instance changing facial expression or changing the colour of clothing.

The range of possibilities within each of these four categories is of course limited, but since they can be combined arbitrarily they amount to quite an extensive array of ways in which the agent can express itself. For example, a walking animation when played quickly while the agent is not moving looks like a frustrated, angry stamping in the ground, especially when supported by an angry face. Figure 5.13 shows a couple of example screenshots from the interaction between the Farmer and the Cow in the PUPPET scenario.

Figure 5.13 On the left the Cow is dancing to the music from the gramophone, ignoring the yelling Farmer (anger showing from behind in the reddish facial colour). On the right the Farmer has obtained the Cow's attention and is waving a stick while moving forward in an attempt to herd the Cow back to the pen.

5.3 Technical Functionalities Supporting Scenario Dramaturgy

After having presented an overview of the core technical aspects of the PUPPET system we now shift our attention towards the actual PUPPET scenario and use various elements from it to showcase the functionalities of the system, and to describe what technical solutions have been designed to support some desired effect in the scenario.

As mentioned in the introduction, the PUPPET scenario is designed for 4- to 8-year-old children. The scenario was meant as a vehicle for exploring children's ability to read characters and interpret their behaviour and motives, to read the drama between characters, and specifically to determine how well children were able to understand and engage in the interaction between characters. More than 100 children have been exposed to the scenario in one form or another, and all children have been accompanied by an adult supervisor/scaffolder. By interacting with the children during sessions and by talking to them afterwards, possibly asking them to re-tell the story as they experienced it, much information has been obtained concerning children's ability to understand and conceptualize the emotion/mood-driven interaction between the Farmer and the Cow.

The scripts for the two main characters in the PUPPET scenario, the Farmer and the Cow, are quite elaborate and depend entirely on each agent being able to continuously perceive the scenario, and especially keep track of the whereabouts and activities of the other agent. Thus the Farmer is constantly checking whether the Cow is inside its pen, and if he finds that the Cow has ventured out, and perhaps gone to read books, he will immediately approach the Cow and take actions aimed at getting the Cow back inside the Pen. What actions he takes depend also on how many times he has tried to persuade the Cow. Conversely, the actions of the Cow depend on what the Farmer is doing and what he has done in the past. Thus, percepts concerning the other agent's current position, as well as current activities, plus a memory of what interactions they have had previously, form the basis for the scripts. A more precise account of the structure of the interaction is presented in Chapter 4.

A session with the system has a number of phases:

1. Explore uninhabited world.
2. Watch Farmer and Cow scenario.
3. Influence the Farmer and Cow scenario by moving a haystack around.
4. Interact with the Farmer and the Cow through an avatar (a sheep).
5. Record lines (utterances) for the characters as the scenario unfolds.
6. Possibly re-record utterances recorded during a previous session.

It is not the purpose of this section to go through each of these phases one by one. Instead, we have taken elements from the scenario and use them as stepping stones for taking a look behind the scenes of the system with reference to the preceding technical overview.

5.3.1 Passively Exploring the Scenario

As described in Section 5.2.1, the PUPPET system supports viewing outdoor scenarios from arbitrary viewpoints and with arbitrary viewing direction. This may seem trivial, but until about a few years ago, when implementation on the system began this was almost unheard of due to the complexity of outdoor scenes, with

Figure 5.14 Initially the child can explore the uninhabited scenario by flying around freely (left). Later the child can, for example, click on the Cow trough (middle) and thus make the Cow appear in the scenario, after which it starts acting according to its script (right).

their potential for viewing very far into the horizon and thus having to deal with a very large number of geometry polygons.

In the initial phase of the PUPPET scenario the child can visually explore the entire terrain, with its mountains, valleys, streams, lakes, and of course the central farm-yard area. Through this exploration the child is gradually accustomed to using the computer mouse to control viewpoint and viewing direction in a mode which is similar to flying an airplane, i.e. the child has full control over six degrees of freedom (position and orientation) for the virtual camera. The left image in Figure 5.14 clearly shows the fog hanging over the scenario, which has the technical func-tionality of hiding the fact that objects very far away are not visualized at all, and it has the aesthetic effect of making it more compelling to venture into the distance to explore what is out there. When flying around in this manner the system is set up to slow down camera movements in the central farmyard area, i.e. the navigation is less sensitive to mouse movements. This makes it easier for young children to perform delicate explorations of the important, and more cluttered, area.

Section 5.2.2 described the collision detection functionality, which can also be applied to the virtual camera used when visually exploring the scenario, making it impossible to "fly through" solid objects. Nevertheless, tests with children demon-strated that the younger children (4–6) had great difficulty mastering the more precise navigation, and got frustrated when trying to move around objects. In response to this, collision detection for the users' navigation was switched off.

After having explored the uninhabited scenario for a while the child is then informed that by clicking objects related to the Farmer and the Cow, the two char-acters will appear in the scene. Figure 5.14 illustrates how clicking on the trough in the shed inside the cow pen causes the Cow to appear. Immediately thereafter, the Cow, or more precisely the agent controlling the Cow, starts executing its scripts. For example, it will start walking to the bookshelf to read.

Clicking, or *selecting*, an object with the mouse is a general functionality in the system. The effect of selecting an object is context-dependent, and the decision about what action occurs in response to the selection is made by a "Scenario Control" module not represented in Figure 5.2. The Scenario Control module is scripted especially for a specific scenario and is not general, as the rest of the system is. In the case of the PUPPET scenario, selecting the Cow's trough causes the Cow to appear, but subsequent selections of the same trough have no effect. Later in the session clicking the Sheep has the effect that the Sheep becomes the child's avatar. Thus overall session control is performed by the Scenario Control module.

5.3.2 Exploring the Scenario Through an Avatar

In the context of virtual environments an avatar is a user's representation, or embodiment, in the scenario. The PUPPET scenario entails a Sheep, which is not an agent in the manner of the Farmer or the Cow. It is a character meant to be controlled by the child. After having watched the struggle between the Farmer and the Cow the child is instructed that by selecting the well a sheep will appear, and by selecting that sheep it will become an avatar.

Having the Sheep as an avatar entails that, instead of exploring the scenario by flying around with a virtual camera, the child is now controlling the movements of the Sheep with the mouse. The Sheep is utilizing the terrain-following functionality in the Server, and thus moves along the ground. Yet in order to study what effect viewpoint has on the child's identification with the avatar as a *me* ("That's me, I am the Sheep, let me annoy the Farmer"), we implemented a selection of avatar viewpoint modes. This is illustrated in Figure 5.15.

For an interesting discussion on viewpoint in interactive games the reader is referred to Rouse (1999). It is generally accepted that first-person perspective is a good vehicle for inducing identification with a character in film and in interactive media. Nonetheless, tests with the PUPPET system clearly showed that children preferred the third-person perspective, as illustrated in the middle image of Figure 5.15. In the third-person perspective the child first of all has a better overview over the interaction between characters, and is also able to see the Sheep, its movements, and its actions. Controlling the Sheep avatar to actually interact with the scenario will be the topic of Section 5.3.4, but first we need to look at a special interaction device employed with the PUPPET system in order to enable young children to control the system.

Figure 5.15 The PUPPET system supports arbitrary viewpoint positions when interacting with a scenario through an avatar. The above images illustrate experiencing the scenario in first-person perspective (left), normal third-person perspective (middle), and a third-person perspective which is very remote from the avatar character (right).

5.3.3 Interaction Device for Small Children

Children in the lower range of the target age group for the PUPPET scenario cannot be expected to possess the motor skills required to interact with a virtual environment through a typical console game interaction device, with its many buttons and joy sticks. As mentioned, our system uses the computer mouse as navigation device (although a PlayStation gamepad can be used instead). But in order for the child to control other degrees of freedom such as viewpoint mode for the avatar, or the actions of the avatar, we employed the so called "concept keyboard" (Concept, 2002). The concept keyboard is a pressure-sensitive pad with 16 × 16 receptive fields. An overlay with icons can be placed on the pad and the pad can be set up to generate arbitrary messages to software applications in response to pressing various areas on the pad. Figure 5.16 shows the icon overlay used with the PUPPET system.

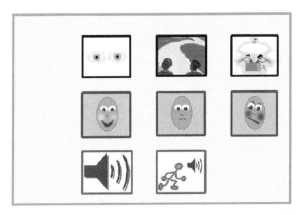

Figure 5.16 Icon overlay for concept keyboard allowing young children to control various aspects of the system. The top row has three icons for choosing viewpoint modes – left to right: first-person perspective for avatar, third-person perspective, and free-flying camera (no avatar). The middle row enables the child to choose the mood of the avatar – happy, neutral, and angry. The bottom row has two icons: one causing the avatar to make a sound, and one causing the avatar to make a sound *and* an animation.

While it can be difficult to design self-explanatory icons for such a device it is still very intuitive, and children quickly master the possibilities offered by the device. By moving the Sheep around using the mouse, and by pressing relevant areas on the concept keyboard, the child is now able to take an active part in the scenario and influence the actions of the Farmer and the Cow.

5.3.4 Are You Talking to Me?

By simply moving the Sheep around in the virtual world the child has the possibility to obstruct the paths of either the Farmer and the Cow. That is, the avatar can be used as a simple obstacle, and with a little training it is possible to annoy the Farmer severely by consistently preventing him from approaching the Cow. But by choosing different moods for the avatar and by causing the avatar to utter sounds it

Figure 5.17 The child has control over the Sheep avatar's mood, which in turn is visualized by using different textures on the sheep body and face. Left to right: happy sheep, neutral sheep and angry sheep.

is possible to provoke a more direct response from the Cow and the Farmer. Figure 5.17 illustrates the various Sheep moods. Given a selected mood, the Sheep will utter a mood-appropriate sound and perform a mood-appropriate animation if the child presses one of the action buttons on the concept keyboard.

In the PUPPET system an avatar is actually an agent for which the autonomous ability to move has been removed and control over movements and actions has been handed over to the user. Being a full-fledged agent the avatar is receiving percepts just as the other agents, which means that should the child choose to relinquish control over the avatar and go for a free-flying camera, the Sheep can act on its own when not an avatar. In the PUPPET scenario the Sheep agent has a very simple script, causing it to return to the well and perform simple idle time actions (occasional sounds and animations). If selected, the Sheep becomes an avatar again, and all movement and actions are then user-controlled.

As explained in Sections 5.2.2 and 5.2.3, percepts play a crucial rôle in enabling the agents to interact with each other. Through percepts each agent has access to information about the actions of the other agents, and can respond consistently. One can say that the agents communicate through a hidden channel, creating the illusion that they in fact perceive and act upon the actions of each other. In this context the avatar is at a disadvantage. There is no way the system can fully interpret what the child is doing or attempting to do though its avatar. For example, the Farmer cannot know if the child (Sheep) is trying to scare him or the Cow.

To this end we needed a way to reason about where the focus of attention of the avatar is. At what agent is an avatar's action directed? The solution in the PUPPET system is to use the spatial reasoning module of the Low Level Agent layer to constantly monitor whether the avatar is *looking at* the agent. Through percepts, the Cow agent, for example, knows the current position and orientation of the Sheep. The Cow is thus able to analyze whether it, or the Farmer, is the primary focus of the Sheep, simply by performing a geometrical analysis of which direction the Sheep is looking. That is, if the Sheep is making a sound, is not too far away, and is looking at the Cow, then the Cow will react to it. This functionality has a side effect also found in real life: if the Cow and the Farmer are standing close together and the Sheep is a short distance away looking in the general direction of the Cow and the Farmer, they will both think they are being addressed and both will

Figure 5.18 On the left the child has chosen to side with the Cow and is using the angry Sheep to scare the Farmer, thus preventing the Farmer from herding the Cow back to the pen. On the right it is the opposite. The happy Sheep is used to lure the Cow in the direction of the pen, thus indirectly assisting the Farmer in his project.

respond. Figure 5.18 shows examples of how the child through the avatar can "help" either the Cow or the Farmer.

5.3.5 Triangle Drama

Augmenting the scenario containing the Farmer, the Cow, and the Sheep avatar to become a true triangle drama turned out to be quite difficult. For example, we wanted the Cow to respond positively towards the Sheep if the Sheep scared the Farmer away. Alternatively, if the Sheep scared the Cow in the direction of the pen, the Farmer should react positively towards the Sheep.

To this end we designed somewhat complex rules allowing each agent to reason about the meaning and effect of the avatar's actions. It would take too long to list and explain these rules and describe how they are employed in the agent scripts, but two examples are given here:

1. **Rule:** If the Sheep is further away from the pen than the Cow, and if the Sheep is luring the Cow towards it, the Farmer should respond negatively towards the Sheep.
   Rationale: If the sheep is luring the Cow *away* from the pen it is against the Farmer's goal, and he should indicate this to the Sheep (and thus the user).

2. **Rule:** If the Sheep interacts with the Farmer (positively or negatively) and the Cow reaches the bookshelf, the Farmer should react negatively towards the Sheep.
   Rationale: If the Sheep is keeping the Farmer occupied and drawing his attention away from the Cow, and if the Cow uses this chance to escape the pen, the Farmer should indicate his frustration with having been tricked into not paying attention to the Cow.

Again we primarily use the agents' abilities to perceive the environment and their abilities to reason about the spatial layout of key objects and the positions of other agents in order to create script rules that can colour the interaction between the three characters of the scenario.

In fact, even the seemingly limited PUPPET scenario contains some action/reaction patterns, or encounters, that are not necessarily immediately obvious when watching them unfold in real time (at least not to a child engaged in navigating and interacting with the agents). To facilitate discussing these encounters with the children we created a functionality to slow down time.

5.3.6 Freezing the Virtual World

In fact, we wanted to be able to bring the virtual world to a complete halt, thus allowing the adult supervisor to discuss situations with the children and to assist the children in reflecting about the motivations and desires of each character.

In support of this we assigned a key on the normal computer keyboard to a "Freeze" function. When the ESC key is pressed the virtual world will stop completely; all moving characters will stop in mid-motion (for example the Farmer's club will hang in mid-air and the Cow will appear as a granite sculpture of a dancing Cow). The really interesting aspect of this functionality, though, is that the user can still navigate the frozen world using a free-flying camera to study the situation from any viewpoint. This allows the child to study the facial expressions of each agent in an encounter, and perhaps to get time to better grasp the meaning of the particular situation.

The freeze functionality is implemented as a temporary halting of the internal loop in the Virtual Environment Server (Section 5.2.2). This causes the percept stream to agents to stop, which in turn stops them from making new actions or from completing ongoing actions. Animations will stop at some frame. The only thing left running is the mapping of mouse movements to translations and rotations on the root node of the scene graph (Section 5.2.1), enabling the user to explore the scene visually from any viewpoint.

Although a simple idea, this functionality turned out to be a great success with the children (and the adults for that matter), as it really allowed for insisting on the PUPPET scenario to be a more thoughtful and laid-back experience than a typical fast-paced computer game.

Another press of the ESC key will bring the virtual world back to life in an instant, and every character will continue as if nothing happened. It is now possible, for example, to see whether what the child thought would happen does actually happen.

5.3.7 Sound Recording and Voice Dubbing

As previously described, each of the three characters in the PUPPET scenario makes extensive use of pre-recorded sounds. The use of sounds and utterances is written into the scripts, which for example will require the sound file named farmerhighminus.wav to be played in a situation where the Farmer is in high

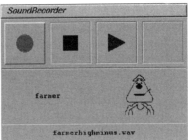

Figure 5.19 On the left is a screen dump from a situation where the Farmer agent desires to utter a sound called `farmerhighminus.wav`. When this happens the virtual world is frozen and a graphical interface to a recording facility appears (right). By operating the interface the child can record a line/utterance that he or she thinks is appropriate, and the agent will then use that sound instead of the pre-recorded one.

status and negative mood. All pre-recorded sounds are word-less and use only intonation and nonsense words to indicate meaning.

To support the children in taking an active part in making the scenario their own experience, and to allow them to express their perceptions of the scenario directly, we developed a sound recording facility and integrated it with the scenario by using the freeze functionality described earlier.

Figure 5.19 shows the interface to the sound recording functionality. If the system is running in sound recording mode (this can be switched on and off at will during a session), and if an agent wishes to make a sound, and if the child has not previously recorded that particular sound, the scenario will freeze and the child can study the situation and make up an appropriate sound. Then the sound can be recorded, heard and either approved or re-recorded. When the child is satisfied with the sound the OK button is pressed. This brings the world back to life, and the agent will now use the newly recorded sound in place of the pre-recorded one.

This is implemented by having two sound directories: one with all the pre-recorded sounds standard to the PUPPET scenario, and a separate sound directory for the child's personal sounds. Initially the child directory is empty and agents will use pre-recorded sounds. By running the system for a while in sound recording mode, gradually more and more child sounds will become available to the agents, and in the end all sounds will be child sounds. When *not* running in sound recording mode priority is given to child sounds if they exist; if not, pre-recorded ones are used.

A sound can only be recorded once during a session. When a sound is recorded a screen dump of the scenario is stored on disk, and when all sounds are recorded, an automatically generated web page contains all screen dumps and all recorded sounds. The child and the adult can now go through all the situations that cause sounds to be recorded; the sounds can be changed if desired, and subsequently the whole PUPPET scenario can be experienced again, this time completely uninterrupted and with a complete set of the child's own sounds.

Again, although conceptually simple, this sound recording facility has been an unimaginable success, extremely popular with the children, and has resulted in numerous entertaining transcripts. It has been a valuable tool in analyzing the children's ability to reflect on the underlying emotional states of the agents, and it has provided insight into the children's ability to use sophisticated dialogue and externalization as a means of understanding the drama.

We also developed another sound-related feature for the system, not one designed for recording sounds, but one meant for real-time verbal interaction with the scenario. The functionality permits the user, when acting as avatar, to utter sounds and speak, and this sound information is captured by a microphone and transmitted into the virtual world so as to enable the autonomous agents to respond to it directly in various ways, for example by running away from a shouting Sheep. Initial experiments indicated that it was not a very suitable feature for the PUPPET scenario for two reasons, one being that the children would get over-excited with the possibility of scaring the other characters, and the other being that it led the children to believe that the agents could actually *understand* what was being said. So the feature was not a part of the final PUPPET scenario, but was exploited for a series of dedicated scenarios with a single autonomous agent, Bouncy (Paggio *et al.*, 2000; Madsen *et al.*, 1999; Pirjanian *et al.*, 1998; Brøndsted *et al.*, 1999).

5.4 Conclusions

This chapter has presented the design of an interactive virtual environment from two perspectives. First we gave a general overview of a design of a system capable of supporting a scenario with autonomous agents interacting with each other and with an avatar. Secondly, we used the case of the PUPPET scenario for children to take a look at how the technology can be used and shaped to support specific intentions with a scenario.

A major challenge has been to enable the system, and in particular the agents, to respond intelligently and rationally to the actions of the user's avatar. It was shown that by having designed the system with an explicit focus on enabling agents to sense and perceive the virtual environment in real time we obtained sufficient flexibility in how agents could be scripted to interact with the avatar.

We also believe that the system's in-session sound recording facility, and the facility to freeze the virtual world, are innovative and greatly assisted in creating an alternative experience for children: an experience focusing on reasoning about the motivations of the computer-controlled characters as an alternative to run-of-the-mill action-packed computer games.

Acknowledgments

The work described in this chapter is all done in fruitful collaboration with numerous people. The author wishes to thank Panteleimon Kampolis, Bo Cordes Petersen, Martin Klesen and Iben Granum, among others, for their invaluable contributions.

Finally, the support of the European research project, PUPPET, ESPRIT Long Term Research EP 29335 under the i3 Experimental School Environments programme and the Danish Research Council research project STAGING is gratefully acknowledged.

References

Angel, E. (2000) *Interactive Computer Graphics: a Top-Down Approach with OpenGL*, 2nd edn. Reading, MA: Addison-Wesley.

Astheimer, P. and Rosenblum, L. (1999) A business view of virtual reality. *IEEE Computer Graphics and Applications*, 19(6), 28–32.

Benford, S. and Fahlèn, L. (1993) A spatial model of interaction on large virtual environments. In *Proceedings: 3rd European Conference on Computer Supported Cooperative Work*, Milan, Italy.

Bjørnstrup, J. (2002) Making 3d models of real world objects. In Qvortrup, L. *et al.* (eds.) *Virtual Space: Spatiality in Virtual Inhabited 3D Worlds*. London: Springer-Verlag, pp. 93–111.

Brøndsted, T., Nielsen, T. D. and Ortega, S. (1999) Affective multi-modal interaction with a 3d agent. In *Proceedings: Eighth International Workshop on the Cognitive Science of Natural Language Processing*, Galway, Scotland, pp. 102–109.

Brooks Jr., F. P. (1999) What's real about virtual reality? *IEEE Computer Graphics and Applications*, 19(6), 16–27.

Carlsson, C. and Hagsand, O. (1993) Dive – a platform for multi-user virtual environments. *Computer & Graphics*, 17(6), 663–669.

Concept (2002), 'Penny+giles computer products'. http://www.conceptkey.co.uk/.

DeLoura, M. (2001) Game plan – on game engines. *Game Developer*, January, p. 4. (This article is a one page "letter from the editor".)

Foley, J. D., van Dam, A., Feiner, S. K., Hughes, J. F. and Phillips, R. L. (1994) *Introduction to Computer Graphics*. Reading, MA: Addison-Wesley.

Granum, E. and Musaeus, P. (2002) Constructing virtual environments for visual explorers. In Qvortrup, L. *et al.* (eds.) *Virtual Space: Spatiality in Virtual Inhabited 3D Worlds*. London: Springer-Verlag, pp. 93–111.

Greenhalgh, C. and Benford, S. (1995) Massive: a distributed virtual reality system incorporating spatial trading. In *Proceedings: 15th International Conference on Distributed Computing Systems*, Vancouver, Canada, pp. 27–34.

Madsen, C. B. and Granum, E. (2000) Aspects of interactive autonomy and perception. In Qvortrup, L. (ed.) *Virtual Interaction: Interaction in Virtual Inhabited 3D Worlds*. London: Springer-Verlag, pp. 182–209.

Madsen, C. B., Pirjanian, P. and Granum, E. (1999) Can finite state automata, numeric mood parameters and reactive behaviours become alive? In *Proceedings: Workshop on Behavior Planning for Life-Like Characters and Avatars*, held in conjunction with the I3 Spring Days, Sitges, Spain.

Martin, K. (1999) Using bitmaps for automatic generation of large-scale terrain models. *Game Developer*, October, pp. 48–53.

Olsen, J. (2002) Game plan – so it's come to this. *Game Developer*, July, p. 2. (This article is a one page "letter from the editor".)

Paggio, P., Jongejan, B. and Madsen, C. B. (2000) Unification-based multimodal analysis in a 3d virtual world: the staging project. In *Proceedings: Twente Workshop on Language Theory, "Interacting Agents"*, Twente, The Netherlands..

Peasley, M. (2001) Terraforming, Part 2. *Game Developer*, April pp. 32–38. (This is part 2I of an article that starts in the March 2001 issue.)

Pirjanian, P., Madsen, C. B. and Granum, E. (1998) Behaviour-based control of an interactive life-like pet. *Technical Report*, Laboratory of Image Analysis, Aalborg University, Aalborg, Denmark.

Rouse, R. I. (1995) Gaming and graphics: what's your perspective? *ACM SIGGRAPH: Computer Graphics*, 33(3), 9–12.

Vince, J. (1995) *Virtual Reality Systems*. Reading, MA: Addison-Wesley.

Watt, A. (1998) *3D Computer Graphics*, 3rd edn. Reading, MA: Addison-Wesley.

Watt, A. and Policarpo, F. (2001) *3D Games – Real-time Rendering and Software Technology*, Vol. 1. Reading, MA: Addison-Wesley.

Watt, A. and Watt, M. (1992) *Advanced Animation and Rendering Techniques, Theory and Practice.* Reading, MA: Addison-Wesley.

6

3D Technology in Design and Production

Anders Drejer and Agnar Gudmundsson

6.1 Introduction

Because of increased competitive pressure on cost and innovation, combined simultaneously with the external dynamics of Information and Communication Technology (ICT) in general, the combined design and production processes in industrial organizations have never attracted more attention in the context of reengineering, organizational change and/or development efforts in general. The application of 3D virtual reality holds promise as one of the most interesting means of support efforts related to transforming design and production. In this chapter, we will investigate how 3D virtual reality technology can contribute to a much needed redefinition of the way we perceive design and production and how we work with design and production in industrial firms.

6.2 One Can Neither Design the Optimal Product nor Produce It

All is not well in the world of production and design. There are many conflicts and challenges inherent in the process of designing and producing – all of which point towards problems that 3D virtual reality can help to solve. Since this is not a chapter about production and design, but one on the application of 3D VR, we shall refrain from discussing design and production *per se*. Instead, we will focus on looking at the problems related to design and production that can be helped, perhaps, by applying 3D VR and similar means.

6.2.1 Definitions

This chapter has the concepts of "design" and "production" in its title. As we shall argue later, it is difficult to separate those two concepts in industrial praxis today, and there is even a great deal of convergence of theoretical perspectives and concepts related to design and production. In fact, some have already argued that "design and production" should be seen as one research and management field rather than two (Andreasen, 1999), perhaps dubbed "the expanded production concept" (Riis *et al.*, 1997) or a number of other terms that we shall return to later. We will follow along those lines and basically see design and production as two entities that should not be kept separate – and allow for comments on how this sometimes still happens.

In light of the first paragraph of this section, our starting point is that the greatest potential for the use of 3D Virtual Reality Technology lies in the link between the traditional concept of design (and product development) and the traditional concept of production (or manufacturing). Since production *per se* has been the subject of research and managerial efforts on performance improvement for some 50 years, there might not be great potential for further improvement remaining. Instead, we believe that there is much greater potential in getting traditionally separated organizational functions to work together on the task at hand – hence the notion of "design-and-production" as one entity.

6.2.2 Problems Related to Design-and-Production

Let us try to define (some of) the problems related to design and production in terms of the vocabulary that has been established for this book. In particular, the notions of habitat as well as truth(s) perceived within different habitats seem to be important.

Consider a standard model for the product development process (Ulrich and Eppinger, 2000) (Figure 6.1). Such models are characterized by a phased approach, stepwise detailing of the design from concept to actual production and the involvement of several functional departments (Drejer and Gudmundsson, 2002). In the case of the seminal model of Ulrich and Eppinger depicted in Figure 6.1 the departments are marketing, design, manufacturing and others.

Generally, a product design (and product development) is thus seen as a process where a sequence of steps transforms a set of inputs into specific output (Ulrich and Eppinger, 2000). The steps or activities of the process are all made in order to receive intermediate results between form, function, performance specification, structure etc. (Hubka and Eder, 1989). The activities or steps are usually grouped into four phases: the conceptual phase, system level designs phase, detail design phase and testing phase (Ulrich and Eppinger, 2000; Cooper, 1993).

Empirical evidence, as well as experience, indicates that much design-and-production is, in fact, organized and managed according to this or similar models, (Andreasen *et al.*, 1999). In Denmark, the equivalent model is the well-known "Integrated Production Development" model (Hein and Andreasen, 1985) that has been adopted, if nothing else by name, by vast number of companies over the years. This kind of model fails to take into account several things. For the purposes of this chapter, we would like to focus on the effects of disposition as well as of decision processes related to design.

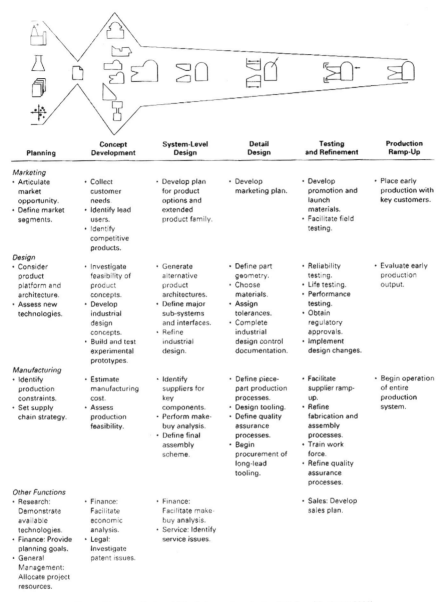

Planning	Concept Development	System-Level Design	Detail Design	Testing and Refinement	Production Ramp-Up
Marketing					
• Articulate market opportunity. • Define market segments.	• Collect customer needs. • Identify lead users. • Identify competitive products.	• Develop plan for product options and extended product family.	• Develop marketing plan.	• Develop promotion and launch materials. • Facilitate field testing.	• Place early production with key customers.
Design					
• Consider product platform and architecture. • Assess new technologies.	• Investigate feasibility of product concepts. • Develop industrial design concepts. • Build and test experimental prototypes.	• Generate alternative product architectures. • Define major sub-systems and interfaces. • Refine industrial design.	• Define part geometry. • Choose materials. • Assign tolerances. • Complete industrial design control documentation.	• Reliability testing. • Life testing. • Performance testing. • Obtain regulatory approvals. • Implement design changes.	• Evaluate early production output.
Manufacturing					
• Identify production constraints. • Set supply chain strategy.	• Estimate manufacturing cost. • Assess production feasibility.	• Identify suppliers for key components. • Perform make-buy analysis. • Define final assembly scheme.	• Define piece-part production processes. • Design tooling. • Define quality assurance processes. • Begin procurement of long-lead tooling.	• Facilitate supplier ramp-up. • Refine fabrication and assembly processes. • Train work force. • Refine quality assurance processes.	• Begin operation of entire production system.
Other Functions					
• Research: Demonstrate available technologies. • Finance: Provide planning goals. • General Management: Allocate project resources.	• Finance: Facilitate economic analysis. • Legal: Investigate patent issues.	• Finance: Facilitate make-buy analysis. • Service: Identify service issues.		• Sales: Develop sales plan.	

Figure 6.1 A standard model for design-and-production (Ulrich and Eppinger, 2000).

The sequence of activities in phases is not sequential and there is an interaction between the phases that result in changes that influence the design and its manufacturing. Generally, development activities are responsible for 70% of all the internal costs generated in an organization (Andreasen and Hein, 2000). Even if this is recognized, it is difficult for engineers and development to understand the overall effect of their efforts in designing and developing products. This is partly because of lack of communication when the focus is on the functionality of the product. The interaction is first put to a test in the testing phase, where the functionality and performance of the construction are in the spotlight before ramping up for production. In the testing phase, errors and mistakes are generally found. Furthermore, errors and mistakes increase the lead time, which is crucial because the market demands newer products, more features and better functionality, customized to their wants (Suri, 1998).

Therefore the design process is complex and difficult to model. There has been one main direction in modelling the design process so far: the so-called consensus model (Pahl and Beitz, 1986; Hubka and Eder, 1989) where the design process is seen as a sequence of activities in different phases (Ulrich and Eppinger, 2000). There are two main characteristics of the consensus model. First of all, it assumes that the problem should be analyzed in abstract terms initially, and that later on in the process it will lead to the particular and concrete. Secondly, it is usually assumed that the overall problem should be decomposed into sub-problems (Kamrani and Salhieh, 2000). What is not discussed is the difficulty of combining different perspectives into the product design.

There are several interest groups, both internal and external within the company. The internal groups generally play a bigger rôle in influencing the design, mainly because they have better access to the development team. External groups could be the government, environmental organizations etc. Therefore the designer has to take different criteria into account when designing a product or component. This generates some difficulties for the designer, who is typically mainly trained to cope with product functionality from a given set of specifications (Andreasen and Hein, 2000). Generally, customers express their needs and wants for a product with phrases like: "easy to travel with". That has to be translated into engineering language, simply because such expressions are useless in given specific guidance for the engineer to follow (Kotler, 2000). They simply leave a broad margin for specific guidance. Therefore the customer's language has to be translated into something that the designer and later manufacturing person understands.

In the vocabulary of this book, we can say that the design-and-production process is a process of interaction between persons in different habitats, who have different languages and perspectives to describe the design with. Typical habitats, as shown in Figure 6.1 could be those of marketing, design (product development) and manufacturing. This corresponds to the seminal model of strategic problems by Miles and Snow (1978) where strategy is seen as comprising the problem of choice of product-market domain, engineering solutions and the administrative problem. Another way of saying the same thing is to focus on the different "worlds" of the management discipline, typically the economic, management, technology, and so on. We see this as yet another way of saying that design-and-production is an activity that needs to integrate a number of different habitats.

The differences in habitat in language and perspective have two effects. First, each habitat tends to arrive at its own model of the reality of the product in question, based on the partial perspective needed for their habitat. For instance, the people in design/product development tend not to focus on ease of manufacturing and handling in their habitat, since this is not necessary or critical for what goes on in that habitat – if the phased model is to be believed. Thus there are several partial perceptions/models of the product being developed in use as the design-and-production process unfolds. There may well be overlap between these perceptions or models, but usually they will be quite different in nature and extent. Second, the different habitats have the curious effect that it is difficult for people to comprehend and hence understand other models than their own. In other words, there are severe problems related to the vocabulary of the different habitats that make it difficult to understand other perceptions of the product being designed. Therefore it is difficult to arrive at better, more holistic, models.

We know the effects of this quite well. People from manufacturing do not understand what marketing people say or the logic of their assertions – and vice versa. The design-and-production process becomes a battlefield between different perceptions, often associated with functional departments, and the resulting product suffers in manufacturability, quality, image, and so on.

6.2.3 Solutions and 3D VR

Elsewhere (Drejer and Gudmundsson, 2002), we have argued that approaches to design-and-production should have three major new characteristics in order to solve the problems outlined above:

- They should be holistic, when it comes to work, rather than functional, splitting work into as many functional parts as possible.
- They should focus on other performance criteria than just cost; preferably also innovation and flexibility.
- They should incorporate the human element both in solutions and in the way solutions are arrived at.

Let us briefly comment upon each of these characteristics. Even before the fashionable concept of Business Process Reengineering, there was much talk of the need for a different approach to how we organize work in or organizations. For instance, Savage made an interesting proposal of fifth generation organizations based on new ICT (of that day) and not building on the principle of specialization as its main principle (Savage, 1990). Such an organization – which might be labelled a network organization – could very well have a more holistic approach to activities of work. Since then, the expanding notion of Business Process Reengineering (BPR) (e.g. Hammer and Champy, 1993), has contributed to a further focus on cross-functional collaboration across the traditional functional organization of this age. This highlights the fact that many activities – seen from the customer's point of view – are something that happens across departments and functional divisions. Hammer and Champy point to three generic activities of some importance to the theme of this chapter – innovation, order handling and production – as three generic business process of organizations (Hammer and Champy, 1993).

The new focus on the cross-functional activities of organizations, has been followed by what we believe is the beginning of a redefinition of the way researchers and managers alike perceive design and production. Some organizations have started to integrate design/product development into the activities of production/operations.

Furthermore, international research has added a new focus on performance criteria of design and production systems. Traditionally, functional departments – the popular saying went – could only be expected to be measured on cost or flexibility or quality (Kaplan and Norton, 1997). However, in recent years notions such as "Mass Customization" (Pine, 1993), "Agile Manufacturing", "Total Quality Management" and several others emphasized that design and production can – and should! – be highly productive, flexible, and innovative at the same time (e.g. Johansen, 1999).

In many areas of management, we have come to realize that the human element of organizations is more important than ever: not just because of the new focus on knowledge as the prime asset of organizations, not even because our employees are of Generation X, but simply because the major obstacle in any organizational change is resistance from employees. The notion of "implementation" of yesterday has been replaced by a major focus on "organizational change" (e.g. Kotter, 1997), or even "revolution" (e.g. Hamel, 1999).

Now, what rôle can 3D VR play in creating such new approaches to design-and-production?

One of the tools that is supportive in creating better integration between development activities and production is a prototype (Ulrich and Eppinger, 2000; Wheelwright and Clark, 1992). The use of a physical prototype as a tool of integrating activities and creating common understanding between functional areas in organization is a very powerful one, because a prototype is an approximation to the actual product (Ulrich and Eppinger, 2000). Therefore the prototype also represents the manufacturability of a given product. The limitation of a given approach for prototypes is the cost involved in making a prototype that is suitable for these purposes. Tools are expensive, and therefore, once tools have been made, only essential adjustments are implemented when the budget has been used up for a specific project (Cooper, 1993)

Ulrich and Eppinger (2000) classify prototypes along two dimensions. The first dimension is the degree to which a prototype is physical as opposed to virtual. The second dimension is the degree to which a prototype is comprehensive as opposed to analytical. The difference from the first dimension is that physical prototypes are tangible, mainly built for testing and experimentation, whereas virtual prototypes are intangible and often build for visualization. Furthermore, the former type of prototype is expensive and requires decisions about manufacturing tools and the product architecture that are difficult to change later on because of the cost.

On the other hand, virtual prototypes represent the product concept in a non-tangible form. Usually non-tangible prototypes are in mathematical form as a 3D computer model. An example of this could be computer simulation: systems of equations encoded within a spreadsheet and a computer model of three-dimensional geometry. The second dimension is about whether the focus is on a fully scaled operational version of the product with all attributes or one with just a few attributes of the product for investigating functionality for example.

Visual, tactile and three-dimensional – in short physical – prototypes are much easier to understand then verbal description, sketches or two-dimensional representations of the product (Ulrich and Eppinger, 2000). The problem is that physical prototypes are expensive and time-consuming. Furthermore, there are many decisions made about the product design that are time-consuming and expensive to change later on in the process. Therefore, virtual prototypes are seen as an alternative to physical prototypes.

In the terms introduced in this book, we can say that 3D VR technology can be used to integrate the traditional model of the design-and-production process along two dimensions. First, 3D VR prototypes can help to integrate different habitats across the functions involved in design-and-production by creating a common language about the final product via more detailed prototypes with a better resemblance to the final product. Second, 3D VR prototypes can integrate activities over time, as a virtual prototype can be built more easily and earlier than a physical prototype. This makes iterations easier and better and can help to speed up the design-and-production process. In other words, we can say that virtual reality technology makes it possible to build virtual prototypes that (1) resemble the actual product better than physical prototypes at earlier stages in the design-and-production process, and (2) can be manipulated and hence alter their design.

6.2.4 About This Chapter

We have now shown that, for many reasons, it is extremely difficult to design products that are optimal from the perspective of the customers, the finance department, suppliers, production department, quality department, designer, manager and so on – especially if you want to satisfy everyone at the same time. As we see it, the major reason has to do with the fact that the design-and-production process consists of a number of habitats that lack the language, the ability and often the will to interact to create an optimal design. Instead we get "over the wall" design, where specifications and documentation are thrown over the walls between functional departments with little or no communication to back it up.

Virtual reality technology can help to remedy this situation by making virtual prototypes that are a better representation of the final product at earlier stages in the design-and-production process than physical prototypes. Furthermore, the virtual prototypes would have an even better effect if it was possible to manipulate them and hence change the design accordingly.

In the next section we will discuss 3D VR and design-and-production by means of a case study of a traditional Danish firm with many challenges related to design-and-production. The firm has, however, engaged in a process where 3D VR has been utilized to improve the design-and-production process in two steps. The first step, which we will focus on in this chapter, is pure virtual reality, as VR has been used to build prototypes of new products that – as a better model of the final product than conventional drawings and text – enabled designers, engineers and production people to discuss the design at an early stage in the design process. The second step, which is a goal of the project and yet to be implemented, is to utilize the first step in a strategic platform for the case company. By using computers and 3D models as decision support, we can say that the second step will end in the other extreme – augmented reality – for the people at the case company. For reasons of space and time, however, this will only be discussed briefly.

6.3 The Case Company

In this section, we will introduce the case company and the challenges related to design-and-production.

6.3.1 Crisplant A/S

In many ways the company, Crisplant A/S, resembles a traditional industrial firm, yet Crisplant cannot escape the effects of the new economy, as its customers are rapidly altering the environment in which Crisplant exists. Founded as a machine shop in 1951, Crisplant has evolved into a major player in the production of sorting equipment for major applications (Figure 6.2). Just two to three years ago, Crisplant was an important player in a fairly stable market, where typical customers included national postal services (e.g. in Germany, Denmark and China) and Freight distributers (e.g. Federal Express).

Crisplant bases its competitive advantage on its ability to help formulate and provide engineering solutions for the specific needs of each client as well as the ability to be very flexible in terms of manufacturing the tailored solutions. All was well for Crisplant. However, in the last few years, several things have emerged to change the market and world of Crisplant. For one thing, the European Union has forced through laws regarding the tendering of large national projects such as sorting equipment for postal services, leading to an increased standardization of the products in this market segment. Second, Crisplant has entered into the market segment of airport sorting. This is a much more dynamic segment with fairly large growth and dynamics in general. Third, and finally, Crisplant is feeling the effects of

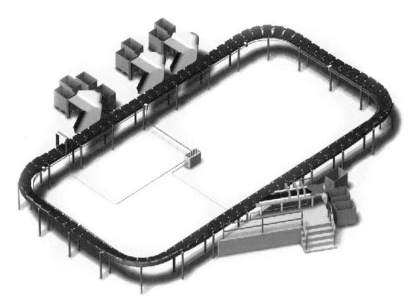

Figure 6.2 An example of a Crisplant product.

the new economy, because sorting is one of the products needed for e-business – and, in short, customers like Amazon.com demand significantly lower delivery times and costs than the national postal services that Crisplant are used to, along with equal quality.

6.3.2 Challenges for Design and Production at Crisplant

In general terms, we can say that Crisplant is experiencing a double external pressure from its environment and competitors. On the one hand, Crisplant has been exceptionally good at making individual solutions for its customers in the past. Much of Crisplant's competitive advantage has been based on that ability, and with the new tender legislation in the European Union there is little evidence that the importance of individual or customized solutions will diminish in the future. On the other hand, Crisplant is being subjected to competitive pressure on cost and price – competitors are able to subject bids that are lower on price than Crisplant and price will of course become an issue in Crisplant's markets. Furthermore, Crisplant needs to start competing on time to market of new projects and solutions. New customers, such as Amazon.com, will not wait a year for the delivery of a sorting installation – six months is more realistic for the future. The latter challenges point towards the need for Crisplant not to work harder, but to work smarter, and to design a set of modular components from which a given, customized, solution can be designed. This will increase speed as well as decrease the cost of new products.

6.3.3 Diagnosis

In order to help Crisplant improve its product development competence, an action research project on strategic platform has been initialized (see Gudmundsson, 2001). As part of this project, an analysis of Crisplant's current product development has been undertaken. The results are presented in this section.

At the present time, Crisplant has a single product focus, where new products are developed without focusing on entire product families. This is because the company started out as a machine shop, focusing on individual orders. There is therefore not much room for development and new products are mostly developed through orders.

The order process of Crisplant – which also serves as its product development process, as each order is treated as one product development project – is illustrated in Figure 6.3.

The process has not changed much through the years and it is standard procedure to sell concepts that are not fully developed. This means that there is not much time to searching for commonalty among other similar products. Therefore the alternative is to engineer the same part again because it takes too long to search for the other part. Furthermore, the database system is from the 1980s, and it is time-consuming to search in the database. Moreover, engineers who have not had experience with earlier similar construction will not try to search in the database.

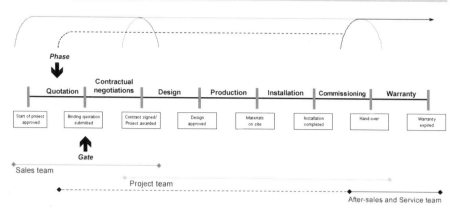

Figure 6.3 Crisplant's order process and project model.

Another important issue is that Crisplant produces for specific orders, and there is a certain fear of declining order flows. Therefore orders are almost never declined. When there are many orders, there are demands on resources from the development department and the development projects are set aside. This gives several problems for the company, and the problem circle can be seen in Figure 6.4.

The internal cost is increased because the project managers create their own solutions owing to lack of time to focus on product families. This increases complexity because of the various product platforms and diverse item numbers.

The design criteria have also, from the beginning, been focused on specific item price. This means that when the engineers are working on developing new things, they try to buy the cheapest part for every new construction without taking into count the cost of producing the item and what it costs to have so many different item numbers and subcontractors.

This process is difficult to change in the company. It is a huge step for Crisplant to change its focus to developing and building an entire family of products that are focused on a specific market segment, instead of focusing on individual orders. This is a leaning process that it is important for the company to go through.

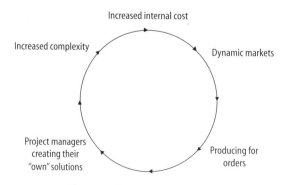

Figure 6.4 The vicious circle for Crisplant.

6.4 Using VR to Build Prototypes

At the operational level, the way in which Crisplant handles order processes as product development projects has serious implications for the quality and cost of the total product. This is, of course, well known as the consequence of the notion of disposal effects – product development is directly responsible for 20% of the total cost of a product, yet indirectly disposes 80% of the cost by its decisions in design and engineering. To motivate employees to take part in this cross-functional project, an analysis of a product in the process of being assembled in Poland was conducted. By means of photographs and other visual illustrations, the analysis showed many examples of low quality, difficulties in purchasing, low manufacturability, and so on. The report, vividly illustrated, from the field trip to Poland motivated employees to take part in a project where 3D VR was to be applied to the challenges of Crisplant.

Thus the analysis revealed that Crisplant had many of the general problems discussed above. Final assembly of the products, to take an example, was made very difficult by the way individual sections of the product were designed. However, there was no learning and/or feedback from assembly to product development. Therefore it was decided to attempt to use VR to facilitate such feedback at an early stage of new product development projects at Crisplant.

The objective of using VR technology was two-fold. First, the idea was to make it possible for representatives from product development, marketing, operations and assembly to meet and discuss a new product design in order to achieve feedback to product development. This is normally close to impossible, because assembly takes places locally, i.e. thousand of kilometres away from Crisplant and its product development people. Second, the purpose of using VR was to try to get feedback from operations and assembly at an early stage of the product development process, so that the design could be improved before it was finalized. The latter objective was, however, seen as a secondary objective at the beginning of the project.

VR technology was seen as an excellent means for facilitating a learning process, where employees from marketing, product development, operations and assembly could easily discuss a new product together. A prototype would be crucial for this purpose, because of the means of communication preferred by employees from operations and assembly. However, at the outset a VR prototype was chosen because it was easier to make than a physical prototype, especially at an early stage of the product development process.

Since many of the problems encountered in the analysis were related to assembly of individual sections of Crisplant's products – and because a section is a separate entity in the design phase – it was chosen to make a VR prototype of a section of a new product that was being designed at Crisplant (Figure 6.5).

Based on newly made engineering drawings and documentation, the Virtual Reality Center at Aalborg University was quick to provide a VR prototype that was used as the basis for organizational learning related to the new design. As such, the objective of the project was reached at this stage, when a number of seminars were conducted and discussions on the new section were facilitated by the VR prototype.

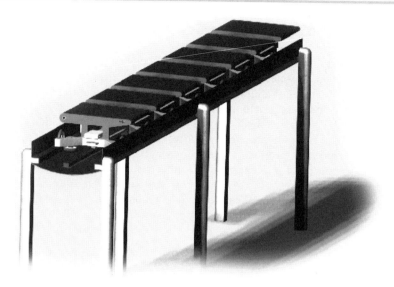

Figure 6.5 The section that was first modelled in VR.

As such, the initial phase of the project was an experiment to see whether 3D VR could yield a virtual prototype that could create a better dialogue than normal at Crisplant. The experiment was a success, but little else could be expected in light of the normal situation with product development at Crisplant. Nonetheless, manufacturing employees from the field felt that the virtual prototype enabled them to make judgements on the ease of assembly and manufacturing of the prototype. This was much better than the traditional engineering drawings and text with which a product (at Crisplant) is documented. Furthermore, the availability of a local prototype (albeit in Aalborg) made it possible for engineering employees to meet in person with assembly employees – for a start – and discuss the new design, communicate about ways to change and improve that design, and to understand each other.

Even though there was made no formal test on scientific principles, there was a strong feeling at this stage of the project that a 3D VR prototype was a much better way to achieve communication in the design-and-production process than traditionally.

6.5 Perspectives – Towards a Strategic Platform

During the first stage of the project, however, the managers of Crisplant were learning that there were other ways to use VR prototypes to improve product development at Crisplant. First of all, Crisplant needs to become better at managing multi-product development in order to standardize its products, thereby lowering costs and accelerating the order process. An obvious means of achieving this is, evidently, modularization, so the new and improved section from Stage 1 was being

Figure 6.6 After the first step – modularization of the section.

used as the basis for designing a modular section that could be used across Crisplant's product range. We may see this as a first step towards working seriously with a strategic platform at Crisplant.

After the VR prototype had been designed and analyzed by a cross-functional group of employees, it was felt that the design could be improved to function as a starting point for all future designs of sections of Crisplant products. With minor variations it is possible to generate a standard design of a section that can be adapted to almost all (perhaps up to 90%) of Crisplant's products across business units and markets. Thus, the result of Step 1 was that Crisplant designed a standard section module (Figure 6.6).

The design of standard modules is a first step towards working with a strategic platform. We will not go into detail about modularization and strategic platform thinking here, but merely note that, in our view, modularization is one means of formulating an architecture for a product, which in turn is a means of achieving a strategic platform for companies (Drejer *et al.*, 2001). In turn, a strategic platform is a means of achieving the above-mentioned combination of individualization/ customization and standardization that is the driver for the development of much of the theory and praxis of product development.

For instance, Ron Sanchez discusses the idea of a product architecture as "the manner in which the components of a computer or a computer system are organized and integrated" (Sanchez, 1996, p. 45). This corresponds to the definition by Ulrich and Eppinger (2000):

> The architecture of a product is the scheme by which the functional elements of the product are arranged into physical chunks and by which the chunks interact.

A strategic platform, hence, is the super-concept to product architecture and is the way in which architectures from several products are related to each other as well as related to operations of the firm (Drejer *et al.*, 2001). Naturally, the strategic platform then relates itself to multi-product development and the achievement of standardization and individualization.

The VR project discussed above made it possible to discuss how Crisplant should work on achieving a strategic platform for the entire company. This leads to the perspectives of the VR technology and project in this case.

Based on the VR project and an ongoing action research project in Crisplant, the top management of the firm realized that Crisplant could change its entire product development process and style completely. This is beyond merely achieving organizational learning via virtual prototypes in the individual projects, as described in Stage 1 of the project. In fact, there are many other ways to utilize VR technology, when Crisplant decides to formulate product architectures and a common strategic product platform for the company.

As mentioned, a product architecture is a means of describing customer needs and wants and linking these with product functionalities and/or components/technologies in the product design. We know this well from the literature on Quality Function Deployment (e.g. Hauser and Clausing, 1989) where methods for breaking a product down into functions and technologies have been suggested. In the more recent literature, this idea is used more proactively to suggest that an architecture can be formulated beforehand and used as a first step in product development (Kim and Cochran, 2000; Meyer and Lehnerd, 1997). Of course this sounds very interesting for many firms, but how can that be supported by technological means?

In this project, the possibilities of visualizing an entire product and its individual parts dynamically are seen as the means of supporting Crisplant's work with product architectures. By showing individual modules, such as the section developed in Stage 1 of the project, and how they are to be connected, it will be possible to discuss and compare different solutions to the fulfilment of customer needs/wants and work with the entire architecture in the virtual space. This will make it possible, it is believed, to oversee an entire product – and its architecture – at the same time, rather than working in a piecemeal and disintegrated manner. At the time of writing, Crisplant is pursuing this as Stage 3 of the project by trying to formulate a product architecture, including standard models, for one of its product families as the basis of a VR model.

There are more options in VR technology. The concept of dynamic simulation and manipulation of an entire product design seems to support the idea of a strategic platform for Crisplant. By dynamic simulation and manipulation, we mean that it should be possible to simulate the actual performance of a product – e.g. speed and accuracy of sorting – as well as manipulating the components or modules of the product at the same time. The latter could be to change existing modules in the model and hence try different solutions to similar problems.

A dynamic model of standard modules and special parts of Crisplant's products will make it possible to discuss how the needs and wants of new customers can be fulfilled by fine tuning existing product architectures, by combining existing architectures, or by adding as little as possible to existing architectures. In that way, a dynamic simulation and manipulation model becomes the means of discussing how good the strategic platform of Crisplant is and whether or not the existing platform can fulfil new customers' needs, or should be supplemented with new modules and/or elements.

In the action research project, a strategic platform has been formulated for Crisplant (Gudmundsson, 2001). However, it is very difficult to work dynamically with this strategic platform and to link the platform to individual product development (and order) projects. This can be done by means of simple rules for designers (e.g. use as few new component as possible), but this is a very static and simple way of utilizing a strategic platform (Sanderson and Uzumeri, 1997; Ulrich and Tung, 1991). Thus there is a great need for the envisioned dynamic simulation and manipulation model at Crisplant. However, building such a model is far from being a simple task. Crisplant needs to define the standard modules and architectures that should form the basis of the dynamic simulation and manipulation model before it even attempts to build the model. This may take several years for Crisplant to achieve. Furthermore, from a technological point of view, building such a model is a complex task for any VR facility in the world. It will take a lot of resources and knowledge in special areas, e.g. movement of high-speed mechanical components in complex systems. Thus, even if Crisplant provides the basis for a dynamic simulation and manipulation model, the VR facility in Aalborg has its work cut out for it.

Furthermore, the research has identified a vast number of barriers to implementing strategic platform thinking in a company. Some barriers are organizational and have to do with resistance from employees and managers, as their traditional habitat and power base are eroded by a common language and regulatory system for design-and-product decisions. Others are more practical and related to the necessary work of redesigning and altering the many existing products of any company. Finally, there are the technological challenges outlined above. In short, Crisplant has five to ten years to go before it can hope to have implemented strategic platform thinking.

6.6 Conclusions

Let us return to the issue of this book – 3D applications – and interpret the case study and the discussion in the introduction according to this theme.

6.6.1 Background of the Chapter

The discipline of product development is evolving these days into what we could call design-and-production. This is because of the competitive and external forces briefly touched upon in the introduction. These forces have serious implications for the way we perceive and practise product development. It is no longer enough to focus on individual product development projects, on singular performance measures (i.e. either low cost or differentiation), or on the product alone. Much more is needed. In short, we are moving towards the concept of "multiple product development" (Drejer and Gudmundsson, 2002), where the ideas of strategic platform and architectures are used as means for managing the entire portfolio of product and product development projects as well as integrating product development with process development and the development of administrative competencies.

Multiple product development is an emerging concept based on several strands of literature: multiple project management, team organization, organizational learning across functional boundaries, and so on (Drejer and Gudmundsson, 2002). We will not discuss this concept in detail here, but refer the reader to existing literature (Gudmundsson, 2001; Drejer et al., 2001).

6.6.2 The Challenges of Design-and-Production

If we are to formulate the challenges of design-and-production in the terms used throughout this book, it seems that one of the major challenges – and, indeed, the challenge that 3D application in this case is to avoid – has to do with the idea of habitats.

Even though the process of design-and-production is one integrated process, the way we organize and manage work in our organizations has a tendency to split up tasks into many sub-tasks and to organize firms according to a functional structure. It is a structure that we also find in the educational system and in society in general. The result is that the process of design-and-production is divided into a number of social habitats or social places that have different perspectives on the product and process related to design-and-production as well as different performance criteria, success criteria and priorities. The habitats are in part defined by the organization and other external factors, such as educational systems, unions and so on. On the other hand, the habitats are also, in our view, partly self-organized. This has to do with the empirical fact that the habitats have often been found to resist attempts to reorganize companies according to, for instance, business processes and, hence, to create new habitats. The forces of social life and identity are very strong and difficult to change and people will act to maintain their usual habitats and avoid organizational change at all cost.

The effect of these habitats, however, is that communication about the products being design and/or produced is made extremely difficult. In short, the habitats create their own languages and find it very hard to understand the languages of the other habitats. Misunderstandings and lack of communication abound.

6.6.3 3D Applications – What Is Needed, Then?

In this chapter we have argued that the application of 3D VR technology is one of the means of remedying this situation. There are many other means, of course, but in light of the purpose of this book, we have decided to focus solely on 3D applications. Given the challenges of habitats, what is needed then? We believe that two kinds of 3D application are needed:

- Realistic applications that correspond to the product being designed and form the basis of communication about the product and its production.
- Regulatory applications that collect experiences from the use of realistic applications and in general, and present these in the form of general guidelines for activities in the design process.

This chapter has given an example of a realistic application. A realistic application needs to be designed and built in the tradition of "pure sense"/reality to use Kant's categories. The application is to simulate something real – the product in its many manifestations in the different habitats – in a realistic or even naturalistic way. But by which criteria will we judge the quality of a 3D application in this case?

Let us start with a word of caution. We do not believe in any list of universal criteria and will merely come up with a list of relevant criteria related to the case study in this paper. Thus pre-modified, let us offer a list of criteria for evaluating the quality of a realistic 3D application:

- *Resemblance*. This means a geometrical likeness to the actual product and its surroundings in its manifestation in different habitats as well as a sufficient level of detail to understand the product. For instance, people from the production habitat need to know something about the product itself as well as how the product is located in their production facility. Is it easy to handle? Difficult to get around? etc.

- *Local*. This means that the application should be available somewhere where representatives from all of the habitats can access it – and, in this case, to communicate about the application. In the case example, we found that a prototype located in Aalborg was excellent as face-to-face communication was much needed, but this need not be the case in other instances.

- *Early*. In short, the earlier in the design process the prototype can be built and evaluated, the better will be the changes of redesigns and iterations in the design-and-production process.

- *Cheap*. The application should be cheaper than a physical prototype, for obvious reasons.

- *Enabling*. An application should enable a dialogue between the different habitats better than traditional means, such as drawings and text, or even physical prototypes.

If we take all of these criteria together, we believe that one of the main advantages of 3D VR prototypes lies in the combination of very good resemblance, at low cost and at an early stage in the design-and-production process. We also feel that 3D applications have the potential of adding "better enabling" to the advantages above. This is due to the fact that the 3D model can include artefacts from the natural habitats involved, for instance the building in which a Crisplant sorter is to be installed, a production facility, a display stand with competitive products and so on. This will be much easier to do in 3D VR than by any other means – not to mention much cheaper.

As for the other kind of 3D applications needed, the regulatory ones, this could well correspond to AR with 3D applications to support design decisions by, for instance, showing standard designs, former designs etc. However, we see these as several steps down the road from the realistic ones. This is because applications supporting strategic platform and standard modules etc., in our view, require that the basic problems of different languages and habitats have been solved. Furthermore, it requires that the motivation for one common frame of reference – the strategic platform that is documented in a 3D application – has been created. Therefore this is an entirely different process that needs to be related to organizational change and learning. As mentioned in this chapter, we believe that it will take a number of years for any organization to reach a state where it is even possible to start implementing a strategic platform and hence apply 3D to AR/regulatory applications.

References

Andreasen, M. M. (1999) Product and production development. In Drejer, A. (ed.) *Production, Learning and Competence*. Aalborg: Aalborg University.

Andreasen, M. M., Hansen, C. T. and Mortensen, N. H. (1996) The structuring of products and product programmes. In Tichem, L. *et al.* (eds.), *2nd WDK Workshop on product structuring*. Delft University of Technology, Delft, The Netherlands.

Andreasen, M. M. and Hein, L. (2000) *Integrated Product Development*. Copenhagen: Technical University of Denmark.

Bettis, R. A. and Hitt, M. A. (1995) *Strategic Management: Competitiveness and Globalization*. London: Thomson Learning.

Cooper, R. G. (1993) *Winning at New Products*. New York: Addison-Wesley.

D'Aveni, R. A. (1994) *Hypercompetition – Managing the Dynamics of Strategic Maneuvering*. New York: The Free Press.

Drejer, A. (1996) *Strategic Management and Competence Development*. Aalborg: Aalborg University.

Drejer, A. (2000a) Integrating product and technology development. *European Journal of Innovation Management*, 3(3), 125–136.

Drejer, A. (2000b) Organizational learning and competence development. *The Learning Organization*, 7(3–4), 206–220.

Drejer, A. and Gudmundsson, A. (2002) Towards multiple product development. *Technovation*, 22, 733–745.

Drejer A. and Riis, J. O. (2000) *Competence Strategy*. Copenhagen: Børsens Forlag.

Drejer, A., Gubi, E., Gudmundsson, A., Hansen, P. K. and Thyssen, J. (2001) *Strategic Platforms*. Aalborg: Center for Industrial Production.

Erens, F. and Verhulst, K. (1997) Architectures for product families. *Computers in Industry*, 33, 165–178.

Erixon, G. (1998) *Modular Function Deployment – A Method for Product Modularization*. Gothenburg: The Royal Institute of Technology, Department of Manufacturing Systems.

Fine, C. H. (1998) *Clockspeed*. New York: Perseus Books.

Galvin, P. (1999) Product modularity, information structures and the diffusion of innovation. *Int. J. Technology Management*, 17(5), 467–479.

Gudmundsson, A. (2001) *The Concept of Multiple Product Development*. Aalborg: Center for Industrial Production.

Hamel, G. (1999) *Leading the Revolution: How to Thrive in Turbulent Times by Making Innovation a Way of Life*. New York: Plume.

Hammer, M. and Champy, J. (1993) *Reengineering the Corporation: A Manifesto for Business Revolution*. London: Nicolas Brealy Publishing.

Hauser, J. R. and Clausing, D. (1988) The house of quality. *Harvard Business Review*, May–June.

Hein, L. and Andreasen, M. (1985) *Integrated Product Development*. IPU, DTU.

Hubka, V. and Eder, W. E. (1989) *Theory of Technical Systems*. Berlin: Springer-Verlag.

Jandourek, E. (1996) A model for platform development. *Hewlett-Packard Journal*, 14, August.

Jiao, J. and Tseng, M. M. (2000) Fundamentals of product family architecture. *Integrated Manufacturing Systems*, 11(7), 469–483.

Johansen, J. (1999) Production development – a futuristic step back in time. In Drejer, A. (ed.) *Production, Learning and Competence*. Aalborg: Aalborg University.

Kamrani, A. K. and Salhieh, S. (2000) *Product Design for Modularity*. Amsterdam: Kluwer Academic Publishers.

Kaplan, R. S. and Norton, D. P. (1996) *The Balanced Scorecard – Translating Strategy to Action*. San Francisco: Harvard Business School Press.

Kim, Y.-S. and Cochran, D. S. (2000) Product variety and manufacturing system complexity. In Cochran, D. S. and Tapia, C. F. (eds.) *The Third World Congress on Intelligent Manufacturing Processes and Systems*, Department of Mechanical Engineering, MIT, Cambridge, MA, pp. 25–33.

Kotler, P. (2000) *Marketing Management*. New York: Prentice Hall International Editions.

Kotter, J. (1997) *Leading Organizational Change*. Boston: Harvard Business School Press.

Meyer, M. H. and Lehnerd, A. P. (1997) *The Power of Product Platforms*. New York: The Free Press.

Miles, R. E. and Snow, C. C. (1978) *Organizational Strategy, Structure, and Process*. New York: McGraw-Hill.

Pahl, G. and Beitz, W. (1986) *Konstruktionslehre; Handbuch für Studium und Praxis, zweite, neuerabeitete und erweiterte Auflage*. Berlin: Springer-Verlag.

Pine II, J. B. (1993) *Mass Customization: the New Frontier in Business Competition*. San Francisco: Harvard Business School Press.

Riis, J. O. (ed.) (1997) *The Expanded Production Concept*. IPS.

Robertson, D. and Ulrich, K. T. (1998) Planning for product platforms. *Sloan Management Review*, 39(4), 19–31.

Sanchez, R. (1995) Strategic flexibility in product competition. *Strategic Management Journal*, 16, 135–159.

Sanchez, R. (1996) Strategic product creation: managing new interactions of technology, markets and organizations. *European Management Journal*, 14(2), 121–138.

Sanchez, R. (1998) *Modular Architectures, Knowledge Assets, and Organizational Learning: New Management Processes for Product Creation*. Copenhagen: Copenhagen Business School.

Sanchez, R. and Mahoney, J. T. (1996) Modularity, flexibility, and knowledge management in product and organization design. *Strategic Management Journal*, 17(Winter special issue), 63–76.

Sanderson, S. W. and Uzumeri, M. (1997) *Managing Product Families*. London: Irwin.

Savage, C. M. (1990) *Fifth Generation Management*. New York: Digital Press.

Sawhney, M. S. (1998) Leveraged high-variety strategies: from portfolio thinking to platform thinking. *Academy of Marketing Science*, 26(1), 54–61.

Suri, R. (1998) *Quick Response Manufacturing*. New York: Productivity Press.

Sundgren, N. (1998) *Product Platform Development - Managerial Issues in Manufacturing Firms*. Gothenburg: Department of Operations Management and Work Organization, Chalmers University of Technology.

Suzue, T. and Kohdate, A. (1990) *Variety Reduction Program*. New York: Productivity Press.

Ulrich, K. T. (1993) *The Rôle of Product Architectures in the Manufacturing Firm*. Massachusetts: Massachusetts Institute of Technology.

Ulrich, K. T. and Tung, K. (1991) *Fundamentals of Product Modularity*. Massachusetts: Massachusetts Institute of Technology.

Ulrich, K. T. and Eppinger, S. D. (2000) *Product Design and Development*. London: McGraw-Hill

Wheelwright, S. C. and Clark, K. B. (1992) *Revolutionizing Product Development*. New York: The Free Press.

The Computer in the World

Introduction

In this section we investigate a specific type of 3D application that exploits physical space. These represent augmented reality applications and pervasive systems rather than pure virtual reality system. The applications are characterized by having a practical and regulative effect on the context in which they are applied.

In Chapter 7, May and Kristensen introduce and motivate the concept of a habitat, characterizing space and environments in the digitally pervasive world. A habitat is seen as specifying some kind of locality (an area that is delimited by some kind of boundary), as containing inhabitants, and as providing support to its inhabitants in the form of opportunities and services that allow its inhabitants to interact and achieve their various goals. The chapter reflects upon the history and possible applications of the habitat concept.

Keldskov (Chapter 8) addresses the design of augmented reality interfaces for mobile computing devices. A central question is raised from this discussion: how can the properties and use of habitats be analyzed and described in a form supporting creative interface design for augmented reality? By addressing this question, it is shown how the rôle of habitats in cooperative work can be formulated in Alexandrian design patterns specifying requirements for human–computer interfaces in a form which identifies the desired qualities of an interface without dictating specific design.

In Chapter 9, Andersen and Nowack characterize the concept of informational and spatio-temporal habitats by illustrating a train and its information system. Different perspectives on habitats and fundamental properties of habitats are discussed and exemplified. The methodological support for the development of software that implements habitats is analyzed and ideas for method improvements are suggested.

May provides, in Chapter 10, an example of an augmented reality system from the maritime domain that involves the practical problem of finding the best technical support for wayfinding, particularly in the context of escape and evacuation situations. Technical support for wayfinding typically involves augmenting the built environment with signs informing occupants of the way to certain places within a building or how to find a way out in an emergency. The chapter discusses non-computerized and computerized augmentation, and *acoustic* media channels are described as an interesting alternative to conventional technology. The example further illustrates the habitat concept.

Finally, in Chapter 11 Kristensen *et al.* present the potential inhabitants of habitats: tangible objects, i.e. objects that are potentially present simultaneously in a conceptual space, a physical space and an informational space. The chapter returns to the problem from the Chapter 7: how to support the development of software that implement augmented reality systems? A fundamental question to any model-based approach (such as object-oriented systems development) is how to model the entities of such systems and how to relate these models. Based on an analysis of abstraction in physical space and abstraction in informational space, a proposal for a combined approach is presented. Hence the possibilities and limitations of abstraction in relation to the understanding of tangible objects are discussed.

Habitats for the Digitally Pervasive World

Daniel Chien-Meng May and Bent Bruun Kristensen

7.1 Introduction[1]

The vision of ubiquitous (Weiser, 1991) and pervasive (Various, 1999) computing that we are moving towards is one where computational capability will make its way into most of the physical objects and space around us. Beyond this, computers are also heading inside us and may be so prevalent as to be disposable (Arnold *et al.*, 1999). We shall move from the perspective of computing in the corner (where computers and our relationship to them are distinct and separate) to our being submerged in computing (where it may be more accurate to suggest that we are embedded in a sea of computation, and it embeds itself within us).

Not only has this involved technological innovation, but it necessitates a grappling with soft issues – among them, social, cultural and political issues. However, the history of pervasive computing demonstrates a bias that has been heavily skewed towards technological and engineering activities (Abowd and Mynatt, 2000). Indeed, there is a persuasive argument that the primary challenges faced by pervasive computing are not technological but human (Thackara, 2001). Yet the technology of pervasive computing has been a powerful catalyst for convergence: pushing together physical materials and information, but also raising questions about how these integrate with *what it is that we do* and the *purpose of our tasks*. Put another way, the question of human interaction in the digitally pervasive world has been raised precisely because the technology has pushed us to the point where we *can sensibly question* how computing should fit into our lives, rather than the other way around.

---

1 Photographs have been used with the permission of Stewart Brand and the University of Southern Denmark. Clip art from the Microsoft Design Gallery Live has also been used.

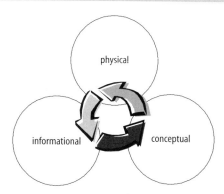

Figure 7.1 A three-dimensional view of the world.

7.1.1 A Holistic Approach

An emphasis on technology to the exclusion of human concerns will cause us to fall short in developing pervasive computing systems, but neither can we emphasize the human element without recourse to real-world practicalities and technological possibilities. Thus our approach to the challenge of pervasive computing is to adopt a holistic perspective. We call our approach *TangO*, for *tangible objects* (May *et al.*, 2001a,b; Andersen and Nowack, 2002; Hallenborg and Kristensen, 2002), for we believe that the objects we create for the digitally pervasive world through this approach will become more real, richer and satisfying in our interaction with them – more tangible. The TangO view of the world is that it comprises three dimensions (Figure 7.1): we need to consider them equally when we are modelling and designing artefacts in the digitally pervasive world.

In the *physical dimension*, we interact with artefacts in their physical form: we can touch them, throw them around and move them around. In the *informational dimension*, we interact with artefacts in their informational form: we can store them, copy them and modify them. These artefacts not only store information, but may have computational ability and also act with autonomy. In the *conceptual dimension*, we interact with artefacts in their conceptual form: concepts shape the way we understand the world and how we will act towards the world. When we are engaged in the design of artefacts, we subconsciously iterate through these different dimensions, as they represent the different aspects of the artefacts we are designing and the contexts in which they will be used.

These three dimensions enjoy interplay: they are not merely related to each other, but they intersect and depend on each other. To model an artefact in any one dimension without considering its connection to the other spaces is to model an artefact that does not take into account the needs of the pervasive world. When we design and create artefacts in any form – physical, informational and conceptual – without combining and managing the interplay of these three dimensions, then we encounter a disconnectedness and incompleteness. Managing the forces between these dimensions is the key to modelling and creating artefacts that are useful and appropriate for the pervasive world.

This is the background to this chapter, which presents the concept of *habitats*. We are using habitats as an abstraction to model spaces and environments in the digitally pervasive world. As an abstraction, we want to be able to apply it in an orthogonal fashion across the different dimensions in our world. In doing so, it is a step towards a better approach to designing for the digitally pervasive world; an approach that is less fragmented than current design approaches, more coherent and integrative of different dimensions of our world.

7.2 Habitats

We have chosen to characterize spaces and environments in the digitally pervasive world as *habitats*. This is deliberate, as we believe that characterizing the spaces we move through as habitats confers certain useful properties. We conceive of habitats as:

- Specifying some kind of locality, an area that is delimited by some kind of boundary.
- Comprising inhabitants.
- Providing support to its inhabitants in the form of opportunities and services that allow its inhabitants to interact and achieve their various goals.

It is no coincidence that this conception draws directly from the biological notion of "habitat", indicating the kind of geographical locality in which particular plants and animals naturally grow or live (Simpson and Weiner, 1989). That a habitat and its inhabitants exist in a close relationship is a given: a habitat nurtures and supports its inhabitants who constantly adapt the habitat to their use, while inhabitants themselves can adapt to their habitat. The notion of *habitat form* is used to describe the form developed by a race or organism in response to its habitat.

For our purposes, an inhabitant is a thing that is capable of acting with some level of autonomy and agency. Typically, living creatures such as humans and animals are considered inhabitants in habitats. If we consider that certain non-living entities are capable of autonomy and agency – such as computer programs, robots and tangible objects (Chapter 9) – then these could also be considered as inhabitants within certain types of habitats. For the purpose of exploring the habitat concept, this chapter focuses on living creatures, primarily people, as inhabitants, and the analysis of tangible objects and other entities as inhabitants will form the basis for a subsequent discussion.

The concept of habitats connotes the organic and dialectic nature of interaction: by thinking of environments in terms of habitats, we avoid thinking of spaces as being clinical and implicitly ignoring the rich interaction therein. By thinking of habitats, we naturally consider the inhabitants, their needs, their goals and intentions and how they interact with the rest of the habitat. Thus, context, situatedness and heterogeneity are up-front considerations when thinking in terms of habitats, capturing the real world as it is rather than over-abstracting away its inherent complexity.

The relevance of this approach to characterizing spaces is considered in relation to a multidisciplinary trend in characterizing things from a more holistic and organic perspective. Such approaches are similarly being adopted across a variety of disciplines that include software (Lehman, 1980; Gamma *et al.*, 1994), architecture and building (Alexander, 1979; Brand, 1994), and business and organizational theory (de Geus, 1997). Such an approach appeals on a number of levels: they are plausible, describing things as they seem to be; there is no shortage of exemplars and we can identify with those; they represent an alternative to "machine thinking" (Taylor, 1911) and an approach to creating longevity and robustness that is difficult to achieve.

7.2.1 Physical Habitats

Physical habitats are probably closest to our intuitive understanding of what a habitat is. Habitats traditionally derive from the study of natural sciences, such as biology, in describing the localities where organisms and life-forms grow and live. However, we might also consider that artificial physical environments could be characterized as habitats – and the scale can vary tremendously (e.g. room section, room, collections of rooms, floors, building, group of buildings, communities etc.). Conceiving of such environments as being habitats, rather than mere "spaces", is advantageous in that it introduces the notion of thinking about how inhabitants and habitats influence each other and *evolve* over time.

The pictures in Figure 7.2 (Brand, 1994) illustrate that it is the nature of constructed physical environments to evolve over time. There is a strong argument that the most effective buildings – those that are shaped to the contours of our needs – are *grown* rather than *constructed*. The latter view posits that we construct physical spaces and their structure is predetermined at the outset; the former view argues that space is in a constant state of evolution and shaping by its inhabitants. Brand (1994) argues that the credo "form follows function" is misleading; form is often designed to *freeze* function. In reality, our needs do not remain static, and we reshape our physical environments after that fact. Eventually, "function melts form". Thus we are challenging the natural flow of growth when we attempt to construct physical spaces that serve for all conceivable uses, and if we try to do this, then our physical spaces will not support our needs – it is better to grow physical spaces.

Brand (1994) describes how one architect prepares the houses he builds for evolution – during the construction process, he takes photographs of the frame of the house and the hidden structure (Figure 7.3). These are keyed to blueprints. The photographs and blueprints form a "book" that is passed to the owners; the book

Figure 7.2 Physical habitats evolve over time.

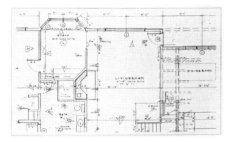

Figure 7.3 Supporting evolution of physical habitats.

acts as a reference for the owners and future builders to use when the house is modified. The alternative is to knock down walls and discover what *really* exists in the structure. Traditional modification usually involves rediscovery of previously known facts about physical habitats.

7.2.2 Informational Habitats

If physical habitats are spaces that are created and exist in the physical dimension of our reality, then informational habitats are those spaces that are created with and exist in information. Here, we are extending the concept of habitats from merely being physical. Typically, if we start discussing "information" and "spaces", then we tend to veer automatically towards virtual reality (Kelly *et al.*, 1989) or collaborative technologies studied by the computer-supported collaborative work (CSCW) research community. Technologies such as chat rooms, ICQ™ and Groove™ and research projects like Worlds (Fitzpatrick *et al.*, 1996) present exemplars of "information spaces". This is a convenient metaphor because thinking of information spaces in this way characterizes them in a way that is similar to physical spaces – chat rooms mirror physical rooms where discourse and conversation take place; virtual collaborative spaces are the informational analogue of project conference rooms; and virtual museum tours try to take us through the museum as if we were there.

While this is not an inappropriate point of perspective, we limit ourselves if our concept of "informational habitat" is prescribed by a view of information space that draws from physical space as a metaphor. If we consider our definition of "habitat", then an informational habitat is some kind of locality with inhabitants, who draw upon the support of the locality and both adapt accordingly – similar to our notion of physical habitat, except that the medium through which interplay occurs is information.

Our everyday information environments can be seen as habitats. Email has been characterized as an informational habitat (Ducheneaut and Bellotti, 2001). There is a topology and structure inherent in our mail folders and mail client software (Figure 7.4) that causes us – the users of the program – to "inhabit" our email, rather than merely to "use" it. We customize the client software, structure and restructure our mail folders, and organize our email in different ways over time. Email is an interesting case in point, as it actually comprises two habitats: mail folders and mail client software. I can use different mail client software to access the

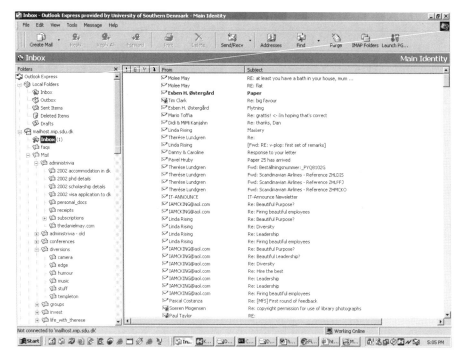

Figure 7.4 Email as habitat.

same set of mail folders, and each time I do so I feel as if I am operating within different habitats, even though I am interacting with the same set of mail folders. For instance, I can use my preferred mail client software when I'm with my notebook computer, but when I'm without my personal computer I use a web mail client from any computer running a web browser. Both mail clients are different habitats, offering different experiences and supporting me in different ways. Mail client habitats can become more complex: a number of them are extensible through programming languages and plug-ins. Thus, over time, my particular mail client can evolve over time in this way.

Classification systems and information architectures can be thought of as habitats (Figyre 7.5). Many libraries worldwide use the Dewey Decimal Classification (DDC) system, first published in 1876, to classify books. The system employs a notational hierarchy (e.g. **6**00 Technology (Applied Sciences) → **63**0 Agriculture and related technologies → **636** Animal husbandry) that has evolved over time to keep pace with the development of general knowledge. We can think of classification systems like DDC as informational habitats: users of books at many schools or public libraries will "inhabit" DDC, navigating through the space to find particular books or just to explore within a subject area.

The proliferation of web sites with large amounts of information, structured in complex ways, can be considered as informational habitats. Interestingly, the collection of methods and techniques for describing the organization of such sites is called "information architecture" (Wurman, 1997; Rosenfeld and Morville,

Figure 7.5 Classification system as habitat.

1998), suggestive of a space-related view of information and drawing an analogy between physical and informational material. Even more pointedly towards a habitat view is that of "information ecologies" (Nardi and O'Day, 2000), which posits an organic characterization of information and its interaction with people.

Environments for programs can be thought of as habitats. Application servers (Figure 7.6) such as iPlanet™ are designed to host and deploy applications over the Internet. Programs are written to exploit the environment provided by the application server (e.g. e-commerce tools, database connectivity, directory services). We can consider the application server as a habitat: programs are inhabitants that draw upon the services and support provided by the application server. Programs evolve over time through programmer intervention or machine generation, all the while being supported by the application server. The application server habitat evolves through customization and the addition of plug-ins; this evolution is mediated through system administrator intervention. Human intervention plays a part in this evolution; we can imagine more autonomous evolution on the part of inhabitants and habitats for systems more similar to multi-agent systems (Bradshaw, 1997).

The example above introduces the additional concept of a program as an inhabitant within an informational habitat. We introduce the possibility of programs being considered as inhabitants, as they may act with some degree of autonomy and

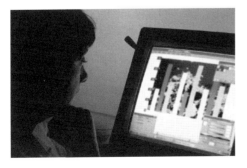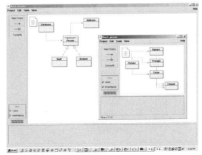

Figure 7.6 Application server as habitat.

agency. Coupled with the richness of informational habitats, thinking of programs as inhabitants of such habitats may be a useful way of understanding and designing informational environments. We choose not to expand on this discussion here, but this is an important point for later work. It is especially pertinent when thinking about programs that will engage in more evolutionary behaviour and have the capacity to perform reasoning.

7.2.3 Conceptual Habitats

In the same way that habitats can be constructed from physical material and information, we can have habitats that are defined in terms of *concepts* and *ideas*. What do we mean by this? In the same way that we as inhabitants can move through physical habitats and interact in informational habitats, we can exist and interact in conceptual spaces. Although much less tangible than physical material or information, concepts and ideas can form habitats that create particular support for us as we think and act in relation to the world around us. Here, the space is being created from "conceptual" material rather than being delimited in terms of physical or information dimensions. Consider one example:

> Cyberspace is the "place" where a telephone conversation appears to occur. Not inside your actual phone, the plastic device on your desk. Not inside the other person's phone, in some other city. **The place between** the phones. The indefinite place **out there**, where the two of you, human beings, actually meet and communicate (Sterling, 1993)

Cyberspace, as a type of conceptual space, is formed by the perceptions of our minds. We believe that we are communing in this space, the place between the phones, as a consequence of conceiving of the interaction in this way. More recent cyberspatial notions of communities, groups and social worlds are also conceptual habitats. Of course, cyberspace is enabled through informational habitats such as servers, connections, storage spaces and accounts, and at the ends of the physical telephone circuit we exist in our physical habitats. There are also many other kinds of conceptual habitat.

We can think of a culture as a habitat. Skansen is an open-air museum (Figure 7.7) on the island of Djurgården, near Stockholm. It was founded for the purpose of

Figure 7.7 Culture as habitat.

Figure 7.8 Group as habitat.

showing how people had lived and worked in different parts of Sweden in the past. As such, it tries to encapsulate aspects of the Swedish culture. Culture is a conceptual habitat, described by beliefs, customs and practices. While a culture expresses itself in concrete artefacts (May, 2001), a culture itself is made of up concepts or "thought stuff". Perhaps to underscore the point further, we can consider a key feature of a culture as what it *excludes* rather than includes. There is a mutual interplay between culture and its inhabitants: the culture supports, sustains and influences its inhabitants, while the inhabitants can also reshape the culture in turn. Those people who do not want to be part of a culture any more effectively leave this habitat, and it will no longer support or sustain them.

Culture is not the only form of conceptual habitat. Arbitrary designations and rules can create particular groupings of people (Figure 7.8) – the space is not defined by a set of beliefs and customs, but by convention and prescription. You may be assigned to a team to complete a certain project, designated by management: management has laid the boundaries for your thinking about your participation in the project; you think about it in terms of your team, your rôle in the team, cooperating with the other team members etc. It is a conceptual space within which you operate. You may elect to join a soccer team: your concept of this team, your place in it, and its practices and activities, is largely determined by the rules of soccer. However, as you start to interact as a team, you start to establish a culture within the team – with customs, beliefs and practices – so you create another conceptual habitat within the original habitat ascribed by the rules. Inhabitants in cultural habitat that do not fit – for example, players who don't join in the customs and practices of the team – may find themselves on the outside, but still nominally part of the team.

We can also see conceptual frameworks, such as philosophies and systems of ideas, as forming habitats (Figure 7.9). For example, a philosophy such as Marxism assumes certain boundaries and assumptions; the notion of a material dialectical process fits within this conceptual space, but not that of spiritual idealism (one which fits into Hegelian space). A conceptual framework such as activity theory (Engeström *et al.*, 1999) assumes that subjects (humans) use mediating artefacts (tools) to interact with the object of an activity (the problem space). Within the space of this conceptual framework is the assumption of an asymmetric

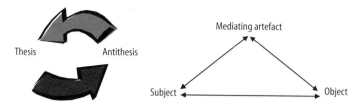

Figure 7.9 Conceptual frameworks as habitats.

relationship between humans and tools. Thus concepts that consider software and hardware as equivalent to humans would not be compatible in this conceptual space.

Again, evolution is an inherent part of conceptual habitats. Ideas change and alter over time; they also cross-pollinate with other ideas from other conceptual frameworks, giving rise to new habitats. For instance, if we look at the history of philosophy, we see the evolution of multiple conceptual habitats, building on pre-existing habitats and splitting off to form new habitats. The same can be said of cultures and subcultures.

7.3 Habitats in the Digitally Pervasive World

Our central thesis in designing for the digitally pervasive world is that it requires a holistic approach to modelling: we need to be able to frame problems and their solutions in a lexicon that can give force to the complexity of the world and bridge traditionally disparate views of the world. Integrating these perspectives is a central challenge of designing and implementing a pervasive system. The digitally pervasive world also challenges us to ask what comprises *the system*. Traditionally, computing has assumed that *the system* is a combination of software and hardware. Pervasive and ubiquitous computing pushes us towards thinking about *the system* as a human activity system that is inherently socio-technical, a combination of people, hardware, software and processes that relate them.

As the previous section illustrates, we find the habitat an appealing abstraction for thinking about spaces because it has properties we can reason about that are *orthogonal* across the different dimensions we move through (Figure 7.1). The following example explores how habitats can be useful in characterizing a human activity system. It is based on an actual subject conducted by a Scandinavian university.

Example: Collaborative Group Project. A university department conducts a subject that is project-based. Students are formed into teams, responsible for individual projects (construction of a hardware device involving software control). The team members are not just drawn from the same local class but include students from a class conducted overseas; students must be able to collaborate in virtual teams. Students carry wireless devices and there is wireless access available in some lecture theatres and meeting rooms. We can explore this example in various ways, but here we will focus on how we can use the concept of habitats to help us analyze, design and structure the system to support students' collaboration and completion of their projects. The following sections consider possible habitats (listed in bold type) that exist in the collaborative group project.

7.3.1 Physical Habitats

Although students will spend much time in their teams collaborating on their projects, the subject also comprises lectures where they learn about how to collaborate, manage projects and discuss technical issues relating to their projects. These take place in the **lecture theatre** (Figure 7.10). The university department also provides **meeting rooms** (Figure 7.10) where teams can physically meet together and work on their projects. Students will also collaborate on their projects from **external locations** such as home, another part of the university or another person's home; we could also think of the students overseas as being located in these other places.

Figure 7.10 Lecture theatre and meeting rooms as physical habitats.

In analyzing the lecture theatre as habitat, we might consider how well it supports the discussion and demonstration of hardware devices that are the students' projects. If the class is large, are there sufficient projection facilities? Should students want to check on their work or communicate using their wireless devices, does the habitat support this effectively or is the signal strength too weak? The meeting rooms are habitats: they should support the teams when they meet to work on their projects. Are the meeting rooms shared with students from other subjects? (This may cause conflict as different subjects have different demands and goals.) Are there computers in the meeting rooms? (Because teams comprise members that are located overseas, team members who meet physically will also want to meet virtually with overseas team members.) Is it possible to partition the meeting rooms into smaller areas so that teams can work with some degree of privacy? (Now we can consider these team areas as habitats themselves.)

7.3.2 Informational Habitats

The main information repository for the subject is a **web site**; the site is an environment where students can seek out information, interact with each other by message

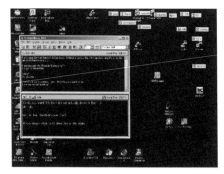 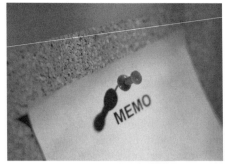

Figure 7.11 ICQ collaboration space and work spaces as informational habitats.

board, and download resources for their project. Team members will collaborate with each other, using some kind of **shared collaboration space**, and they may do so synchronously or asynchronously. Such a collaboration space could be any combination of tools, such as a web site, ftp site, shared directories, basic talk and messaging tools, Lotus Notes™, CVS, ICQ™, Groove™ or NetMeeting™. Products from their work-in-progress are stored in this space. Assessment is performed periodically by the subject coordinator in order to ensure that teams are on-track with their projects. Because team members are distributed around the world, project teams meet the subject coordinator using a chat/conference tool over the Internet, where he or she can perform a **team assessment**. Throughout the subject, students will have **work spaces**; these represent information environments where a student is engaged in getting some work done. A work space can be a student's email, but also a collection of documents that he or she is currently working on (Figure 7.11). Work spaces need not be digital – they could be a memo board or a shared project journal – and they may involve *ad hoc* collaboration with other people and their work spaces.

How should we support these? Students may access virtual collaboration spaces from university computer laboratories, so there needs to be consideration of how the physical space supports such collaboration. Support for work spaces includes physical areas where documents and other information may be stored, as well as virtual work spaces where electronic documents can be stored. Policies regarding this ought to be considered: are these work spaces shared, or are they considered public areas? Should informational habitats be strictly regulated so as to encourage students to have physical interaction? Should shared collaboration spaces be allowed to be accessed during lectures? We can see that the regulation and management of informational habitats derives in a significant way from policies and principles regarding the way the subject is run. These are conceptual issues, which include philosophical and cultural principles.

7.3.3 Conceptual Habitats

Conceptually, the **subject** tries to cover a set of competencies (Figure 7.12) – namely, learning about project management, team dynamics, virtual collaboration,

Figure 7.12 Areas of competency/theory and groups as conceptual habitats.

hardware and software implementation. We can consider that there are two main **disciplines**: project management and computing. Topics that are not central or complementary to these competencies have been excluded from the course schedule. There is a different **class** each time the subject is run, and from each class different **teams** are formed.

The notions of *subject* and *discipline* describe groupings of knowledge that will define such practices as what will be taught, how students will think about their work, and how they differentiate themselves from other students taking other subjects and students in other departments. Within subjects and disciplines, there may be social culture that is passed on by lecturers and researchers (e.g. the culture of a humanities department is different from that of an engineering department). Physical habitats can be structured in a way to support the culture of a discipline or subject. For instance, some work places have corridors that support people running into each other, with whiteboards that allow people to stop, discuss and work on problems. There are alcoves where people can sit and talk.

The notions of *classes* and *teams* describe organizational groupings. It could be possible to create social habitats (a type of conceptual habitat, perhaps) where class and team members interact and bond together as a group. These organizational groups can be structured and reinforced through physical habitats (dedicated classrooms and work areas for classes) and informational habitats (collaboration spaces for the class, separate collaboration spaces for the groups, noticeboard for the class).

7.3.4 It's the Big Picture

The discussion of the preceding examples illustrates the element of mutuality between the three dimensions. As each type of habitat is considered, it becomes natural to consider the relations between it and the other types of habitat. One cannot design a conceptual habitat without considering how and where it will manifest in physical and informational dimensions. Nor can you think of physical habitats without recourse to its conceptualization and attached information. That we consider the informational dimension of our world is a comparatively recent activity in our history. While information has always been an aspect of our history since sign systems were conceived, we have not focused on it as explicitly as we have in recent history. The consideration of conceptual and physical dimensions of artefacts has proceeded in a more conscious fashion than has our consideration of the informational aspects of artefacts.

With the advent of the information revolution, it is the informational dimension that is now the dominant factor under consideration in the creation of many artefacts and spaces that we inhabit, perhaps too much so. Yet it is also the informational dimension that is pushing us towards an understanding of the world as the convergence of these three dimensions, a more integrative view of the world around us. And it is in the interaction of habitats – both types and instances – and their inhabitants that we find the focus of the systems that we are contemplating and creating, rather than the static relationships and structures. "The play's the thing" (*Hamlet*, Act 2, Scene ii) is perhaps quite close to the reality of the situation.

7.3.5 Properties of Habitats

When reasoning about habitats, we can think of them as having particular types of properties. (The properties that habitats possess can be characterized in different ways (Chapter 9).

- *Intention*. The insides of habitats are not context-free. Because of the relationship between a habitat and its inhabitants, the habitat must act in relation to the inhabitants, supporting their needs and their intentions. So although a habitat may not act with the same level of agency as an inhabitant nor could be thought of as having its own "intention", it must be aware of and support the goals and telos of the inhabitants. In doing so, this will affect the purpose and behaviour of the habitat itself, how it relates to its inhabitants and to other habitats. It is an open question whether it is useful to consider habitats themselves as possessing intentions and goals.
- *Context*. Because habitats are supporting the activities and life of their inhabitants, they must be aware of context within their boundaries. Beyond their boundaries, habitats are not islands unto themselves. Habitats are always placed in context with other habitats. In fact, habitats are not wholly self-sufficient, often relying on connectivity to a surrounding environment for support and also to make sense. This could just be seen as habitats being capable of being enclosed within another habitat – in this way, habitats can be treated as *objects*, not just as surrounding space.
- *Ontology*. One of the fundamental facts of a habitat is that it prescribes a locality: separating *what is* and *what is not* the habitat (and therefore delineating what is within or without the habitat). As illustrated by the various examples in this chapter, the delineation of this boundary can vary for all kinds of reasons, but what is within the boundary exists within its own ontological space. The same rules do not apply outside the boundary of the habitat. Thus habitats and their inhabitants share a certain expectation of how each other behaves, in terms of ontology. This distinguishes inhabitants from entities that enter habitats but are not capable of fitting into the ontology of the habitat.

- *Abstraction.* We can apply principles of conceptual abstraction and modelling to habitats (Chapter 11). In other words, we can apply principles of classification, generalization and aggregation. In this way, we can describe habitats at different levels of granularity and different levels of abstraction, according to need. We can also compose more complex structures of habitats containing other habitats, and other habitats in relation to each other. This makes habitats useful for describing aspects of the world and constructing artefacts in the world.

7.4 Habitats and Tangible Objects

As the previous section discusses, thinking of spaces as habitats confers certain advantages: we think of environments as evolving rather than being static, and we consider the design of human activity systems from the perspective of both environment and inhabitants (rather than emphasizing one to the exclusion of the other). Such an approach is conducive to thinking about the digitally pervasive world, which is supposed to comprise technology and environments that are highly responsive to all manner of tasks in all kinds of contexts.

We consider habitats from the perspective of tangible objects: the digitally pervasive artefacts that we can create. An example of a digitally pervasive artefact is a smart badge that reveals its location or a PDA. We also envisage tangible objects such as those discussed at length in Chapter 11. We expect tangible objects to have properties that complement those that are present in a habitat. Both are based on principles of growth and evolution, rather than specification and completeness, and as such complement each other. There are a couple of key points in relation to pervasive computing from the perspective of tangible objects and habitats.

Firstly, tangible objects and habitats are about a "big picture" perspective. Tangible objects actively engage with each other but also with the habitat; the habitat supports tangible objects in their activity and also actively engages with them, evolving over time as a consequence of this interaction. Such interactions between inhabitants and habitats are a consequence of the TangO philosophy of seeking to capture the totality of the system's aspects. The implication for us is that systems begin to be considered less as highly structured, fixed and predetermined structures, and more as constantly interacting, dynamic and organic entities. In this way, they are closer to the original notion of a system as conceived by systems theorists (Bertalanffy, 1968). This idea of a system focuses on the totality of interaction and the rich behaviour between all the elements – habitats, inhabitants, tangible objects. Again, it draws us to a view of a system as an ecology rather than a machine.

Secondly, if we consider that tangible objects and habitats are really systems engaging in complex behaviour, then we expect to encounter emergent phenomena. Assuming we have tangible objects that possess adaptive behaviour and some level of autonomous behaviour, and that these objects are situated in habitats that evolve and support activity between tangible objects, then we lay ourselves open to generative behaviour with the possibility of emergent properties. Domains such as art, generativity and emergence (McCormack and Dorin, 2001) can be highly desirable outcomes, as the purpose is to surprise and create novel experiences for the observer. However, in the digitally pervasive world, art is only one such domain and there are many domains that pervasive computing will not be prevented from entering. Domains such as business, manufacturing and medicine seek artefacts that display a greater measure of adaptability and intelligence than is typically experienced today, and yet often do not tolerate less than mission- or safety-critical performance (which may be difficult or impossible to guarantee in a system where emergence is a side-effect *or even a feature*). It seems an interesting and open question as to whether we are able to have our cake and eat it.

7.5 Concluding Remarks

There are significant questions that arise if one takes a habitat-based view of the world around us. What consequences do we reap if we take an organic approach to designing and growing environments? Evolution and growth take time. Biological systems – which have long practised organic models of growth – are robust, but factor this in over many generations. This seems to challenge notions of creating physical and informational systems that are rapidly prototyped, highly tailored and developed in a short amount of time. There seems to be a clash of priorities and values. Habitats may also exhibit some kind of generative and emergent behaviour; this may be undesirable in the context of industrial and mission/safety-critical systems. People and artefacts may need to perform to precise specification, otherwise undesired consequences may arise. Perhaps habitats may need to be more rigorously defined in some contexts than others.

The interaction between inhabitants and habitats is a crucial point. We may be in the process of constructing a variety of complex habitats, intersecting each other and between the different dimensions. Such a lattice of habitats must be considered in relation to the trajectory of inhabitants through these habitats, for – unlike biological habitats – the inhabitants of artificial habitats leave and enter habitats as a matter of course. Inhabitants of biological habitats make the habitat their "neighbourhood", where leaving it is leaving a locality that provides life-sustaining features. As we have tried to expand the notion of what a habitat is, we must also expand the notion of inhabitants and what they can do. For if we consider inhabitants in the everyday world – biological or artificial agents – then they can pass through and make use of many kinds of habitats.

The habitat is a useful abstraction for describing and understanding the different types of space we move through in our world. In designing systems for the digitally pervasive world, it is these spaces that we are trying to model and construct. In using orthogonal abstractions such as habitats to unify aspects of design, we are not merely catering for the designer but creating a common language that we can use to communicate with *all stakeholders* in the design process. Because the notion of a system in the digitally pervasive world implies *an activity system*, users, agents and other stakeholders are vital – not just as people who will use the system, but as inhabitants or actors in habitats that are part of the *system in evolution*. In the same vein, designers are also part of the evolving system.

The habitat abstraction does not capture something completely novel about the world and its different dimensions. It is an abstraction that tries to distil a fundamental set of characteristics about the spaces through which we move. It can describe ideas and concepts, but also informational environments and physical spaces. In doing so, it yields a measure of comprehension that bridges perspectives borne of different disciplines, perspectives that are traditionally disparate. The habitat also encourages us to think in a certain way: of context, situatedness and connectedness. It encourages us to think of the spaces we create as changing, mutable, heterogeneous and complex. It encourages us to be careful about making the mistake, often made by many technologists, of abstracting to pure forms. As such, the habitat tries to give force to our view of designing for the digitally pervasive world, that in order for us to design effectively – for people, by people – then we need to be speaking the same kind of language that can adequately express the world around us.

References

Abowd, G. D. and Mynatt, E. D. (2000) Charting past, present, and future research in ubiquitous computing. *ACM Transactions on Computer-Human Interaction*, 7(1), 29–58.

Alexander, C. (1979) *The Timeless Way of Building*. Oxford: Oxford University Press.

Andersen, P. B. and Nowack, P. (2002) Tangible objects: connecting informational and physical space. In Qvotrup, L. (ed.) *Virtual Space: The Spatiality of Virtual Inhabited 3D Worlds*. London: Springer-Verlag.

Arnold, D., Segall, B., Boot, J., Bond, A., Lloyd, M. and Kaplan, S. (1999) Discourse with disposable computers: how and why you will talk to your tomatoes. *Usenix Workshop on Embedded Systems (ES99)*, Cambridge, MA.

Bertalanffy, L. v. (1968) *General system theory: Foundations, development, applications*. New York: George Braziller.

Bradshaw, J. (ed.) (1997) *Software Agents*. Cambridge, MA: AAAI Press/The MIT Press.

Brand, S. (1994) *How Buildings Learn: What Happens After They're Built*. London: Orion.

de Geus, A. (1997) *The Living Company*. Harvard Business School Press.

Ducheneaut, N. and Bellotti, V. (2001) E-mail as habitat. *interactions*, 8(5), 30–38.

Engeström, Y., Miettinen, R. and Punamäki, R.-L. (eds.) (1999) *Perspectives on Activity Theory*. Cambridge, Cambridge University Press.

Fitzpatrick, G., Kaplan, S. M. and Mansfield, T. (1996) Physical spaces, virtual places and social worlds: A study of work in the virtual. *ACM Conference on Computer Supported Cooperative Work (CSCW '96)*, Boston, MA.

Gamma, E., Helm, R., Johnson, R. and Vlissides, J. (1994) *Design Patterns: Elements of Reusable Object-Oriented Software*. Reading, MA: Addison-Wesley.

Hallenborg, K. and Kristensen, B. B. (2002) Pervasive computing: mapping TangO model onto Jini technology. *6th World Multiconference on Systemics, Cybernetics and Informatics*, Orlando, FL.

Kelly, K., Heilbrun, A. and Stacks, B. (1989) Virtual reality: an interview with Jaron Lanier. *Whole Earth Review*, 64, 108–119.

Lehman, M. M. (1980) Programs, life cycles, and laws of software evolution. *Proceedings of the IEEE*, 68(9), 1060–1076.

May, D. C. (2001) Building the cultural artefacts of the organization. *Proceedings of the European Conference on Pattern Languages of Programs*, Irsee, Germany.

May, D. C., Kristensen, B. B. and Nowack, P. (2001a) *Tangible Objects – Modeling in Style*. Aalborg University.

May, D. C., Kristensen, B. B. and Nowack, P. (2001b) TangO: modeling in style. *Proceedings of Second International Conference on Generative Systems in the Electronic Arts (Second Iteration – Emergence)*, Melbourne, Australia.

McCormack, J. and Dorin, A. (2001) Art, emergence, and the computational sublime. *Proceedings of the Second International Conference on Generative Systems in the Electronic Arts (Second Iteration – Emergence)*, Melbourne, Australia.

Nardi, B. A. and O'Day, V. L. (2000) *Information Ecologies: Using Technology with Heart.* Cambridge, MA: MIT Press.

Rosenfeld, L. and Morville, P. (1998) *Information Architecture for the World Wide Web.* Sebastopol, CA: O'Reilly & Associates.

Simpson, J. A. and Weiner, E. S. C. (eds.) (1989) *Oxford English Dictionary.* Oxford: Clarendon Press.

Sterling, B. (1993) *The Hacker Crackdown: Law and Disorder on the Electronic Frontier.* New York: Bantam Books.

Taylor, F. W. (1911) *Principles of Scientific Management.* New York: Harper Bros.

Thackara, J. (2001) The Design Challenge of Pervasive Computing." *interactions*, 8(3), 46–52.

Various (1999) Pervasive computing. *IBM Systems Journal*, 38(4).

Weiser, M. (1991) The computer for the twenty-first century. *Scientific American*, 265 (September), 94–104.

Wurman, R. S. (1997) *Information Architects.* New York: Watson-Guptill Publications.

8

Lessons From Being There: Interface Design for Mobile Augmented Reality

Jesper Kjeldskov

8.1 Introduction

Virtual 3D worlds used to be accessible primarily through display systems separating the users from the physical world and immersing them in a parallel computer-generated virtual reality. Today, virtual 3D worlds are being merged into physical space, creating not only *virtual* but also *augmented* realities (AR). In contrast with virtual reality, augmented reality facilitates mobility in the real world as well as a close relationship between physical space and virtual objects. This makes AR an interesting approach for human–computer interfaces in mobile use contexts.

Based on the lessons learned from developing "Being There" – an experimental prototype for distributed cooperative work – this chapter addresses the design of augmented reality interfaces for mobile computing devices. Augmented reality is discussed in relation to the concept of *context awareness* in mobile computing and is presented as an interface approach in which designers must take into consideration the rôle of physical space on a very high level of contextual detail. One central question guides the discussion: how can the properties and use of physical space be analyzed and described in a form supporting the creative design of new and fundamentally different human–computer interfaces such as augmented reality? Addressing this question shows how the rôle of physical space in cooperative work can be formulated in Alexandrian design patterns specifying requirements for human–computer interfaces in a form that identifies the desired qualities of an interface without dictating a specific design. The implemented prototype exemplifies how design patterns as interface requirement specifications can be converted into creative interface design for augmented reality.

8.2 Interface Design for Mobile Devices

The use of mobile computing devices imposes several challenges on the design of human–computer interfaces.

Providing highly relevant input to designers and developers within the mobile device industry here and now, much research on interface design for mobile devices is focused on exploiting the potential of existing technology better. This means coming up with new solutions which overcome the obvious limitations of present mobile technology: small displays, low network bandwidth and limited means of interaction. A number of approaches to these challenges are being explored, such as the use of spoken interaction for reducing visual attention and tactile contact with the physical devices, and guidelines for graphical interface design being reconsidered in the context of small screens on mobile devices (see, for example, Bergman (2000)). In particular, the latter sometimes results in new design more or less contradicting the recognized trends within interfaces for desktop computers: the quality and resolution of images and graphical information representations for use in mobile device interfaces are being *reduced* to the limit of losing their semantic value and information is being squeezed into displays by *removing redundancy* and sometimes cutting it up it into a *more complex* structure or hierarchy of subsections. Existing information content (e.g. on web pages) is being *filtered* and cut into smaller pieces in order to fit on the displays of handheld PCs or WAP phones and to reduce data transfer. These solutions all contribute to making data and communication accessible while being mobile.

Mobile computer use is, however, more than just a question of communication and information access while being separated from one's desktop, and the usability of mobile devices is not only influenced by technical limitations such as small screens, but also by the relation between their design and their use context. As opposed to desktop computing, users of mobile devices are typically characterized by moving through physical space and interacting with a series of objects and subjects that are autonomously moving in and out of the user's proximity. This results in use contexts in which demands for information and functionality change in accordance with contextual factors such as time, place and social constellations.

The implications of the use context are increasingly being taken into account within mobile HCI. Devices are being equipped with sensors to make them react to how they are being held, touched and moved (Hinckley *et al.*, 2000). Spatial, temporal and social *context awareness* are being explored as means of input for customizing interfaces to specific situations or locations in time and space (Izadi *et al.*, 2001) and displays build into spectacles are providing mobile users with computerized graphical overlays on the real world, typically referred to as *mobile augmented reality* (Feiner *et al.*, 1999). While the properties and use of physical space are often downgraded or left out in interface design for existing mobile technology in favour of more technical issues, the design of context-aware and augmented reality interfaces is demanding an explicit focus on such contextual factors, as these interfaces are inherently related to the physical space in which they are used.

8.2.1 Context Awareness and Augmented Reality

Whereas small displays and restricted means of interaction are obvious *limitations* on mobile technology, challenging designers to come up with new solutions, the dynamic use contexts of mobile computing do not necessarily constitute a problem that needs to be solved through design. On the contrary, continuously changing contexts can be viewed as a rich *potential* for interface design.

By making computer systems sensitive to or aware of changes in their use context, interfaces can be designed for adaptation to specific contexts or *habitats* (see Chapter 9) defined spatially by location in space, temporally by location in time and socially by the presence of other people. Designing interfaces for adaptation to different habitats will not only facilitate reduction or simplification of the information and functionality available in specific situations when moving between habitats, but in doing so will also minimize the need to explicitly focus on and interact with the device. When viewing context changes as a means of input to mobile devices, physical space becomes a part of the human–computer interface, providing the user with information and functionality "just-in-place" (Kjeldskov, 2002).

Mobile information services adapted to habitats do not have to run exclusively on mobile phones or pocket-sized PCs, but can appear in various forms. In some museums for example, visitors are equipped with infrared headphones providing contextually adapted spoken information related to the works on display in specific rooms. On RDS-enabled car radios, broadcasts are interrupted with spoken traffic messages or supplemented with text-based information on the radio's graphical display related to a delimited geographical area. Another example is the ability to charge mobile phone users different rates (e.g. at home or at work) according to their presence within specific GSM network cells.

Using mobile augmented reality, habitats (whether spatially, temporally or socially defined) can be represented even more sophisticatedly through visual augmentation of the user's physical surroundings. Specific locations, objects or persons can be complemented with visual information, such as written text, icons, computer graphics, pictures and video, facilitating the reception of and interaction with virtual objects, information and actors, resembling that of their physical counterparts and thus demanding only a limited additional cognitive load. This has great potential in situations where moving one's visual focus away from the physical world should be avoided (such as when driving or walking down the street) or in situations where interaction with computers is naturally related to interaction in physical space (such as in synchronous cooperative work). Other application areas include situations in which central information related to interaction in the physical world may be visually hidden or obscured (such as when manoeuvring a ship through thick fog).

By taking into consideration the rôle of physical space in computer use, context awareness and augmented reality challenge our usual notions of usability and involve the fundamental traditions of graphical interface design being reconsidered and new paradigms for interaction and interface design being explored.

8.2.2 Level of Contextual Detail

From the examples above, it is clear that while context-aware mobile information services do not have to have augmented reality interfaces, augmented reality interfaces, in contrast, depend on a close relation to their physical context. This consequently means that mobile augmented reality cannot be viewed as an *alternative* to context awareness, but is inseparably a subordinated specific variation of this.

Differentiating context aware information services with reference to their relation to physical space, context-aware information services and tools can be plotted on a continuum of *contextual detail* within spatially defined habitats, describing in how much detail the interface reflects changes in the user's physical location (Figure 8.1). At one end of this continuum, augmented reality represents a high level of contextual detail, while GPS driven navigation systems, for example, represent a lower level of contextual detail. At the other end of the continuum, SMS-based advertising broadcast when entering specific GSM network cells and broadcast traffic information interruptions on RDS radios represent a low level of contextual detail.

Additional dimensions could be added to this continuum, reflecting for example the level of *temporal* and *social* contextual detail and refining the picture of relations between existing context-aware information services further.

How accurately physical space and computer interfaces should be related in a specific habitat depends on which rôle physical space plays in that habitat. If a context-aware information service or tool is to provide general information and functionality adapted to a specific room or building, it may be accurate enough to know in which room of a building or which building of a city a user is located, and to provide an interface adapted for that room or building.

In designing a context-aware mobile device interface for a cinema, for example, facilitating movie information and ticket acquisition, this level of contextual detail could be achieved by making movie information and ticket acquisition available on small-screen devices in the physical space of the lobby and specific halls of the cinema (see Figure 8.2, left and centre) using wireless network cells or infrared beaming. Creating a meaningful relation between the interface and physical space at this level of accuracy would not demand an augmented reality interface. However, if a service or tool is to provide highly detailed computer-based information and functionality adapted to specific and delimited areas and objects in a room or building, a higher level of contextual detail is needed concerning the user's whereabouts in physical space and the placement of the interface within this space. When designing a context-aware

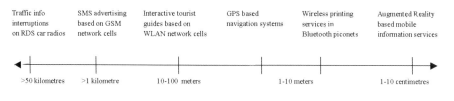

Figure 8.1 Level of contextual detail in context-aware information services for physically defined habitats.

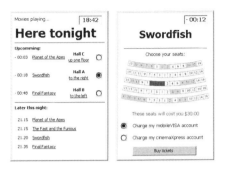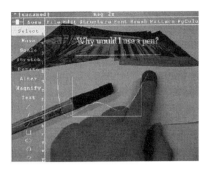

Figure 8.2 Context-aware interfaces for a cinema information service available when entering the lobby (left) and waiting outside the hall (centre) and augmented reality interface for a drawing tool enhancing the user's physical desk through a computerized graphical overlay (MIT MediaLab, 1999).

drawing tool, for instance, this level of accuracy could be achieved by spatially tracking the user, superimposing the computer interface on a physical desktop, and facilitating interaction through the use of spatially organized physical tools and objects such as paper, pens and scissors (Figure 8.2, right).

Compared with context-aware mobile information services for low-level contextual detail, creating a meaningful relation between a computer interface and physical space at the higher level of contextual detail exercised in augmented reality, increases the demands for knowledge about the user's contextual surroundings on two levels.

On a *technical level*, the user's location and orientation in space, proximity to objects and subjects surrounding him or her etc. have to be registered by the computer system with a very high level of precision. While several technologies for motion tracking are already available for virtual reality, appropriate technologies have yet to be developed for mobile augmented reality involving additional demands for facilities such as wireless operation, mobility and range.

On a *cultural and social level,* the properties and use of physical space have to be identified, analyzed and described in order to capture qualities and limitations, which should be exploited or supported in the specific interface being designed. In relation to this analysis, it is important to notice that physical space does not have to be replicated in every detail in order to make a useful augmented reality interface. On the contrary, many significant properties of physical space, such as gravity and distance, are neither necessary nor appropriate in the majority of augmented reality interfaces in order to make them useful.

Apart from the analysis of the relation between physical space and mobile computing, converting this knowledge into a specific interface design constitutes a major issue for the designers of such systems.

8.3 Analyzing the Use of Physical Space for Interface Design

When designing context-aware or augmented reality interfaces, designers are faced with two general problems of HCI research.

Firstly, whereas guidelines for traditional WIMP (windows, icons, menus, pointers) based interfaces are widespread (Preece *et al.*, 1994; Dix *et al.*; 1998; Shneiderman, 1998), the literature on human–computer interaction does not provide much input on how to design interfaces closely merged with their physical surroundings. Neither is there much experience with the usability of such interfaces reported. General guidelines for graphical user interfaces, concerning concepts such as mental models, mapping and feedback are of course also valid and valuable in relation to context awareness and augmented reality. However, most concepts and notions of HCI research only superficially address the rôle of physical space and the relation between interfaces and their physical surroundings. Secondly, HCI research may be criticized for primarily supporting *retrospective* measures and explanations of the quality (or lack of quality) in *existing* systems, and not providing a fruitful foundation for the development of *new* good interfaces (Nardi, 1996).

Designing human–computer interfaces that differ fundamentally from the WIMP paradigm, such as context awareness and augmented reality, thus challenges both the scope and applicability of existing HCI research and calls for new approaches to design to be explored. In order to support innovative design, such approaches must provide:

> ... (1) a broad background of comparative understandings over many domains, (2) high-level analyses useful for evaluating the impact of major design decisions, and (3) information that suggests actual design rather than simply general design guidelines or metrics for evaluation. To be able to provide such expertise, we must develop an appropriate analytical abstraction that "discards irrelevant details while isolating and emphasizing those properties of artefacts and situations that are most significant for design". (Nardi, 1996, pp. 69–70)

One of the problems with this perspective on HCI is the potential conflict between converting theoretical and analytical insight into suggestions for actual design without ending up in the pitfalls of either *dictating* specific solutions, thus limiting creativity and innovation, or leaving it all to creativity, with the risk of losing control of the process and focus. To balance these, an analytical abstraction will be appropriate only if it captures the essence of the design problem in a form both *general* enough for innovation and at the same time *concrete* and *structured* enough for directing the creative efforts.

When designing for context awareness or augmented reality such analytical abstraction must specifically be able to capture and differentiate the essential properties and uses of physical space in mobile computing in a way that inspires interface design merging the two, without simply just replicating the characteristics of physical space.

Inspiration for such analytical abstraction on design can be found in the works of architect and design philosopher Christopher Alexander. In his early work *Notes on the Synthesis of Form* (1964), Alexander presents a perspective on design of general value not limited to the architecture and design of physical artefacts but also applicable within other areas, such as computer interface and system design. In his principal work *A Pattern Language* (Alexander *et al.*, 1977), this perspective is elaborated further into a method for describing and categorizing design on a level of abstraction that captures the essence of existing form–context relations relevant for new design, while also supporting systematic structuring, interpretation and creativity.

8.3.1 Form and Context

According to Christopher Alexander, good design is a matter of creating the right *fit* between form and context – form being the solution, the part of the world we can control and manipulate, and context being the part of the world defining the problem and making demands on form. Design is thus not a question of form (or context) alone but a question of addressing the creation of *ensembles* fitting the two together. Ensembles of form and context exist on multiple levels. In a game of chess, some moves (form) fit the stage of the game (the context) better than in other stages of the game. In city planning, improving the city constitutes an ensemble of, for example, the form of expansion fitted to the context of the way the city works, the physical limitations and potentials, and the necessity for such expansion (Alexander, 1964, p. 16). From this perspective, it is clear that the world cannot be definitively divided into categories of form or context, as both form and context in themselves can be considered ensembles of form and context. What is form in relation to a given context may be viewed as context of other forms and vice versa. Subsequently, fit (or misfit) can be obtained either by modifying the form to the context or by modifying the context (including existing forms) to the form. The latter, however, carries the danger of breaking down the existing fit in other ensembles. According to Alexander, design is typically situated between these two extremes, involving a mutual adaptation of form and context. Because form in itself also influences its own as well as other contexts, fit will consequently always be a dynamic rather than static property of form–context ensembles, making design a potentially infinite task.

The dynamic relation between form and context requires designers to introduce a borderline between form and context in a given design case or ensemble and to specify what defines the problem and what constitutes the domain for possible solutions. Such a borderline will, of course, always be superficial in the sense that it could have been drawn elsewhere. But another borderline also implies another relation between form and context and thus demands another form. In relation to this, Alexander (1964, p. 17) emphasizes the tendency among designers to stretch the form–context boundary and to want to redesign large proportions of the context rather than simply focusing on the objects that they are supposed to improve. While this, on one hand, may be extremely impractical, it is, on the other hand, stressed as a fruitful way for designers to keep their eyes open to alternative solutions, other than the immediately obvious.

Pushed to the extreme, the development of a new form perfectly fitted to its context demands either a complete description of the context or that a number of forms are tried out until a good one is found. Neither approach is realistic in itself. If the context could be described completely there would be no issue of design, only a question of construction. Randomized non-reflected experiments with different forms, on the other hand, cannot be characterized as a process of design. According to Alexander, understanding context and experimenting with form are instead inseparable elements in design, as insight into the context influences the creation of form and experimenting with form influences the understanding of its context.

In relation to augmented reality user interfaces for mobile devices, an Alexandrian perspective on design helps in understanding the ensemble of devices and use better. First of all it is clear that shifting the use context of computing towards being mobile requires corresponding form changes in order to maintain fit. Design that may have fitted very well into the context of desktop computing may be less appropriate in the context of being mobile. Supporting text input on mobile phones exemplifies this problem. Furthermore, the use of augmented reality displays implies a displacement of the form–context border, as display and means of interaction, which usually belong to the context of interface design, now become a part of the form domain. Apart from displacing the borderline between form and context, designing augmented reality interfaces for mobile devices also extends the scope of the context domain to involve the use of physical space and other objects and persons in the user's physical surroundings, which was not necessarily relevant for design previously.

Extending the context may involve additional demands on the form, but at the same time may also widen the horizon of possible solutions.

Through the process of design, it is of course important to be able to evaluate and elaborate on form. According to Alexander, when people are exposed to a misfit between form and context in poorly designed artefacts they are typically capable of both identifying these and expressing how they are perceived to be defective. Fit, on the other hand, is neither easy to identify nor to describe because forms fitting their context appear transparent. This has the abrupt consequence that fit cannot be described independent of misfit, but must be defined as a *form without misfit,* making it problematic to characterize the desired positive properties of a new form without having to refer to the elimination of known misfit. In this way, misfit becomes a driving force in design through motivation and focus, subsequently introducing a demand for knowledge about the fit/misfit of similar form–context relations (either through practical experience or theoretical insight) among designers.

When designing something fundamentally new, such as augmented reality interfaces, however, examples of misfit can be hard to come up with due to lack of precedent. In this situation, experiments with form play a significant rôle, not only as a way of creating fit but also as a way of generating misfit, challenging the designer and providing forces pointing towards solutions and extending her insight into the context.

Concrete cases of fit and misfit, combined with insight into the context, describing when and why forms fail or perform well, can be systematized as *patterns* of design (Alexander *et al.*, 1977), having the potential to direct designers towards the creation of new solutions, recreating the qualities of existing forms without replicating the form as a whole.

8.3.2　Design Patterns

The concept of design patterns deals with some of the challenges of creative design discussed earlier in relation to interface design: how to capture the essence of existing form–context relations (fit and misfit) while supporting creativity and facilitating a systematic approach to the problem domain.

Following Christopher Alexander's (1977) design methodology, a problem domain can be divided into a hierarchy of interrelated "patterns", collectively constituting a "pattern language" for designers across competences and demarcations. Every pattern within this hierarchy potentially relates to the implementation of one or more general patterns and typically points towards a number of more specific, subordinated patterns supporting its own implementation (if such patterns exist). Each pattern itself represents an empirically based formalized description of central properties and dynamics in the relation between the form and context of a specific ensemble. Patterns identify and accentuate known examples of fit and misfit, and guide the designer towards the creation of new forms through general examples useful for *inspiration* rather than *duplication*.

Alexander (1977) provides such a hierarchy of 253 interrelated patterns concerning architecture at three levels of abstraction: towns, buildings and constructions.

Although potentially related to a larger theoretical framework, design patterns are not in themselves abstract principles hard to apply in practical design. At the same time, patterns are not so specific that they lose value in development of new forms. On the contrary, design patterns are general concrete guidelines for the creation of fit, unifying insight into form and context and pointing towards new forms (as illustrated in Figure 8.3) but without dictating specific design.

Similar to grounded theory, design patterns emerge from empirical observations. But contrary to grounded theory, design patterns do not make up theory as such, but are merely structured *descriptions* of form–context relations having been observed in the field. The process of identifying design patterns in a problem domain, however, very much resembles the process of generating theory from empirical data grounded in the real world. Identifying design patterns thus requires designers to observe a number of representative and reliable ensembles of form and context in a problem domain and to generate abstractions from this data which capture the essence and explain the phenomenon on a level of general validity. Like generating theory from empirical data, identifying patterns of design

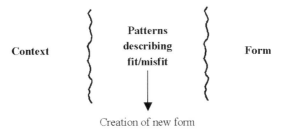

Figure 8.3　Design patterns merging knowledge about context and form towards new design.

is a long process, requiring designers/researchers to take a step backwards and elaborate on their understanding and ideas or even returning to the field for further observations and more focused studies. The methodology of Alexander (1977) does not provide much operational input on how to manage this process. However, the structure and interrelation of Alexandrian design patterns provide a valuable template, aiding the formulation of patterns from one's empirical observations.

Alexandrian design patterns follow a uniform structure and graphical format, which makes them highly consistent. Each pattern is headed with a brief name and a photograph exemplifying its application. Following the photograph, the pattern is related to possible parent patterns, which it may contribute to the realization of. This is followed by a concentrated problem statement, describing the essence of the problem addressed by the pattern in one or two short sentences (formatted in bold). Subsequently, the empirical background of the pattern and detailed insight into the context, along with examples of fit and misfit, are presented. This part is often accompanied by further pictures, drawings, diagrams etc. substantiating the empirical foundation. Finally, the solution to the problem (the essence of the pattern) is described in a few brief sentences (also formatted in bold) often supplemented with a general graphical representation. Each pattern is terminated with references to possible subordinated patterns. A single design pattern typically takes up 3–5 pages.

The uniform format of Alexandrian design patterns has a number of advantages in the design process. First of all, the graphical layout and consistent use of photographs and text formatting makes collections of patterns (or pattern languages) easy to browse and be inspired by without having to read them all word by word. Secondly, the structured format facilitates design patterns being read on several levels of abstraction according to the need for input at a given time.

For browsing and overview, patterns can be read primarily through their names and photographs, pinpointing design issues and capturing possible applications of the pattern. For this use, the photographs heading each pattern play a significant rôle, often saying "more than a thousand words" and stimulating the user's memory of a pattern. Selecting good photographs illustrating one's design patterns is thus critical and should not be down-prioritized (or left out).

For a brief summarized insight into the design issue addressed by a pattern, design patterns can be read exclusively through the short statements describing the problem and pointing out solutions. For this use, it is important that these sections are both brief and clear and do not concern themselves too deeply the background of the pattern.

Finally, for a full description, covering the empirical and theoretical foundations of a pattern, design patterns can, of course, be read in their full length. For this level of abstraction, it is important that the pattern provides insight that substantiates both the problem statement and the suggested solution.

In practical use, designers will most likely shift back and forward between these levels of abstraction during the design process and e.g. (1) browse headings/photographs for a quick overview, (2) read the problem and solution statements of those patterns which seem immediately interesting, (3) read selected patterns in their full length for additional insight and finally (4) implement selected patterns using primarily their problem statements and suggested solutions, browsing between them using their headings and photographs.

8.3.3 Design Patterns as User Interface Requirement Specifications

Whereas the concept of design patterns has received much attention within software engineering and object oriented programming, less focus has been brought to this approach within human–computer interaction. Though several references to the work of Alexander exists within mainstream HCI literature (Norman and Draper, 1986; Norman, 1988; Winograd, 1996), only a few examples exist of HCI researchers actually applying the concept of design patterns and pattern languages in interface and interaction design. This is the case even though the concept of design patterns as originally intended within architecture has much more obvious relations to user interface design than to software engineering, with respect to the focus on users and design meeting the demands and potentials of a use context. Among the most central research on design patterns for HCI is the work of Tidwell (1999) and Borchers (2001), illustrating the potential of design patterns as user interface requirement specifications.

Through a comprehensive collection of interrelated patterns, Tidwell (1999) shows how the overall concept of a highly interrelated web of patterns can be applied to interactive software, describing highly specific issues of interaction design with a broad range of applications such as "going back to a safe place" and "disabling irrelevant things", while leaving out issues about implementation and user interface technologies. Exemplifying the strength of a pattern approach for capturing "timeless" examples of fit and misfit in interaction design, the majority of these patterns successfully balance the edge of being neither too specific nor too general for application outside the context within which they were identified.

Whereas Tidwell, however, does not strictly follow the format of Alexandrian patterns described earlier, making her patterns less inspiring to browse and rather superficial regarding their empirical background compared with the patterns of Alexander, Borchers (2001) carries the format of Alexandrian design patterns all the way through. In his patterns on the design of interactive exhibitions, dealing with more general interface issues than Tidwell such as "domain appropriate devices" and "immersive display", Borchers shows how patterns for HCI can benefit from following both the structure and the level of abstraction characterizing Alexander's design patterns for architecture, facilitating a high level of interpretation.

While the work of both Tidwell and Borchers, however, focuses primarily on the *identification* of patterns of interaction and interface design from existing HCI design, the actual *applicability* and *usefulness* of such patterns in the creation of new interface design still needs to be investigated and reported.

In the following sections, the practical applicability of design patterns for human–computer interaction is explored through a specific design case, dealing with the design of an experimental augmented reality prototype for distributed cooperative work. A number of empirically identified design patterns for computer-supported cooperative work are presented, followed by a description exemplifying the actual application of these patterns in an augmented reality interface.

Compared with the HCI patterns of Tidwell and Borchers, the patterns described in this chapter are more closely related to the use of physical space than to experience with specific design solutions of existing well-performing human–computer interfaces. The reason for this is twofold. First of all, the use of physical space plays a significant rôle in the type of interface being designed. Secondly, the prototype developed explores interface design within an area with limited precedents. The design is thus not aiming at recreating specific qualities of existing tools as much as it aims at recreating the qualities related to the use of physical space and solving some general misfit in existing tools.

8.4 Design Case: Augmenting a Habitat for Cooperative Work

Work spaces for cooperation, such as offices, meeting rooms and workshops, can be viewed as spatially, temporally and social defined habitats, facilitating specific cooperative activities at different times according to the people present or not present. Such work spaces often involve people in a workgroup moving around and artefacts being closely related to specific physical locations at specific times. Furthermore, physical space is frequently being reconfigured for a variety of use purposes: working individually or in groups, conducting presentations, holding meetings, organizing and storing shared resources, socializing etc. When a workgroup is physically distributed, many of these properties and potentials of physical space are lost.

A variety of computer-based tools for supporting cooperative work (CSCW) exist for supporting the creation of distributed shared work spaces facilitating sharing of files and applications as well as video-based interpersonal communication on ordinary desktop computers. While overcoming some of the problems of distributing a workgroup physically, these tools typically fail to support users being mobile in, and taking advantage of the properties of, physical space, which usually characterizes cooperative work. Instead of providing the user with a transparent virtual space within which cooperation can exist, CSCW tools thus typically constitute new tools to be operated in order to facilitate cooperation. This consequently results in an additional layer being introduced between the users and objects of a workgroup, creating demands for an intuitive representation of the system's conceptual model, restricting interaction and introducing a rather solid boundary between objects in physical and virtual space respectively.

Using mobile augmented reality interfaces to augment habitats for cooperative work through the creation of distributed virtual work spaces merged into physical space introduces new potentials for the design of CSCW tools. By potentially relieving some of the problems of existing CSCW tools, mobile augmented reality interfaces for supporting distributed cooperation could enable a stronger relation between information systems and physical space as well as a higher level of mobility in the physical world while also being present in a distributed virtual 3D space.

To explore this hypothesis, an experimental augmented reality prototype for distributed cooperative work was designed and implemented. The interface design of this prototype was based on requirement specifications in the form of design patterns, describing the use of physical space in cooperative work in relation to examples of fit and misfit in existing CSCW tools.

8.4.1 Identifying Design Patterns for CSCW

During 1999, 12 design patterns were identified and used as interface requirement specifications for an augmented reality interface supporting a physically distributed workgroup. The basis of analysis leading to the identified design patterns was three-fold (Figure 8.4):

1. Literature studies on the rôle of physical space and artefacts in our daily lives generally (Hall, 1966; Tuan, 1977; Tillich, 1933) and in cooperative work specifically (Kaptelinin, 1996; Kuutti, 1996; Obata and Sasaki, 1998) provided a theoretical background for the empirical observations and analysis of collected data.
2. Empirical observations of cooperative work activities in physical space at the University of Aalborg (meetings, presentations, workshops etc.) with and without the use of computer-based tools provided specific insight into the use of physical space and artefacts.
3. Usability evaluations of a broad range of tools for computer-supported cooperative work (Microsoft NetMeeting, Teamwave Workplace, SGI InPerson, VirtualU, FirstClass etc.) pointed out examples of fit and misfit in existing tools.

From the empirical observations, a number of distinctive characteristics and properties of cooperation in physical space were extracted and organized in a simple list

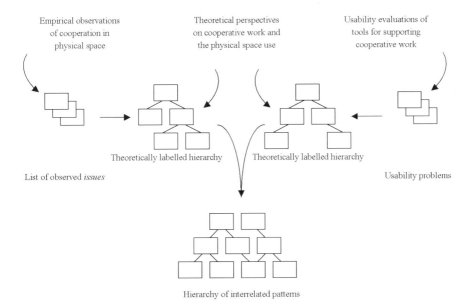

Figure 8.4 The process of identifying patterns of cooperative work.

of issues. Each issue was then discussed and reconsidered in relation to the others, resulting in some being merged and others being left out. The remaining issues were then organized in a hierarchy and related to the theoretical perspective on physical space and labelled with a number of theoretical concepts. Similarly, the identified usability problems as well as examples of successful design in existing computer-based tools for supporting cooperation were listed, grouped and subordinated to each other. Where possible, usability issues were related to the corresponding use of physical space and labelled with theoretical concepts from the literature. Subsequently, the two lists were merged into a hierarchy of preliminary outlines of 12 interrelated design patterns associated with the physical distribution of a workgroup, formulated in terms of physical space use with references to specific design. Finally the outlined design patterns were refined further, reformulated and supplied with an extended body discussing the problem addressed by the pattern and pointing out avenues for possible solutions. Photographs capturing the focus of each pattern were then added.

8.4.2 Outlines of a Pattern Language for CSCW

From the original 12 design patterns identified, the six shown in Figure 8.5 had the most significant impact on the interface design of the implemented prototype, and are presented in this chapter in summarized form (Figures 8.6–8.11).

Within the context of augmented reality-based interfaces for cooperative work these patterns can all be subordinated the realization of Borchers' (2001) pattern H8 on Augmented Reality:

> In situations where your system aims to recreate a real experience, use as much real instead of virtual environment as possible. Instead of trying to recreate all aspects of reality inside an artificial environment, augment the real environment with interactive technology that is not usually available otherwise. (Borchers, 2001, pp. 127–128)

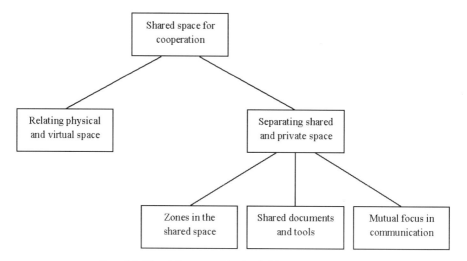

Figure 8.5 Hierarchal structure of the identified design patterns for CSCW.

1. Shared space for cooperation

When a group of people are working together, it is important to have access to a shared space for cooperation facilitating members of a workgroup relating to each other, sharing documents and engaging in communication, presentations, meetings, etc. When a workgroup is distributed physically, this space for cooperation is lost.

Observing cooperative work, it is obvious that the joint activity of a workgroup can be coordinated. Coordination typically takes place in three different ways: *scripted* through means such as plans, calendars and timetables, *communicatively* through written or spoken language or *instrumentally* through knowledge of each others actions. These ways of coordination requires that members of a workgroup have access to shared resources concerning their joint activities, can communicate and interact with each other and are aware about the actions and activities the workgroup as a whole. The closer a workgroup cooperates the more it depends on means for coordinating. Under normal circumstances, physical space plays a vital role as highly versatile medium for such mechanisms. When a workgroup is distributed physically, this medium is lost. Observing the use of tools for distributed cooperative work indicates that while scripted and asynchronous communicative coordination is typically supported very well through access to e.g. shared folders, e-mail based communication and discussion forums, it is hard to support instrumental and synchronous communicative coordination. While chat relays, video communication and application sharing have potentials in this direction, current implementations of these technologies are still rather limited.

Therefore:

Create a computer-based shared space for cooperation by connecting the individual workspaces of people in a distributed workgroup to each other. Within this space, facilitate information access and flexible communication and interaction among the group. If possible, support the maintenance of peripheral awareness about the presence and activities of others.

Create such shared space for cooperation by *relating physical and virtual space (2)* and *separating shared and private space (3)* with reference to *zones in the shared space (4)*, *shared documents and tools (5)* and *mutual focus in interpersonal communication (6)*.

Figure 8.6 Pattern of shared space for cooperation.

2. Relating physical and virtual space

The use of computer-based tools or media in distributed cooperative work introduces a hard boundary between virtual objects and physical space, restraining the relation between the two. Each member of a workgroup consequently has to maintain an informational (virtual) space and a physical space, as well as an arbitrary relation between the two.

While physical space facilitates objects being spatially organised and related to each other in a meaningful way, according to their location in space, this facility is restricted when dealing with a mixture of physical and virtual objects.

Observing the use of tools for computer supported cooperative work indicates that physical and virtual spaces are highly separated, and that user's spend considerable efforts on maintaining a relation between the two, displacing the focus of activity away from the cooperation itself.

The lack of relation between physical and virtual space often results in a messy, confusing and unnatural organisation of the elements in the interface. In tools for supporting a distributed workgroup, shared objects, representations of other members of the workgroup, control panels, etc. are typically crowding the user's desktop in a very unstructured fashion without any relation to the physical space surrounding the tool. Such badly organised interfaces limits the usability of the shared space for cooperation, because fundamental operations such as changing focus from one object to another (whether virtual or physical), interacting with shared tools or communicating with remote users cannot be done without consciously focusing on interaction with *system*.

The problem can be described as lack of context awareness, making interaction in the physical world surrounding the system "invisible" to the system and visa versa. How accurate interaction in physical space should be reflected in virtual space depends on the specific context of use. Some applications such as augmented reality may require a very close relation while others may require only a superficial relation in order to support interaction.

Therefore:

Strengthen the relation between physical space and virtual objects by making the computer system context aware on a level of detail matching the specific need of the cooperative work activities being designed for. Design the means of interaction in a way that makes interaction in physical space a part of the human-computer interface.

Figure 8.7 Pattern of relating physical and virtual space.

3. Separating shared and private space

In a shared space for cooperation, it is important that members of a workgroup are not forced to be together at all times, but can separate from each other and retrieve to a space of their own. The separation of shared and private spaces is critical. Lack of separation breaks down the private space while too much separation isolates people from the workgroup.

According to Tillich (1933), the presence of private space constitutes a significant foundation for people's ability to act in shared space. Without private space, people have nowhere to retrieve to and feel secure but are constantly public, resulting in a feeling of root- and restlessness. Goffman (1959) addresses the same issue through the concepts of front- and backstage, while Tuan (1977) describes the problem as a matter of facilitating the creation of a *place* as opposed to *space:* a secure base, in which people are their own masters, in charge of the spatial layout and organisation of space and artefacts.

Observing the use of shared physical workspaces confirms the fine balance between shared and private space and furthermore indicates, that the separation is often dynamic, exemplified by e.g. people keeping the doors to their office open or closed towards the hallway at specific times.

In cooperative work, the importance of separating shared and private spaces is not only related to the individual need for a place of ones own. It is also simply a matter of facilitating individual work activities, relatively undisturbed by the presence and activities of others.

The separation of shared and private space is traditionally not an issue taking up much focus within CSCW, as the problem may remain invisible until private space is threatened by e.g. the creation of distributed shared spaces, exposing it to other people.

Therefore:

Provide each member of a workgroup with a private space facilitating individual work, clearly delimitated from the shared space. Make the private workspace half-open towards the shared workspace so that peripheral contact to the other members of workgroup can be maintained without people being able to keep a private workspace under surveillance.

Figure 8.8 Pattern of separating shared and private space.

4. Zones in the shared space

In cooperative work, it is important to be able to organize the shared space of a workgroup in a simple and comprehensible way, facilitating differentiation of objects belonging to the individual members and objects being shared by the group as well as easy exchange of private and shared objects among the members of the group.

In physical meetings around a central table, space is often divided into a number of zones, having a number of properties for organizing the shared space. Objects located within a person's intimate distance (15-45 cm) (Hall 1966) are considered belonging to this person while objects located within a person's personal distance (45-120 cm) but not within other people's intimate distance are considered shared by the people surrounding these objects. Objects within the social distance of a person (1,2 – 3,65 m) are also considered shared by the group while objects or persons within a person's official distance (3,65 m –) may belong to other groups. The division of shared space into zones supports an implicit reduction of complexity, clearly distinguishing between private and public objects as well as persons within close or remote proximity. The figure below illustrates such division of space in a physical meeting into specifically named zones (Obata and Sasaki 1998).

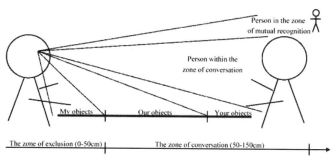

Therefore:

Divide the shared workspace into a number of zones corresponding to the zones of physical meetings facilitating intuitive identification of my objects, our objects, your objects as well as close and remote persons. Make the objects belonging each member of a group visible to other members within close proximity and facilitate easy exchange of objects between persons within close range.

Figure 8.9 Pattern of zones in the shared space.

5. Shared documents and tools

Cooperative work typically involves the use and organisation of a large amount of shared documents, diagrams, archives, drawings, etc. and the joint interaction with tools for modifying these. When a workgroup is physically distributed, the access to shared documents is limited and the cooperative use of tools is made difficult.

Cooperating in a shared physical space, shared documents etc. constitute a common frame of reference and a central means of asynchronous communication within the workgroup both through their informational content and their spatial relations, grouping, location, etc.

When a workgroup is distributed physically, the members of such group usually end up with multiple outdated versions of shared documents, and the common spatial relation between shared documents is lost, breaking the common frame of reference. In tools for supporting a distributed workgroup, it is thus important to support not only access to shared documents but also facilitate the members of a group jointly organising these documents in an appropriate way.

In relation to shared documents, tools for modifying these documents, whether individually or in groups, also plays a significant role in cooperative work as "mediating artefacts" (Kuutti 1996), supporting the transformation of the objects of cooperation and the instrumental coordination of activity. Observing the joint use of shared tools in physical as well as virtual space reveals a significant problem related to the regulation of turn taking: who is in control of the shared tool at a given time and how is the control taken by or passed on to another? In physical space, turn taking is usually regulated by cultural rules and cues, facilitating quick and easy handover. In tools for supporting distributed cooperative work, turn taking on the opposite, often involves a structured procedure to be carried out, facilitating control but limiting flexible use.

Therefore:

Within the shared workspace, make it possible to store, organise and retrieve shared information, and support the use of appropriate tools for modifying these individually or in groups. Make it possible to organise shared documents in a flexible way similar to the way one would organise physical documents: spatially, in stacks etc. If a shared tool can only be operated by one at a time, facilitate an easy regulation of turn taking.

Figure 8.10 Pattern of shared documents and tools.

6. Mutual focus in interpersonal communication

In physically distributed meetings, it can be difficult to maintain the mutual focus in interpersonal communication, which is implicitly established in physical space by virtue of visual orientation and body gestures.

Observing communication and interaction in physical meetings, the importance of visual orientation and body gestures of others becomes very clear. Establishing an implicit mutual focus and facilitating instrumental coordination of joint interaction among the members of a group, these means support the basic control of communication and joint interaction such as e.g. turn taking (passing the word on to another speaker) and indexicality (looking or pointing at someone or something while talking or interacting).

When people are physically distributed, the mutual focus characterising interpersonal communication in physical space is impeded, making it difficult to maintain a common frame of reference among members of a workgroup. This not only restricts interpersonal communication through a distributed shared space due to lack of properties such as mutual gaze-direction, but also lower the usability of shared tools and documents in synchronous cooperation.

Reducing the means of instrumental coordination, people consequently have to compensate for the lack of mutual focus and body gestures through other modes of operation such as meta-communication like "I now do this while looking at that…" or "do you see where I am pointing now…?" etc. This need for meta-communication further strains the channel of verbal communication and moves the focus of activity away from the objects of cooperation towards conscious operation of the tool itself.

Therefore:

Design the shared space for cooperation so that the gaze-direction and gestures of the distributed users such as pointing is reflects and represented in a natural and meaningful way. If possible, introduce into this representation some kind of reciprocity of gaze-direction, resembling the feeling of face-to-face contact in physical space.

Figure 8.11 Pattern of mutual focus in interpersonal communication.

8.5 Applying Patterns to Augmented Reality Interface Design

This section describes how the six patterns of design presented above were applied to actual interface and interaction design. "Being There" is an experimental prototype, exploring the use of mobile augmented reality interfaces in relating a spatial habitat to a virtual information space at a high level of contextual detail. The prototype exemplifies how the visual augmentation of a private office for distributed cooperative work could be designed for access through a mobile device interface, exploiting the potential and use of physical space in cooperative work. The illustrations show the user's perspective on the interface in an office already rich on physical objects and artefacts.

8.5.1 Creating a Shared Space for Cooperation

The pattern for *creating a shared space for cooperation (1)* motivates the overall creation of tools for supporting distributed cooperative work. In the implemented prototype, such shared space for cooperation was created by augmenting the physical offices of each member in a workgroup with a computerized graphical overlay of a virtual 3D world, running on a central server and shared over a high-speed network. This design first of all facilitated a much larger graphical interface than on traditional desktop monitors, leaving room for much more information without cluttering the interface. Wearing lightweight, semitransparent head-mounted displays, users at the same time remained mobile in the physical space of their offices while simultaneously also being present in the virtual shared space of the workgroup.

The specific design of this shared space was realized through *relating physical and virtual space (2)* and *separating shared and private space (3)*.

8.5.2 Relating Physical and Virtual Space

Supporting the relation between virtual objects and physical space, the implemented prototype was made context-aware at a high level of spatially contextual detail, generating an impression of computer-based documents and tools being present alongside their physical counterparts. This is illustrated in Figure 8.12,

Figure 8.12 Physical desk populated with physical as well as virtual objects.

showing the user's view of his physical desk, populated with both physical and virtual objects.

By turning his head, the user can change the view of the virtual world in the same way that he would orientate in the physical world, preserving a consistent spatial relation between the two. In the lower left corner is a self-view, showing the video feed being transmitted to the other users of the system.

Blurring the boundary between physical and virtual space further, the interface design facilitates virtual objects being spatially organized in all three dimensions, being grouped, stacked, pushed further away or dragged into closer proximity. Additionally, virtual objects could have been directly related to physical objects, creating an even stronger relationship between physical and virtual space. This, however, was not implemented.

Interaction is done by means of a dataglove, allowing virtual objects to be grabbed, moved and modified with one's hand in more or less the same way one would interact with physical objects. To rectify some of the limitations of interaction in physical space, the user is, however, equipped with "stretchable" virtual arms, making him capable of reaching objects in virtual space at a greater distance than in physical space.

8.5.3 Separating Shared and Private Space

To implement the pattern of *separating shared and private space (3)*, the virtual space merged into the user's physical office is divided horizontally into two overall areas. The area of the virtual space surrounding a user's physical desk is considered private and is not visible to the other users in the system, while the area facing away from the desk is shared among the group. This is illustrated in Figure 8.13, showing a view of the private space on the left and the boundary between private and shared space on the right. Physically this boundary is marked by the end of the desk. In the computerized overlay this location is marked/enhanced with a vertical line.

The implemented layout of the interface to a large degree resembles the typical division of physical space in both private and shared offices, supporting peripheral contact with the workgroup while working in one's private space and facilitating an easy transition between private and shared spaces by simply turning round on

Figure 8.13 The boundary between private (left) and shared space (far right).

one's chair. To exploit this design further, documents can easily be exchanged (copied) among the group by simply dragging them from private to shared space and vice versa.

The specific design of the shared space is realized through *dividing the shared space into zones (4)*, and *supporting shared tools and resources (3)* and *mutual focus in interpersonal communication (6)*.

8.5.4 Dividing the Shared Space Into Zones

The layout of shared space (facing away from the physical desktop) is organized vertically in accordance to the pattern describing *zones in the shared space (4)*. The implemented design more or less directly resembles the zones characterizing a physical meeting.

When looking down at her lap, the user has visual access to documents within the shared space, corresponding to the documents located right in front of her in a physical meeting (Figure 8.14, left). This resembles the zone of exclusion, containing documents belonging to a specific person but visible to others in proximity. Looking upwards, the user has visual access to the shared documents of the workgroup, corresponding to the documents located in the zone of conversation between people in a physical meeting (Figure 8.14). These documents can be organized and manipulated simultaneously by all users. Further upwards in the interface, the user sees the documents belonging to other members of the group: your documents (Figure 8.14, right). The representations of the zone of exclusion of remote users are located immediately below their respective live video image (see section 8.5.6), supporting a natural mapping between the two.

Though designed in accordance with the zones of proximity in mind, the design of the shared space does not aim to resemble physical space in every aspect. Contrary to physical space, all users see the shared space from the same visual perspective, preventing users having to compensate for the mutual displacement characterizing a "real" 3D world and directly facilitating the use of spatial indexicality in communication, such as referring to "the document down to the right".

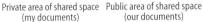

Private area of shared space   Public area of shared space   Public area of shared space   Private area of shared space
(my documents)   (our documents)   (our documents)   (my documents)

Figure 8.14 The division of shared space into zones.

Figure 8.15 Private and shared tools embedded into physical space.

8.5.5 Supporting Shared Documents and Tools

In accordance with the pattern on *shared documents and tools (5)*, the shared space for cooperation merged into the user's physical office supports the joint spatial organization and interaction with computer-based documents and tools.

In reducing the traditional boundary between documents and tools in computer artefacts, the interface design of the prototype facilitates documents (e.g. web pages or word processor documents) being editable in their corresponding tools by simply dragging them into closer proximity (Figure 8.15).

While tools in the private space (Figure 8.15, left) are not visible to the group, tools in the shared space (Figure 8.15, right) are by default shared among the users. As the multi-user tools available in the prototype (word processors and web browsers) can only be operated by one user at a time, regulations of turn taking have been implemented. Resembling turn-taking in physical space, control over a shared tool is taken by another user simply by starting to interact with it. While this regulation of turn-taking may result in anarchy and a constant battle for control, on the other hand it facilitates turn-taking being controlled by cultural rules rather than through formalized procedures.

8.5.6 Supporting Mutual Focus and Interpersonal Communication

When looking straight into the shared space, the user has visual access to the other members of the workgroup facing the shared space through live video feeds (Figure 8.16). In accordance with the pattern on *zones in the shared space (4)*, the vertical location of these video images resembles the location of other people's faces in a physical meeting.

To implement the pattern on *mutual focus in interpersonal communication (6)*, a remote user's gaze direction in the shared space is reflected by the horizontal location of his video image in the shared space, thus causing video images of remote users to slide from left to right according to their orientation. This is illustrated in Figure 8.16.

Figure 8.16 Gaze-direction represented by the horizontal location of live video in shared space.

Figure 8.17 The gaze direction of remote users represented through the orientation of avatars.

While very different from the way in which physical space works, this design has a number of advantages. First of all, it supports a simple cue for revealing the visual orientation of other users, making it possible to determine what remote users are looking at in the shared space. Secondly, an approximation of face-to-face contact is supported by the reciprocity of video image locations, meaning that if I look towards the video image of you, you will also be faced with the video image of me, providing valuable assistance in the establishment of interpersonal communication. This reciprocity is not available in traditional video-based communication tools. Thirdly, if a user is not facing the shared space, no video image will be available, preserving the privacy of private space. In accordance with the pattern on *zones in the shared space (4)*, remote users facing away from the shared space are represented as distant avatars in the zone of mutual recognition (at the top of the interface), supporting peripheral awareness (Figure 8.17).

Providing each user with a distinctive pointer in shared space supports the representation of pointing in shared space, but does not represent actual body gestures.

8.6 Lessons from Being There

The prototype presented exemplifies what a mobile augmented reality interface for distributed cooperative work *could* look like in order to support the properties and use of physical space, described earlier. The lessons learned from developing Being There can be divided into three sections:

1. Augmented reality interface design
2. Mobile augmented reality
3. Using patterns in interface design

8.6.1 Augmented Reality Interface Design

Apart from being tested extensively by the developers, the design was evaluated through interactive exhibitions at Intermedia Aalborg in August/September 1999, during which a total of 25–30 people unfamiliar with such interfaces tried out the system for approximately 10 minutes each. During use, people were asked to "think aloud" communicating their comprehension and intentions when interacting with the system. Following use, people were informally interviewed about their experience with the system.

The evaluation showed that even though the graphical performance of the system was not optimal, the design demanded little instruction to be done. Users typically had no problems understanding the relation between physical and virtual space and using the system for spatially organizing virtual objects in physical space, as well as orientating in virtual space by moving physically. They often walked right up and used the system. Some users, however, expressed a wish to link virtual and physical objects, while others expressed wishes for real 3D representation and stereoscopic projection, which was not facilitated in the prototype.

Users had little or no difficulty in differentiating between private and shared space and exchanging documents with each other. Some, however, expressed a wish for a clearer graphical identification of the boundary between the two, which might have been affected by the lack of natural demarcations of private and public areas in the physical space of the exhibition area. The division of shared space into zones was also easy to comprehend. Users expressed that they found the location of video images straight ahead of them natural and easy to use, and that the location of documents virtually in their lap supported a feeling of ownership.

While users engaged easily in interpersonal communication through the video links, the representation of gaze direction was, however, reported by first-time users to be difficult to understand and rather confusing. Suggestions of other designs were made, e.g. indicating viewing direction through a small compass below each video image. Users communicating through the system for a longer period of time, however, found the representation of gaze direction very practical and easy to use, expressing that it actually supported their communication and interaction.

Although very intuitive at first, direct manipulation of virtual objects using the dataglove was reported to be demanding, as it required large physical arm movements for even simple operations. While this might be related to the relatively low frame rate and high response time of the prototype, similar problems have also been reported in the use of high-end virtual reality installations without these limitations (Kjeldskov, 2001), indicating that absolute input devices may simply be problematic for some types of interaction in virtual space. In both cases, using a relative pointing device would demand smaller physical movements.

The evaluation of Being There indicates that augmented reality interfaces exploiting the potential and use of physical space and populating it with virtual objects have a high level of immediate usability, although they are fundamentally different from traditional human–computer interfaces. The virtual implementation of qualities found in physical space do not, however, demand physical space to be replicated in all aspects, but can be achieved through design inspired by it, leaving designers room for creativity, exemplified by the unnatural representation of gaze direction. In contrast, implementing the natural properties of physical space may result in limited usability, as exemplified by the glove-based interaction technique.

8.6.2 Mobile Augmented Reality

Although not suitable for mobility outside a dedicated physical office because of the use of stationary electromagnetic tracking devices, the implemented prototype provides input on the design and usability of spectacle-based mobile augmented reality, relating physical space and user human–computer interfaces at a high level of contextual detail.

Addressing the challenges of mobile HCI described in the beginning of this chapter, Being There shows how separating the computing device from the graphical interface and embedding the display into the user's spectacles can increase the limited screen real estate of mobile computers. Covering a large percentage of the user's visual field of view at all times does, however, not necessarily mean that it should be completely filled with graphical information at all times. In most mobile use contexts e.g. when walking down the street, the primary advantage of the relatively large screen real estate of an augmented reality interface is not the amount of information potentially squeezed into the interface. It is rather the ability to capture the user's visual attention and locate small bits of information at the appropriate spatial location within her visual view, enabling her to receive information without having to pull out and hold a physical device. As physical space is typically already abundantly populated with objects, artefacts and people (illustrated in Figures 8.12–8.17), the designers of mobile augmented reality interfaces must balance the weight of embedding virtual objects into physical space without creating an explosion of complexity.

In exploring the potential of context awareness in mobile device interfaces, Being There shows how virtual information can be merged successfully into specific locations surrounding the user, preserving a dual focus on the computer interface and the physical world. While the prototype primarily exemplifies how a *spatially* defined habitat could be represented through a context-aware mobile information service, mobile augmented reality could also facilitate the representation of temporally and socially defined habitats through similar design, taking these contextual factors into consideration.

In relation to the limited means of interaction characterizing mobile devices, the use of augmented reality in Being There does not indicate an obvious path for solutions. On the contrary, one could claim that the problem of interacting with mobile device interfaces is in fact increased in the light of augmented reality by removing the usual relation between the physical input device and the visual output device. While walking down the street, how does one interact with virtual objects floating in space? Apart from the use of simple pointing devices, interesting areas of research include the use of speech (Sawhney and Schmandt, 2000), eye-movements (Duchowski and Vertegaal, 2000) and even brainwaves (Hjelm and Browall, 2000) as means of input potentially applicable within the context of mobile augmented reality.

8.6.3 Using Patterns in Interface Design

The employment of Alexandrian design patterns in the development of Being There exemplifies how the properties and use of physical space can be analyzed and described in a form supporting creative interface design for augmented reality. In the specific design case, the methodology of Alexander constituted an appropriate analytical abstraction by describing interface requirement specifications through a series of design patterns, balancing the need for facilitating creativity in a new design while approaching the design problem in a systematic and structured way. The identified patterns specifically played a threefold rôle as *design tool, communication tool* and *structure tool.*

As a *design tool,* the patterns reduced the complexity of the specific form–context ensemble in focus and pointed towards new solutions by identifying and describing key issues of the context and existing forms relevant for design while discarding irrelevant details. As no specific solutions were dictated, the patterns challenged the designers to be innovative within the frame of the patterns.

As a *communication tool,* the patterns supported the accumulation of the problem domain analysis and mediated this knowledge on to the process of design. During design, the patterns worked as a common frame of reference in communication within the design team, supporting a high degree of subjective interpretations within a common frame of understanding.

As a *structure tool,* the web of patterns divided the form–context ensemble into a series of interrelated tangible design problems to be addressed explicitly. Each isolated pattern furthermore supported the structure of the design process by dealing with a clearly delimited area of the form–context ensemble.

While design patterns are great for supporting communication and a structured approach to creativity, they are in themselves, however, too general for implementation without further efforts being made. At some point of the design process, patterns must thus inevitably be complemented with additional and more detailed requirement specifications, specifying exactly *how* the interface should look and work and *how* it should be constructed in order to do so. In this perspective, design patterns may be most valuable in the *early* phases of a software development process.

8.6.4 Limitations of This Work

As the primary focus of this project was a preliminary study of the design potential and problems of mobile augmented reality, the prototype was never intended to make up a fully implemented system suitable for real-world use, but should rather serve as a *proof of concept*. Full-scale usability studies of the interface design in real distributed cooperative work setting were thus not conducted, naturally limiting our ability to assess whether or not the design really has the intended qualities of physical space and would perform well over a longer period of time.

8.7 Conclusions

In this chapter, I have presented mobile augmented reality as a possible human–computer interface approach for context-aware information services with a very detailed relation between physical and virtual space. In the light of a number of limitations within HCI research in relation to the creation of new interface design, I have presented the concepts and methodology of Christopher Alexander, suggesting the relations between ensembles of form and context being described as patterns of design. Using this approach, I have shown how a mobile augmented reality interface for supporting distributed cooperative work can be designed from empirically identified design patterns, capturing the rôle of physical space in cooperative work.

The implemented prototype shows that physical and virtual space *can* be related in a mobile augmented reality interface and that locating virtual objects in the user's physical surroundings *can* be useful in a mobile device interface. The evaluation of the prototype indicates that such interfaces *can* be comprehended and utilized by ordinary users.

Acknowledgements

The author thanks Tom Nyvang who participated in the identification of the original 12 design patterns and the development of the prototype. Acknowledgements are also paid to Ellen Christiansen and Erik Granum for engagement and enthusiastic supervision of the project and their participation in constructive discussions.

References

Alexander, C. (1964) *Notes on the Synthesis of Form*. London: Harvard University Press.
Alexander, C., Ishikawa, S. and Silverstein, M. (1977) *A Pattern Language*. New York: Oxford University Press.
Bergman, E (ed.) (2000) *Information Appliances and Beyond*. London: Morgan Kaufmann.
Borchers, J. (2001) *A Pattern Approach to Interaction Design*. New York: John Wiley & Sons.
Dix, A. Finlay, J., Abowd, G. and Beale, R. (1998) *Human–Computer Interaction*, 2nd edn. London: Prentice Hall.
Duchowski, A. and Vertegaal, R. (2000) Eye-based interaction in graphical systems: theory and practice. In *Course Notes no. 5*, Siggraph 2000, New Orleans.
Feiner, S., MacIntyre, B. and Höllerer, T. (1999) Wearing it out: first steps toward mobile augmented reality systems. In Onto, Y. and Tamura, H. (eds.) *Mixed Reality – Merging Real and Virtual Worlds*. Berlin, Springer-Verlag.
Goffman, E. (1959) *Presentation of Self in Everyday Life*: Garden City, NY: Anchor.
Hall, E. (1966) *The Hidden Dimension*. New York: Doubleday.

Hinckley, K., Pierce, J., Sinclair, M. and Horvitz, E. (2000) Sensing techniques for mobile interaction. In *Symposium on User Interface Software and Technology, CHI Letters*, 2(2), 91–100.

Hjelm, S. and Browall, C. (2000) Brainball – using brain activity for cool competition. *Demo at NordiCHI 2000*, Stockholm, Sweden.

Izadi, S., Fraser, M., Benford, S., Flintham, M. and Greenhalgh, C. (2001) Citywide: supporting interactive digital experiences across physical space. *Proceedings of the Mobile HCI 2001 Workshop on Human Computer Interaction with Mobile Devices, IHM-HCI 2001*, Lille, France.

Kaptelinin, V. (1996) Computer-mediated activity: functional organs in social and developmental contexts. In Nardi, B. (ed.) *Context and Consciousness: Activity Theory and Human–Computer Interaction*. Cambridge, MA: The MIT Press, pp. 45–68.

Kjeldskov, J. (2001) Combining interaction techniques and display types for virtual reality. In *Proceedings of OzCHI 2001*. Churchlands, Australia: Edith Cowan University Press, pp. 77–83.

Kjeldskov, J. (2002) "Just-in-place" information for mobile device interfaces. In Paternò, F (ed.) *Human Computer Interaction with Mobile Devices. Proceedings of 4th International Symposium, MobileHCI 2002*, Pisa, Italy. Berlin: Springer-Verlag.

Kuutti, K. (1996) Activity theory as a potential framework for human–computer interaction research. In Nardi, B. (ed.) *Context and Consciousness: Activity Theory and Human–Computer Interaction*. Cambridge, MA: The MIT Press, pp. 17–44.

Mackay, W. E. and Fayard, A. (1998) Designing interactive paper: lessons from three augmented reality projects. In Behringer, R., Klinker, G. J. and Mizell, D. W. (eds.) *Augmented Reality: Placing Artificial Objects in Real Scenes: Proceedings of IWAR '98*. Natick, MA: A. K. Peters, pp. 81–90.

MIT MediaLab (1999) *The Wearable Computing Project.* http://www.media.mit.edu/wearables/lizzy/augmented-reality.html

Nardi, B. (ed.) (1996) *Context and Consciousness: Activity Theory and Human–Computer Interaction*. Cambridge, MA: The MIT Press.

Norman, D. A. (1988) *The Design of Everyday Things*. New York, Doubleday

Norman, D. A. and Draper, S. W. (eds.) (1986) *User Centered System Design*. London: Lawrence Erlbaum Associates, Inc.

Obata, A. and Sasaki, K. (1998) OfficeWalker: a virtual visiting system based on proxemics. In *Proceedings CSCW 98*, Seattle, WA, 14–18 November 1998. New York: ACM, pp. 1–10.

Preece, J., Rogers, Y., Sharp, H. and Benyon, D. (1994) *Human–Computer Interaction*. Wokingham: Addison-Wesley.

Sawhney, N. and Schmandt, C. (2000) Nomadic radio: speech and audio interaction for contextual messaging in nomadic environments. *ACM Transactions on CHI*, 7(3), 353–383.

Shneiderman, B. (1998) *Designing the User Interface: Strategies for Effective Human–Computer Interaction*, 3rd edn. Reading, MA: Addison-Wesley.

Tidwell, J. (1999) *A Pattern Language for HCI Design.* http://www.mit.edu/~jtidwell/interaction_patterns.html

Tillich, P. (1933) Dwelling, space and time. In *On Art and Architecture*, New York: Crossroad, pp. 81–85.

Tuan, Y. (1977) *Space and Place – The Perspective of Experience*. Minneapolis, MN: The University of Minnesota Press.

Winograd, T. (ed.) (1996) *Bringing Design to Software*. New York: ACM Press.

Modelling Moving Machines

Peter Bøgh Andersen and Palle Nowack

9.1 Introduction

In the old days computers didn't move; today they do. This means two things. On the one hand, you want access to the information services you need in whatever place you are. You want to plug your computer into whatever socket is close at hand, receive emails, access files and watch video. And you want the service at any time of the day: banking should be possible at one o'clock in the night if that suits you. On the other hand, you want your car's computer to take its point of departure from the exact location you are in when it gives you driving directions. It should not tell you how to get to the ferry in Dover if you are leaving Cologne. In addition, we want it to be sensitive to the time. Our calendar should alert us to a deadline two days before, not one month after is has passed.

Apparently these are opposite demands: on the one hand, the computer should be immune to its physical and temporal location; on the other hand, it should be sensitive to it.

It is as if the computer is located in two independent spaces. In the *physical* space the requirement is *local mobility*. However, in the *informational* space the requirement is also *global connectivity*, besides the context sensitivity connected to mobility. Being the workaholics we are, we want the computer to maintain its connection to the data we normally need as well as connecting to information sources relevant at our current location and time.

A computer is thus an empty shell, suspended in two spaces from where it gets its only reason for being: the informational space furnishes it with information material, and its space–time coordinates enable it to select those chunks that will please its spoilt owner. The computer is nothing in itself; it is a placeholder, a parasite of the surroundings that provide the goods that prevent its owner from thrashing it. Like postmodern humans, the computer is nothing but the associations it contracts with other computers and people. It/I is/am what others make me.

The life of modern computers (and people) is very different from that of older tools (and people). The affordances of a saw or a hammer are, so to speak, innate; a hammer is good for hammering and not for sawing because of its physical shape. The hammer is not supposed to maintain ephemeral relations to do-it-yourself books on hammering, and neither is it required to adapt itself to the particular nail its owner wants to hit, or to the time of the day. A hammer is something in itself because of the way it was born. Relations to other tools are of no importance to it. It couldn't care less.

But modern computers parasitize their surroundings. One may say that for such leeches it is more important which *associations* they can contract than what they are in themselves. Modern computers are media whose purpose is to pass information from one place to the other. The more information they can pass, the more associations they can contract, the more successful they are, as the history of Microsoft shows. Some theories even claim that you can only have one medium of this kind. This explains why we have only one video standard today, even if several ones competed some decades ago, and it explains why Microsoft has acquired monopoly in the market for desktop operating systems. The reason is that the benefits of a medium increase with the number of people that use it. It is no fun to own the only telephone in the country; the investment is much more rational if there are thousands of people you can phone. Media are amoral in the sense that quality does not matter as long as sufficiently many use it. After some critical number has been reached, one medium wins and the other loses. As Nokia correctly claims, the function of media is *connecting* people, and communication requires standardization.

The gist of these arguments is that good relations with other computers are the most important property of the modern computer. The value of a computer is the sum of the associations it can contract.

From this initial analysis two concepts are important. The first is the notion of the dual space, the *informational* and the *spatio-temporal* space; the second is the notion of *relation* or *association*.

We shall use the term "habitat" to characterize the dual space (May *et al.*, 2001; Andersen and Nowack, 2002; and also Chapters 7 and 11 of this volume). The general concept is defined as follows:

> A habitat is a *container*. *Inhabitants* can move into a habitat, live there for a while, and move out again. The *action possibilities* (and as a consequence the *information needs*) of the inhabitants depend upon the habitat they currently inhabit. Habitats evolve. When the inhabitants act, the habitat is modified to make their actions easier. But this enables a new set of action possibilities, and a new set of supporting modifications are superimposed on the old ones. Habitats are *crystallized actions*.

We distinguish between *spatio-temporal* and *informational* habitats. This is exemplified in the next section.

The purpose of the rest of this chapter is to describe existing habitats in order to get a feeling for their nature and the problems associated with them; then we discuss whether standard analytical techniques in the object-oriented analysis (OOA) tradition are able to deal with the phenomenon; finally, we propose a few amendments to the OOA tradition that can hopefully become useful in designing mobile technology. In particular, we propose a map annotated with software objects as a possible diagramming technique.

9.2 The Train as a Spatio-Temporal Habitat

In this section we use the train as an example of a habitat. The data was collected in a one-day trip on the Danish rail network.

The train is clearly a spatio-temporal habitat, since it is a container you enter and leave. If one observes the passengers in the compartment, two or more distinct behaviours can be seen, including the *travel* and the *office* behaviours.

The travel behaviour includes *entering, taking a seat, sitting, showing tickets, consulting timetables, rising* and *leaving*.

The train information system supports this travel behaviour by offering timely information. The main loop of the train information system in a Danish Intercity train is shown in Figure 9.1.

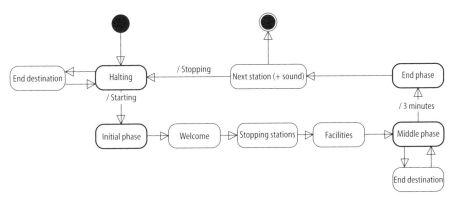

Figure 9.1 The main loop of the Intercity train information system. Round rectangles: State. Fat line: train state; thin line: state of display. Arrows: transition from state to state. Labels of arrows: events causing the change of state.

The default display shown in the middle phase informs the passengers of the end destination of the train: it predicts a potential question from the passengers: *Will it bring me to where I want?* and answers it (Figure 9.2).

Figure 9.2 The default display.

Three minutes before the train stops at the station, information about the station is displayed (answering the question *When should I begin collecting my things?* Figure 9.3).

Figure 9.3 Next station.

This message is also spoken and accompanied by a sound in order to interrupt whatever the passenger is doing, and return his or her attention to the travel process: the travel behaviour interrupts whatever behaviour the passenger is engaged in. Speech is also used to inform passengers of connecting trains.

The reason is that people tend not to look up from what they are doing, so important messages must be conveyed in an intruding modality. In the trains we visited, predictable speech was computer-generated whereas unpredictable speech was produced by the railway staff.

When the train starts again, it informs the new passengers of the end destination, welcomes them, and lists the stopping stations ahead and the facilities offered by the train. Then it returns to its default state. Apart from this loop, relevant messages about delays, for example, can be sent (Figure 9.4).

Figure 9.4 *At which stations does the train stop?*

It is possible to make a more fine-grained analysis of the train in terms of habitats.

There are different compartments with special behavioural constraints: smokers/non-smokers, ordinary compartments versus "silent" compartments, where loud talk is prohibited and where people can work. In night trains, there are special compartments for sleeping. The aisles are for walking and for assembling before disembarkation, whereas the seats are for sitting.

Thus the same spatio-temporal habitat is decomposed into parts, each with its own behavioural repertoire associated, and some habitats support intertwined different behavioural repertoires.

There are various ways of displaying information relevant to passengers. In the Intercity example above, the bits of information are presented in a temporal sequence where one piece of information replaces the other. On the one hand, this enables the system to display information at the time it is needed, but since the information is not persistent, it does not give the passenger an overview of the journey. This is done in the S-net in Copenhagen (see Figure 9.5). Here the whole route is displayed simultaneously, and the passengers can continually assess

Figure 9.5 S-net display. *How long has the train got on its scheduled route?*

whether they are heading in the right direction and how long there is until disembarkation.

What this display does not offer is information about connections at future stations, which is relevant if the passenger is to change train. The old-fashioned displays are far better at this (Figure 9.6).

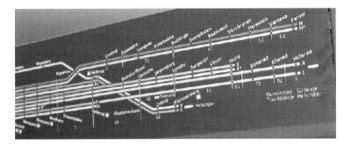

Figure 9.6 S-net display: old-fashioned track diagram. *What are the possible connections in the S-net?*

But the drawback of the older display is that it does not provide "run time" – information about the current position of the train. Passengers have to figure this out themselves by looking out of the window at the stations. Between stations, passengers just have to bite their nails.

The S-net system tries to provide connection information by displaying a ticker-tape in the lower left part of the display before entering a station (sequential information). However, the pace of the ticker-tape was so fast that it was virtually useless (Figure 9.7).

Figure 9.7 S-net display: ticker-tape in the S-net.

The Intercity system offers a dynamic map showing the position of the train and the future stopping stations by means of LEDs (Figure 9.8).

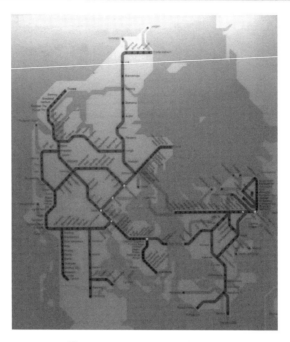

Figure 9.8 Intercity train: map plus LEDs.

9.3 The Train as an Informational Habitat

A very characteristic feature of the train information system is that it is *self-referential* and *deictic*. It refers to itself both textually (the word "toget", *the train*, in Figure 9.4) and graphically (the moving dot in Figures 9.5 and 9.8). In many messages "I" or "this" is presupposed. For example, Figure 9.9 must be interpreted as "I am (this wagon is) number 91" and Figure 9.2 must be understood as "(This train is) going to Copenhagen".

It is deictic in that it refers to other objects in relation to itself, its history, and the time of speaking. The message "Next station" in Figure 9.3 means "The station

Figure 9.9 *This* wagon is number 91.

Figure 9.10 Trains leaving *x* minutes from *now*.

immediately *after the one we have just visited*", and the sign in Figure 9.10 (from a Copenhagen platform) describes departures in terms of "*x* minutes from *now*".

Self-referentiality is a necessary feature of systems whose behaviour must be sensitive to the spatio-temporal habitat they are located in. For example, the sign in Figure 9.3 requires the program to execute code equivalent to:

```
MyPosition = read PositionSensor
Myspeed = read SpeedSensor
if EstimatedTimeToStop(MyPosition, MySpeed, Schedule)
    < 3 then DisplayText ("Next station" +
    Nextstation(MyPosition, Schedule))
end if
```

9.4 Defining the Concept of Habitats

In Section 9.1 the general notion of *habitat* was defined as follows:

> A habitat is a *container*. *Inhabitants* can move into a habitat, live there for a while, and move out again. The *action possibilities* (and as a consequence the *information needs*) of the inhabitants depend upon the habitat they currently inhabit.

Habitats, like other artefacts, have *affordances* (Gibson, 1986), i.e. they afford action possibilities to particular kinds of people, devices and software objects. Thus a habitat can only be defined with respect to specific types of inhabitants, in the same manner as the Gibsonean concept of affordances is a relation between an environment and a specific type of animal. To the fox, a steep mountainside is an obstacle; to the bird, a safe place for nesting. Similarly, a wireless ethernet habitat is only a habitat for devices that can receive and send the signals and that support specific kinds of protocols.

Some habitats maintain *boundaries* and allow only specific objects to enter. This is true of both informational and spatio-temporal habitats. In the former case, we have firewalls to protect the habitats from intruders and passwords to restrict access to specific information. The train itself is a good example of the latter: you must have a ticket to physically enter the train; if not you are thrown out or you have to pay a fine.

Habitats can be active phenomena with *reactive* and/or *proactive* behaviour. The former means reacting to external events generated by users and/or external systems. Examples are automatic door openers, automatic light systems or burglar alarms that react to moving bodies. The ATC system uses sensor stations along the tracks to react to moving trains. The train system described in Sections 9.2 and 9.3 is a good example of a proactive habitat: it tries to preview the information needs of the passengers and supply the needed information.

Proactive behaviour is becoming more interesting with the shift from traditional to pervasive computing: the habitat of a pervasive system can try to guess what the users or external systems in the habitat want to do. However, this is only possible in spaces that already have a well-codified set of behaviours associated with them, such as airports, trains and other public places. We can make good guesses at the behaviour needs of the flight passenger when in the entrance hall, in the departure hall, and at the gate.

9.4.1 Informational Habitats

The informational habitat is a subclass of the general habitat class:

> An *informational (or computational) habitat* is a habitat providing a computational context offering services to the applications running in the habitat. Informational habitats can coincide with a spatio-temporal habitat, but need not.

Although both spatio-temporal and informational habitats are spatial, the nature of their space is different. In Andersen (2001), spatio-temporal habitats are said to have a *Euclidean* space, whereas the space of informational habitats is a *connectivity* space.

The train example shows that informational habitats can be *nested* inside each other. On the one hand, the train is itself a container that provides services to its mobile objects. For example, the business compartment may offer Internet connections to laptops, and the train's information system offers services to the passengers moving inside the train.

But the train itself moves through other habitats. One technique for updating the information system of the train with respect to booking seats is to update it when stopping at stations. In this case, the station is a computational (and spatio-temporal) habitat for the train.

The same phenomenon can be observed with ships. Information about weather conditions, prohibited areas, defect buoys etc. is sent via radio and fax and can be received within a certain area. However, in this case the informational and spatio-temporal habitats are not congruent; many messages are irrelevant to the captain's actions, since they concern locations many nautical miles away. Important information may drown in noise.

In some cases, thinking in terms of informational habitats would improve the information services. For example, the pilot station in Bremerhafen has a very good radar surveillance system monitoring all in- and outbound ships in the river Elb (Andersen *et al.*, 2002). The data goes to the screens at the pilot station where pilots guide the ships via monotone radio messages: "You are exactly on the line", "You are to the right of the line", "you are to the left of the line". If the ship's computer system had access to this information, the captain could use it himself to steer the ship into harbour.

Although computational and spatio-temporal habitats do not necessarily coincide, they do in many cases for security reasons. Employees may have remote access to the mail servers of the organization but not to any other servers. If they want full access to the organization's facilities, they must connect to it via stationary computers inside the building. Moveable laptops can be connected via special sockets that give only restricted access.

Inside the individual computer, the operating system constitutes the computational habitat for applications by offering access to necessary computational resources and by enforcing standards. Whoever comes to control this informational habitat controls the *survival conditions* for software, and in this way gains potentially total control over all software. This is a real liability, as the legal action against Microsoft has clearly shown.

Thus computational habitats form *the* environment that determines the survival of computational objects.

9.4.2 Behavioural Repertoires and Spatio-Temporal Habitats

The other important habitat subclass is the spatio-temporal variant:

> A *spatio-temporal habitat* is a slice of physical time and space whose inhabitants tend to exploit a particular *behavioural repertoire* or *set of repertoires*. The habitat offers informational and physical support for these behaviours.

This definition covers the normal biological notion of habitats that support a particular animal species in finding food and reproducing itself. Even in the biological version, a habitat needs to incorporate time as a dimension, since birds, for example, may use the northern hemisphere in the summer for reproduction and the equatorial areas in the winter to find food. The temporal coordinate is even more pronounced in human habitats. For example, shops only afford buying and selling during opening hours.

Behavioural repertoires can sometimes be divided into subsets, each of which can be found in other habitats. In this case, the habitat is said to house many behavioural repertoires. As mentioned above, a train houses at least two main groups of behaviours:

- The *travelling* behaviour, which includes entering the correct train, finding the right seat, moving out into the corridor a couple of minutes before arrival, and leaving the train at the right station.
- But intertwined with this behaviour is another set of behaviours. During our train journey we observed passengers *writing on their PCs*, *talking into mobile phones*, *writing on paper*, *reading the newspaper*, *drinking*, *eating*, *sleeping* and *looking out of the window*.

Some of these behaviours occur nearly unchanged outside the travelling habitat, for example working on a PC. Therefore the most economical analysis of this is to say that two distinct repertoires of behaviour are *overlaid* or *intertwined*.

The informational habitat of the carriage must be so designed that it supports both repertoires at the same time. The business behaviour for example would need proper email connections to support modern office behaviour.

Of two overlaid repertoires, one can be *subordinate* to the other. In the train habitat, the office behaviour is subordinate to the travel behaviour, since it is the travel that determines when to interrupt the office behaviour: you must interrupt working when the attendant comes to check your ticket, and you must stop completely when arriving at your destination station. Interruption in the other direction is not allowed: you cannot ask the attendant to wait five minutes for the tickets because you are deeply engaged in writing a memo.

Orthogonal to the above characterizations of habitat is the distinction between a *paradigmatic* habitat, providing all behavioural elements and constraints simultaneously, but no order among them (the web is good example of a paradigmatic computational habitat) and a *syntagmatic* habitat, imposing a sequence on the behaviours. The Intercity train information system is one good example of this; the chains of emergency signs on passenger ships described in Chapter 10 are another example. In the latter case, the arrow signs indicating the direction to the muster stations must be read in sequence as the passengers move, and each sign must tell them the direction in which to go next.

9.5 Habitat Crossing

Habitat crossing means that the occupant of a habitat changes information services, physical location and behavioural patterns. Habitat crossing is a basic human accomplishment we perform every day. I display one behaviour when moving around in a public space, but quite another when secure behind the four walls of my house.

Habitat crossing is often carefully prepared. For example, in an airport train waiting for permission to drive on, the following written message was issued: "The train is waiting at the moment for permission to drive on" followed by a verbal comment: "We are waiting for permission so that we get to the Kastrup airport on time". The train personnel know that many passengers are anxious to catch a plane, and try to reassure them that they will arrive at the airport on time.

Crossing from the train to the platform is also prepared: "Disembark on the left side".

Inside the airport the arriving passenger is guided towards buses and trains by means of signposts (Figure 9.11).

But change of informational habitat is not always seamless: for example, the GPS signals may be useless in the transition between two sets of satellites, as every

Figure 9.11 Signs at an airport referring to buses leaving: "Bus 9, Nordhavn st. 14.47, Bus stop A".

maritime officer knows, and owners of mobile telephones have the same experience with the mobile net.

9.6 Modelling Habitats

In the previous sections we have offered empirical observations of several habitats. Although in the past decades computer gurus with severe Platonic inclinations have preached their grand visions of virtual realities and information spaces that allow us access to unlimited resources of information and free us from the confines of our earthly bodies, the fact seems to be that we still chop up information and behaviour into small manageable chunks and associate them likewise with human-scale chunks of space and time, for the very good reason that we want to lead a comfortable life and avoid going crazy.

In order to account for this phenomenon, we needed the following list of distinctions:

- *Types of habitat*: informational versus spatio-temporal habitats.
- *Properties of individual habitats*: containers, boundaries of containers, and inhabitants of containers; being located, moving into, and moving out of.
- *Relations between habitats*: congruence/incongruence between informational and spatio-temporal habitats, nested habitats, habitat crossing.
- *Habitats, inhabitants and behaviours*: affordances, behavioural repertoires, subordinate and superordinate behaviours, intertwined behaviours, reactive and proactive habitats, stability versus mobility, survival conditions, and associations.
- *Properties of displays*: paradigmatic versus syntagmatic displays, self-referential and deictic displays.

We claim that these (and other) distinctions are necessary in order to model mobile computer systems adequately. It is therefore relevant to find out whether existing methods support these distinctions, and, if not, how one can improve upon them. We shall limit ourselves to object-oriented methodology, since it is very widespread and, we must confess, also the only one we know well.

9.6.1 A Brief Overview of Object-Oriented Modelling

Object orientation sees the world as consisting of interacting objects, where an object is a stable association of properties and behaviour. Objects (signifying phenomena) can be classified into classes of objects, and these classes can be generalized into larger classes sharing properties and behaviour. Classes can also be decomposed into parts belonging to different classes.

As a textual genre, object-oriented programs belong to the *descriptive* genre, since they are organized around objects, and actions are only described in relation to these objects.

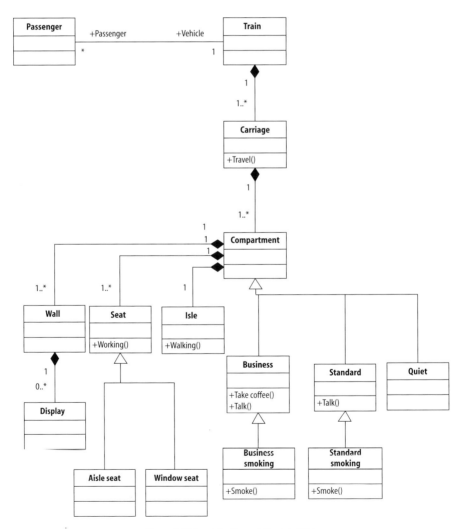

Figure 9.12 Specialization and decomposition.

An object-oriented model will typically at least include a description of specializations and decompositions, a diagram of the behaviour of the individual classes, and a description of the ways in which objects interact with one another by sending messages. Figure 9.12 shows an example of classification and decomposition. ——◆ means *decomposition* (part–whole) and ——▷ means *specialization* (class–subclass). The diagram says that trains consist of one or more (1..* means "one or more") carriages that consist of compartments that consist of walls, seats and aisles. Walls have displays attached to them. One can exhibit travel behaviour everywhere in the carriage, but work behaviour is associated with a seat. There are various subclasses of compartments with different behaviours allowed or disallowed.

There exist tools that allow you to draw diagrams like Figure 9.12 and, in return, will generate code that can run on a computer (Figures 9.13 and 9.14).

The *behaviour* can be described by state diagrams that show how the object changes state as a result of events. In Figure 9.15 we model the behaviour of the passenger.

```
class Carriage
{
  public:
    // methods
    Void Travel();
End of user code.
};
```
```
Void Carriage::Travel() { }
```

Figure 9.13 C++ code generated by the `Carriage` node.

```
class BusinessSmoking : public
Business
{
  public:
    // methods
    Void Smoke();
};
```
```
Void BusinessSmoking::Smoke() { }
```

Figure 9.14 C++ code generated by the `BusinessSmoking` node.

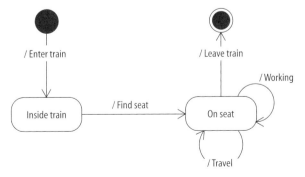

Figure 9.15 State diagram.

The event of entering the train makes the passenger change state to "inside train", and the event of finding the seat changes his state to "on seat". In this state three events can happen. The working and travelling events do not change his state, but the "leaving train" event does. Figure 9.1 uses the same formalism to describe the behaviour of the display object.

The question we want to address is: can this kind of object-oriented methodology describe our findings in a *simple, adequate* and *exhaustive* way? The last qualifications are important: a descriptive apparatus can in many cases describe anything, so the interesting question is whether it highlights the features that the writer and reader consider important. It is of course possible to write a detective novel in an object-oriented way, but since these novels get their interest from their narrative structure, object-oriented methods will yield extremely boring novels. Compare Texts 1 and 2. Text 1 is narrative since the objects are only presented when needed by the action. Text 2 is descriptive, since all the actions belonging to one object are collected in the same paragraph. Although both texts describe the same events, Text 1 is clearly better than Text 2.

Text 1

It was a typical foggy evening in London. Mr Sherlock Holmes looked nervously through the yellow mists hanging over the docks, and suddenly discovered a dark furtive shadow moving along the quay. A hundred yards away a slender female shape was standing in the shadow of an old warehouse, anxiously watching the dirty waters of the Thames. The dark shadow stopped, snarled, and was obviously moving towards the female figure. It lingered for a moment, then hurled itself towards the lonely shape. A faint muffled shriek reached the ears of Holmes, and in the next moment both shapes disappeared in the fog. When he reached the scene he saw that Lady Snodgrass had met a horrible death.

Text 2

London is a town containing a harbour by the river Thames. A yellow dark fog often hangs over the docks.

Sherlock Holmes is a detective. He follows Lady Snodgrass and watches her. As she is assaulted and killed by her depraved son, he runs to her and discovers the crime.

Lady Snodgrass is a rich window with a furtive depraved son. She has a slender figure. She was lured by him to the harbor, assaulted at a warehouse, snarled at, and horribly killed.

9.6.2 Types of Habitat

An important distinction is that between, on the one hand, the *informational/computational habitat* characterized by the computational services it offers visiting objects, and on the other hand the *spatio-temporal habitat* characterized by the behavioural affordances it offers its inhabitants. The former is a software concept, while the latter concerns the application domain. The main thesis is that they are subclasses of the same general class, namely the habitat. The software domain is normally described by class diagrams like Figure 9.12, whereas the application domain, i.e. the interaction between the tasks of the user and the services offered by the system, is described by so-called use cases. But class diagrams and use cases are not specializations of a common class, and OOA therefore cannot see informational and spatio-temporal habitats as subclasses of the same superclass.

One reason for this is that the software models are sharply distinguished from their implementation. There are perfectly good reasons for this. The software models reduce complexity by capturing the essentials of the software and disregarding details of implementation. This means that software models are not located in space and time. But if the location of computational objects in space and time is essential, then it ought not to be relegated to implementation, but must have a systematic place in the model.

A similar problem is encountered in Chapter 7, which discuss the notion of *tangible objects*, i.e. associations of informational and physical objects. The problem consists in developing good abstractions that enables us to view the tangible object as a unity, not as a split Cartesian personality divided into a spiritual (here: informational) and a material (here: physical) world. The same desideratum is voiced by Kjeldskov in Chapter 8 in the form of a design pattern for augmented reality systems: the relation between physical space and virtual objects (= informational space) should be strengthened, for example by designing interaction methods that makes interaction in physical space a part of the human–computer interface.

It is worth emphasizing that we are concerned with *modelling* the relation between software objects and space; however, a description of *what* the system is to accomplish does not necessarily coincide with *how* it should achieve it. For example, *spatial computing* (Grønbæk *et al.*, 2001, p. 409) aims at using a whole room as the interface to computational objects and supporting the movement of information objects from walls to tables to PCs. However, this can be implemented by means of traditional servers keeping track of the location of the display of the objects and does not imply that the objects themselves will move.

9.6.3 Properties of Individual Habitats

As mentioned in Section 9.4, a habitat is a container with boundaries within which inhabitants can live. Inhabitants can move in and out and reside inside the container. Some boundaries only tolerate objects with certain properties to pass their boundaries.

OOA has essentially two ways of modelling containers with inhabitants. The *decomposition* (part–whole) relation is used to represent stable "inhabitants" of objects, and the *association* is used to model transient ones. Figure 9.12 therefore uses decomposition to model the relation between trains and carriages, since trains always have one or more carriages. However, it uses the association to model the relation between passengers and trains, since trains may have no passengers, and passengers may not be on board trains.

Language makes the same distinction; the verb *to have* and the genitive denote both relations, and both come in two variants: *non-alienable* (parts: "My eyes") and *alienable* (e.g. possession "My car"). But *have* has a third function, namely to denote general relations described elsewhere in the sentence. The phrases *She has a teacher* and *her teacher* neither mean that the person is a part of her nor that she possesses him; it means that a specific relation obtains between them, that of *teaching*: *he teaches her*. This general meaning of "relation" seems to be the basic one, since the other two can be reduced to it: "She has two legs" can be rephrased as "Two legs are parts of her body" or, somewhat morbidly of a murderess, "She possesses two legs (from her victims)".

The term "passenger" is also a relational term on closer scrutiny. Only when I have bought the ticket and entered the train do I assume the rôle of passenger with the rights and obligations it entails. When my travel has ended, my rôle as passenger also ends, although I persist as a person. To say that I am a passenger of the train means that the train is obliged to bring me to my destination.

The relation of a habitat to its inhabitants seems in fact to be of the relational kind. The behaviour afforded by a habitat is, as Gibson knew, a relation between a particular species of animal and its surroundings. Similarly, the relation between a passenger and a train is neither part–whole nor possession; rather, it can be described as a kind of protocol specifying the interaction between train personnel and passenger: the passenger is entitled to enter the train; he is entitled to a specific seat if he has a reservation, otherwise he may have to stand up; the attendant has the right to check his ticket; etc. To claim that the concepts of habitat/inhabitant are relational is to claim that we can predict very little about the events taking place if we only inspect the habitat or the inhabitant. As said at the beginning, they are just the end points of relations.

If this is true, then it seems somewhat inconvenient to make the decomposition relation primitive. Instead, we would need a concept of *rôle* connecting two objects and specifying the protocol for their interaction.[1]

9.6.4 Relations Between Habitats

As we saw in the maritime example, informational and spatio-temporal habitats may be incongruous. A sensible design objective would therefore be to design the two habitats so that the former fits the needs of the occupants of the latter. Can we express fitness between habitats systematically in OOA? The answer is *no* if the claim in Section 9.6.1 is true, namely that we cannot deal systematically with the two phenomena in the same model.

What about *nested habitats*? We need this concept in the transportation domain: the means of transportation is a habitat for the passengers, and is itself transported in and out of other habitats. It turns out that nesting is in fact well supported in OOA, since one can define objects within other objects.

The final important relation between habitats we came across is *habitat crossing*. We need to model the gradual transition of an object from one habitat to another in order to design the information support we observe in the real world (e.g. Fig. 9.11

---

1   This problem has in fact been noted, and a design pattern that circumvents the problem has been invented, namely the *rôle* pattern.

that supports movement from the airport habitat to the bus habitat). Can we express the notion of something continuously changing rôle and location? Not immediately, at least.

We need to model the habitat as a spatial structure which the object can move into and out of. But associated with this movement must be a change of the rôle relationships that define the habitat and whose strength changes. When we are in the airport it is strong, but as we move out of the airport, the airport's responsibilities weaken and are finally handed over to the bus company. We gradually cease to be an airport passenger and start becoming a bus passenger. Therefore we need to associate strength with the rôle relationship, a kind of variable *glue* that glues the participants to the rôle and defines the habitat's *sphere of influence*. The strength of the glue may be calculated on the basis of the distance between the person and spatial habitat, but other definitions may also be useful.

If the glue ceases abruptly as the passenger leaves the habitat, the airport is not invited to think about the passenger's fate once outside the doors of the airport, since the airport's responsibility stops here. The result is missing information and confused passengers that cannot find buses, hotels, taxis and trains.

If instead the glue decreases gradually, and retains some of its strength a hundred metres or so away from the buildings, the designer will think of this area as still within her responsibility, although to a lesser degree. She will consider it her obligation to support the passenger in his rôle-shift, from airplane passenger to bus passenger, and may eventually hit upon the idea of designing Figure 9.11. If the bus company feels the same, there will be an area of shared responsibility where the object is weakly both an airplane passenger and a bus passenger, and where supporting information facilities will therefore be motivated.

This means that the informational habitat will be larger than the spatio-temporal one, and that the two informational habitats will overlap. Figure 9.16 shows one

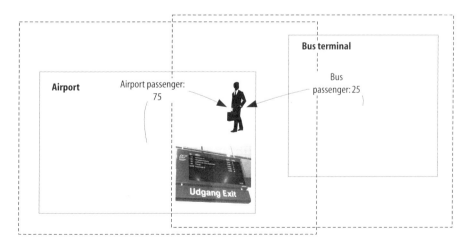

Figure 9.16 Habitat crossing. Solid lines: spatio-temporal habitats; dashed lines: the sphere of influence of informational habitats. Arrows define rôle relationships and their strength. They lead from the center of the informational habitat to the passenger. Note the location of the bus sign.

way of diagramming this. Although the spatio-temporal habitats (solid lines) are disjunct, the spheres of influence of their informational habitats (dashed lines) are overlapping. The two rôle relationships and their strength are represented by two labelled arrows anchored inside the two habitats and directed towards the passenger.

9.6.5 Habitats, Inhabitants and Behaviours

The distinction between *reactive* and *proactive* habitats is easy to express. In the former, there is a direct connection between sensor information and the reaction of the habitat. The following piece of code could control the doors in the airport.

```
If something moves in the vicinity then
    open the door
    wait for 20 seconds
    close the door
end if
```

The proactive habitat does not react directly, but makes statistical guesses that a certain situation obtains. It tries to estimate the future evolution of this situation and to present information that will hinder undesired outcomes and enhance the desired outcome. Here is an example:

Situation assessment:

```
If a new PDA enters the airport and
    contains an electronic ticket and
    the flight-number is boarding
then there is x% chance the owner wants to catch the
    flight and y% chance that he will miss it
end if
```

Avoidance of non-desired outcome:

```
If there is x% chance that someone wants to catch a
    flight and y% chance that he will miss it
then alert him
    display the route to the gates on his PDA
    alert the gate that the passenger will arrive
    late
end if
```

This system tries to avoid the plane leaving without the passenger by alerting the gate, and supports him in getting quickly to the gate by displaying the route to him. The distinction between reactive and proactive objects is well known in agent theory, which distinguishes between reactive and deliberative agents.

The notion of *intertwined* behaviours is also well known in programming. Most modern languages support more than one thread of execution; conceptually, these threads run concurrently, and one thread can interrupt another, one acting as superordinate to another.

9.6.6 Behavioural Repertoires

It is a bit more difficult with the notions of affordances and behavioural repertoires. We have argued that the habitat/inhabitant distinction is really an association between two entities entering a specific rôle relation. Thus affordances and behavioural repertoires take the form of protocols regulating the interaction between the two parties. As noted in Section 6.4, these protocols must be sensitive to the strength of the rôle relations, which again depend upon the physical location of the inhabitant. Some (syntagmatic) protocols execute differently depending upon the time of day and the location of the inhabitant. Finally, the same person can enter more than one rôle relation when located at a particular position.

Clearly these ideas can be described by a normal class diagram, such as Figure 9.17. It says that inhabitants can be associated with zero or more glue objects that are associated with exactly one rôle and inhabitant each. Rôles are associated with zero or more glue objects, and with one or more spatial/temporal and informational habitats. Finally, informational habitats can be associated with one or more spatio-temporal habitats, and vice versa.

The last requirement can clearly be questioned: it asserts that the train passenger rôle is always associated with the informational habitat of trains and with a location in relation to the train territory. Thus it asserts a strong association between rôle, spatial location and informational context.

It is easy to find examples where this association does not exist. For example, you can sit at home as a potential passenger and book a seat via the Internet. In this case, you have a rôle in the informational habitat of the railway company, but no rôle in relation to its physical territory. Figure 9.17 is a false model of this situation, and we have two options for correcting the situation: the first one is to modify the model to fit the situation, e.g. by removing the demand that a rôle and an informational habitat are obligatorily connected to a spatial habitat. This option is chosen by May and Kristensen in Chapter 7; on the one hand it gives a wider area of application, but on the other hand, it runs the danger of emptying the habitat concept of content. The other option is to claim that not everything is a habitat. A habitat is a *special* way of organizing social rôles, physical surroundings and information.

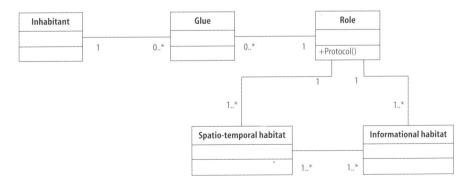

Figure 9.17

Some ways of doing this are habitats, others are not. The railway station and the trains are habitats, the WWW services are not.

9.6.7 Maps Annotated by Software Objects

In this section we shall suggest one way of conceptualizing physical and informational space.

Figure 9.17 is a traditional diagram that tries to capture the relation between informational and physical space, but it does give us an immediate impression of the important part of the system, the relation between informational and physical objects. The reason for this is the diagram type. It belongs to the class of *conceptual diagrams* where space is used to denote conceptual relations. However, we have just decided that spatial relations are important in the habitat concept, and would like to have a representation that emphasizes this. One such representation is the old-fashioned *map*. A map is a graphical representation that uses space to represent space, although all maps superimpose additional information called *signatures*: place names, types of roads, icons for types of buildings, bus and train routes, etc. However, the strength of a map lies in its iconic relationship to its denotation: what is to the left in the map is also to the left in reality. However, real maps will always have symbolic material attached to them, such as signatures and names. Thus, maps are basically iconic signs with symbolic material superimposed (May and Andersen, 2001).

This suggests a solution: in so far as space is important in habitats, maps decorated with pieces of code, parts of protocols and information needs are a natural model. Thus, software objects, protocols and information needs correspond to the signatures and names in ordinary maps. Figure 9.18 shows an example. It models a railway station which is predominantly a paradigmatic habitat and annotates the map with information needs (the balloons) associated with specific behavioural

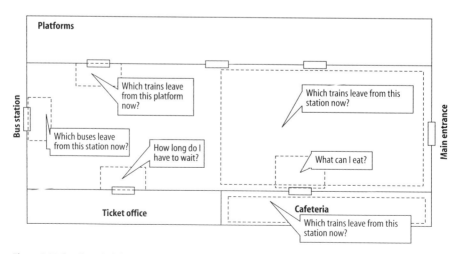

Figure 9.18 Paradigmatic habitat modelled by a two-dimensional map decorated with information needs in balloons. Informational habitats are shown by dashed lines.

habitats (dashed rectangles). In the main hall, passengers may need information about all trains leaving the station within the next half hour, while they only need to know about trains leaving a particular platform when they are placed at the entrance of the platform. Passengers seated in the cafeteria still need to know when their train leaves, even if they are eating. At present, these information needs are fulfilled by stationary monitors, timetables and menus. The ones shown in the figure can be observed in any railroad station.

Another map would show the pieces of protocol that motivate the information needs: with the platform entrance will be associated the part saying that the company is obliged to transport a passenger with a valid ticket but is not required to wait for her – it is the passenger's responsibility to be at the right place at the right time; at the ticket counter belongs the part saying that the passenger is obliged to buy a ticket, but has to stand in a queue until it is her turn.

Can the same be done with software models? Figure 9.19 shows a sketch of a diagram that captures some of the concepts. It is basically a map of an airport that is decorated with informational habitats and inhabitants and by the rôle relations that motivate the informational habitat. Within an informational habitat, the corresponding service is offered. For example, when a person enters by the rightmost door, arrival and departure information plus warnings are offered. The user can configure his PDA to accept only some of these services. Balloons show the services requested by the user. The topmost PDA, for example, is in the airport to welcome a friend, and therefore only requests arrival information. The rightmost one has requested access to four pieces of software: the Wayfinder, the Liquor Store, Warnings and Departure Information. At the moment only the latter two requests have been fulfilled, shown by the pluses and minuses. If the PDA contains an electronic ticket, it would be possible for the airport system to turn on the Warnings and Departure System automatically, since it can figure out that they will probably be needed by the passenger. If given access to the ticket, the Warnings system could inform the individual passenger of the flight he is about to take, since it would know the flight number. Finally, the leftmost PDA is offered a *passenger* relationship to the Wayfinder and a *customer* relationship to the Liquor Store, which it has in fact accepted. The Warnings and the Departure Information are no longer available in this constructed example.

Figure 9.19 is one way of localizing software models. It uses a kind of market model: inside the sphere of influence of the informational habitat, information services are supplied. If an offer is accepted the two parties enter into a temporary specific rôle relation ship, e.g. salesperson–customer. The supplies are represented by the names of the informational habitats; the demands by the text in the balloons; and the concluded bargains by the minuses and pluses in the balloons.

9.7 Philosophical Implications

We hope to have shown that the habitat concept is a useful one: it can be used to analyze the existing usage of spatial information systems and to plan future ones.

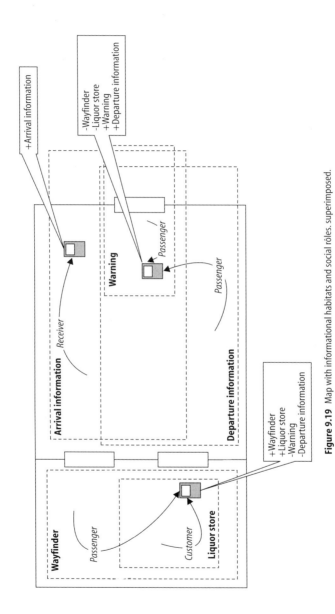

Figure 9.19 Map with informational habitats and social roles. superimposed.

However, it also has more general implications. It essentially claims that humans are not fixed entities, but change attitudes, action potential and language as they move from one context to another.

Let us treat the implication as a scientific theory; are there anomalies in traditional theories that it can explain better? One of the authors, who is a linguist by education, has always been vexed by the following problem: according to dictionaries, most words have multiple senses. For example, Microsoft Word's thesaurus yields six senses for the word *move*: *go, reposition, change, attempt, shift, cause*. Now, if each word has six senses, then a sentence of 10 words will have 6^{10} senses. This is indeed a large number! And in a split second, the listener has to choose the one intended from this huge number.

This is simply not possible, so where did we go wrong? The six senses are a fact: check it yourself. Therefore, we must conclude that we do not ourselves use Microsoft's lexicon when we understand sentences. But then what *do* we do? The riddle can be solved if we hypothesize that language is used in habitats too. A linguistic habitat would be a *situation type*, associated with a specific time and place, with a delimited number of action possibilities, information needs, *and linguistic resources*. Situationally bound linguistic resources are called *registers*, and they are assumed to offer exactly those distinctions needed in the habitat, and none else. In a particular register, *move* may have only 1 or 2 senses, so the problem of disambiguating sentences has been made exponentially easier. The implication is that national languages, as we see them in lexicons, are a fiction. What exists in reality is registers, or, to use the vocabulary of this volume: *habitats*.

References

Andersen, P. B. (2001) Pervasive computing and space. In Stamper, R., Liu, K. and Abou-Zeid, E.-S. (eds.) *Proceedings of IFIP WG8.1 Working Conference. Organizational Semiotics: Evolving a Science of Information Systems*. Concordia University, Montreal, Quebec, pp. 106–125.

Andersen, P. B. and Nowack, P. (2002) Tangible objects: connecting informational and physical space. In Qvortrup, L. (ed.) *Virtual Space: Spatiality of Virtual Inhabited 3d Worlds*. London: Springer-Verlag, pp. 190–210.

Andersen, P. B., Carstensen, P. and Nielsen, M. (2002) Means of coordination. In Liu, K., Clarke, R. J., Andersen, P. B. and Stamper, R. K. (eds.) *Coordination and Communication Using Signs. Studies in Organizational Semiotics*. Boston: Kluwer, pp. 32–58.

Gibson, J. J. (1986) *The Ecological Approach to Visual Perception*. Hillsdale, NJ: Erlbaum.

Grønbæk, K., Gundersen, K., Mogensen, P. and Ørbæk, P. (2001) Interactive room support for complex and distributed design projects. In Hirose, M. (ed.) *Human–Computer Interaction. INTERACT '01*. Amsterdam: IOS Press, pp. 407–414.

May, D. C., Kristensen, B. B. and Nowack, P. (2001) TangO: modeling in style. *Proceedings of the Second International Conference on Generative Systems in the Electronic Arts*. Melbourne, Australia.

May, M. and Andersen, P. B. (2001) Instrument semiotics. In Kecheng, L., Clarke, R. J., Andersen, P. B. and Stamper, R. K. (eds.) *Information, organization and technology. Studies in organizational semiotics*. Boston/Dordrecht/London: Kluwer, pp. 271–298.

10

Wayfinding, Ships and Augmented Reality

Michael May

10.1 Introduction

The focus of this chapter will be on the practical problem of finding the best technical support for wayfinding in the maritime domain, especially in the context of escape and evacuation situations. Technical support for wayfinding can in general take many different forms, but it usually involves augmenting the built environment with signs informing occupants of the way to certain places within a building or how to find a way out in an emergency. These signs will usually be *graphical* signs and they will often be *static* signs, as we know them from street signs on buildings, telling us of the name of a particular street, or city maps giving us an overview of the layout of a part of the city. Inside buildings and other built environments, such as ships and aircraft, we often find a third type of sign, besides *symbols* naming objects or *maps* locating objects relative to each other; namely, a *network* of graphical arrows indicating the direction to the nearest exit.

Symbols, maps and networks are different ways of representing information – different *types of signs* (May and Andersen, 2001) – and they are traditionally all expressed in graphical media, or (in other words) in the graphical *channel of communication*. Signs in the graphical media channel are however not *a priori* restricted to being *static* signs. Graphical signs could be *dynamic* and have interactive properties. A nice classical example, independent of computer technology, is the electromechanical interactive maps found in subway stations in many large cities around the world: when a traveller pushes a button representing her destination, one or more routes from her present location light up on the map, making the choice between different metro lines an easy task. An example of a non-interactive dynamic map is the dynamic map found in the Danish Intercity trains to indicate to passengers the present location of the train and its future stopping stations (Chapter 9).

Just as architects, engineers and designers have a choice of representational forms (sign types), they also have a choice of media channel. Symbols, maps and networks are not only expressed in the graphical media channel, but can also – within certain constraints – be expressed in the *acoustic* media channel, i.e. as acoustic symbols, acoustic maps and acoustic network diagrams, or even in the *haptic* media channel (touch media). The problem of choosing between these different possibilities in the context of emergencies is the problem of how to *design for safety and efficiency.*

Designing for the safe and efficient escape and evacuation of occupants from buildings or from trains, aircraft and ships involves the application of many types of knowledge about how human beings interact with the space of the built environment, how they interact with each other during an emergency and how they respond to graphical signs and acoustic alarms. These are the questions that will be discussed in the following in the context of *wayfinding* of passengers on ships and the problems of maritime evacuation during emergencies at sea (such as fire, collision, grounding or flooding). Special attention will be given to the possibilities provided by the use of *directional sound* as an alternative to the traditional graphical means of augmenting the reality of the built environment. From a theoretical point of view traditional graphic signs are already a form of *augmented reality*, a way of *drawing and writing directly on the reality of the environment*, even though it is not as safe and efficient as electronic computer-supported forms. Using directional sound to further enhance this augmented reality creates a *virtual acoustic display* superimposed on the built environment of the ship.

This superimposition of a virtual acoustic display on the physical space of the ship creates the *dual space* discussed in Chapter 9, i.e. an *informational space* and a *spatio-temporal space*, and this dual space is *partitioned* in different *habitats* with different action possibilities provided for their "inhabitants" – in this case the passengers moving around on the ship.

10.2 Signs as Technical Assistance for Wayfinding on Ships

During emergencies on ships, trains and aircraft – as they are addressed through emergency plans – the primary assistance to passengers is given by human agents who have been trained in emergency procedures and evacuation of passengers. In trains, aircraft and small vessels the *spatial arrangement* is very simple to overlook, and if no panics arise the crew can easily direct passengers to the nearest exits. The major hazard is when a fire occurs, because smoke will reduce visibility and will put an added pressure on evacuation because of the reduced time available for safe escape. Under these circumstances panics can also arise if passengers get trapped in closed areas or if they judge that there is not enough time for orderly escape. We will return to the question of panic and escape later. In an orderly escape from trains, aircraft and small vessels passengers are guided towards and verbally ordered to go to the nearest exits without delay, and under these circumstances wayfinding problems are not an issue.

Technical assistance for wayfinding becomes important in large buildings and passenger ships, where the spatial layout is more complex. Here we find many different signs (symbols, maps and networks) in use to direct occupants and passengers under normal conditions of wayfinding as well as specialized signs for wayfinding in emergencies.

Graphical *symbols, maps* and *networks* are generally used to assist wayfinding in buildings, and they serve three distinct functions (O'Neil, 1999):

- to *identify places and routes*
- to *map the spatial layout of an area*
- to *direct occupants and passengers to routes*

It has been demonstrated that a system of graphic signs (pictographic symbols for places and directions) is generally more effective than maps ("you-are-here" maps) in assisting wayfinding of newcomers in complex buildings (Butler *et al.*, 1993), and to be effective signs should be placed at decision points in the environment (Best, 1970). The reason for the superiority of pictographic symbols over maps is that *local signs place the directional information directly in the environment*, whereas the directional information of maps has to be inferred by reasoning from map information and from mental manipulation of the map. This is why we should actually conceive this use of graphic signs in the built environment as an early form of "augmented reality", even if it is not implemented through the use of computer technology. The cultural invention of augmented reality has its origin in *the technique of writing and drawing* directly on the perceived reality of the environment. An example could be the Bedolina petroglyph (2000–1900 BC), which is a graphical inscription in stone from the Bronze age in northern Italy: it is considered to be a map of a village and could be the earliest known map augmenting the local reality of the past village with information about the location of houses and cattle and routes between them.

On a ferry or a passenger ship many passengers will not know the spatial layout in advance, although some will already be familiar with the general layout of decks from previous journeys. The built environment of ships will typically use *pictographic symbols* to direct passengers in case of emergencies and *"you-are-here maps"* to assist passengers in emergencies as well as in general wayfinding tasks.

You-are-here maps (Figure 10.1), however, depend upon examination in order to be useful for wayfinding (Wickens, 1992), and they will require some *manipulation of a mental model* of the ship layout to make the depicted schematic map *congruent* with the visual experience of the passengers. Imagine a passenger moving along a ship from bow ("front") to stern ("back") and also changing sides from starboard ("right") to port ("left") side. His location could be indicated on you-are-here maps as shown in Figure 10.2. He might be confused in consulting the two maps, however, because of the apparent collocation of his indicated positions. A passenger in distress could easily overlook the fact that the ship layout diagram on top has been flipped in order to adapt the map below to starboard and port views respectively. This *rotation* is a design solution to the burden of *mental rotation* of the map that would otherwise be imposed on the passenger had the maps been consistent and decontextualized from the location of the observer. On the other hand, passengers might not expect the map to adapt to their local point of view, because this is not how ordinary static graphic maps behave: we have to turn a city

Figure 10.1 A "you-are-here" map embedded in directional signs giving information about important places on the ship (restaurant, perfume shop etc.) during a normal voyage. In an emergency this type of complex sign would not be very useful.

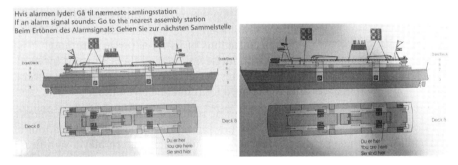

Figure 10.2 Two "you-are-here" maps from the Safety on Board signs displayed on deck 8 (starboard) and deck 8 (port side) on a Danish ferry. Notice that the orientation of the ship is different in the two maps.

map ourselves – either the physical map or the mental map constructed from it – in order to obtain congruence with our visual experience.

Notice that passengers, according to the text annotating the ship diagram (Figure 10.2, left), are expected to *initiate mustering on their own* upon hearing an alarm, by going to the nearest assembly station (called a "muster station" before 1997). This is partly in conflict with the instructions that passengers will typically be given by the captain over the public address system: they will in most cases be *instructed to await further instructions* from the crew. The crew needs to assemble first and the captain needs time to evaluate the emergency and decide on the best course of action.

Although a system of signs combining symbols and networks has been proven to be more effective than maps for wayfinding, a questionnaire and interview survey with over 1200 passengers on board four different Danish ferries found disturbing errors of interpretation in reading the system of signs used in maritime emergencies (May, 2000).

10.3 Graphic Symbols and Networks for Wayfinding on Ships

There is a set of graphic symbols that have been approved for assisting passengers on ships in finding their way in emergencies (Figures 10.3 and 10.4). Some of these label *places* (or "habitats") that may go unnoticed by passengers during a normal voyage, such as the *assembly stations* where passengers will receive their lifejackets in cases where evacuation might be necessary. Other signs naming places are signs for emergency exits, and at the assembly stations annotated graphic symbols will signify the location of lifejackets.

It cannot, however, be assumed that passengers understand the meaning of assembly signs or that they will spend time to get acquainted with ship diagrams and safety instructions. In a large-scale passenger survey (May, 2000), one elderly female passenger travelling alone claimed to have noticed signs on the ship, but she did not know the meaning of the assembly sign pointed out to her in the reception hall where she was sitting: "People are coming from all directions" she remarked. Ignoring the arrow next to the assembly sign, she believed it to state that a lot of people could gather in the reception hall, where the sign was located. This is a true statement about the reception hall, but not the meaning of the assembly sign indicating the way to an assembly station in an emergency. Another typical example of this *decontexualized sign reading* of passengers was given by a young male passenger, who was travelling with his wife and their baby. He did not notice signs on the ship and did not take any interest in safety instructions. Asked about the assembly sign and the adjoining arrow, he pointed to the stairs and claimed: "It means that the stairs are going up". After a while, he seemed to realize that it did not make much sense to have a sign state the obvious and then added the literal reading

Figure 10.3 Pictographic symbols (in green) naming places and locations of important objects (lifejackets, emergency exits) during an evacuation on board a ship. The assembly sign discussed in the text is the leftmost sign. The sign is not always annotated with the explanatory text.

Figure 10.4 Pictographic symbols (in green) used in a network of local arrows representing the escape routes through a ship; often used in combination with the assembly sign.

of the sign: "People are coming from all directions", but with no added interpretation.

Passengers lack "lexical knowledge" about the meaning of the individual graphic symbols used on board ships. Some passengers even associated the green colour with an "ecological" context (pollution etc.) and not with emergencies.

On top of these *lexical* problems, there are a series of *visual, syntactic* and *semantic problems* with traditional graphic signs for wayfinding (May, 2002). Visual problems include problems with:

- Visual *access* to signs
- Visual *occlusion* of signs
- Visual *masking* of signs

Visual access to relevant signs can be impeded by the *imposed viewing angle* (as with the hidden up-arrow in Figure 10.7); signs can be *occluded* by passengers in situations of crowding; and signs and exits can be *masked* by visual noise; see May (2002) for more examples.

Many syntactic and semantic problems in interpreting groups of signs and sequences of signs were discovered, among them problems with:

- Decontextualized reading of sign groups and sign sequences
- Ambiguity of signs
- Confusion of similar signs
- Confusing "gestalt effects" (proximity of signs etc.)

The "decontextualized" sign reading already referred to arises as a problem because of the implicit syntax of graphic symbols combined into groups of adjoining symbols (Figure 10.5) and then again into larger sequences of symbol groups. An example of such a sequence is the network of arrows with adjoining assembly signs that are found throughout the ship along the many different emergency routes to the assembly stations. Usually these assembly stations are found on the highest upper deck, but assembly stations can also be found on lower decks, where some of the passengers have to assemble to get lifejackets before being evacuated (an example is given later in Figure 10.9).

The "syntagmatic" sequence of graphical symbols (forming a "syntagmatic habitat" in the sense of Chapter 9) will correspond to phrases in natural language. The assembly sign with the adjoining arrow shown above (Figure 10.5, left) would either correspond to a descriptive phrase like "*An assembly station is found... by*

Figure 10.5 Graphic symbols are often grouped together like phrases and in larger syntactic sequences forming a network of signs (e.g. the network of arrows). Two unrelated examples of this grouping are shown here.

going this way", i.e. in the direction of the arrow, or to an imperative phrase embedded in a hypothetical statement like "*In case of a call or an alarm for assembly... go this way!*". In the second interpretation there is a conditional statement involved ("In case of..."), which is a natural way to express *relevance*. The descriptive statement simply informs passengers of the way to an assembly station, but this information will generally not appear as relevant to a passenger. This is of cause part of the problem of evacuation: passengers do not generally take much interest in safety before they have to, i.e. in the case of an emergency. It is reasonable to expect that passengers under normal conditions will not notice these signs unless they take a special interest in safety.

Another important aspect of the assumed interpretation of graphical signs for evacuation is the understanding of *deictic* reference structures (cf. Chapter 9). The sequence of graphical symbols and their corresponding phrase structure relies on an understanding of the contextual use of "*this* way" in the pointing of the arrow. The preposition "this" has a deictic function that can only be understood with reference to *the location of observers* HERE and NOW and oriented in space by looking THIS way. We could in fact conceive of signs like these as *anamorphic* signs in the sense that they include the position of the observer in their meaning. If you for instance look at the sign from far away, the imperative meaning of the sign could change, since another sign might in fact be closer to the observer, thus indicating another escape route to follow. The full contextual meaning of the sign – including the syntagmatic reference to the *next similar sign* in the sequence – is therefore more complex and can be paraphrased in the following way (imagining that the sign could explain its own meaning to the passenger observing the sign):

> *If* you are standing close to *this* sign *and if* you have been informed of an evacuation emergency by call or alarm, you *should go in the direction of the arrow* and *look for the next similar sign*.

The decontextualized reading of the system of signs turned out to be the rule rather than the exception. In a test study, passengers walking towards an area with two subsequent arrows with adjoining assembly signs, were asked about the meaning of the first couple of signs located next to a hallway (to the right in Figure 10.6). The horizontal arrow was here interpreted by all but two passengers as *pointing* to the

Figure 10.6 Panoramic view of two assembly signs supposed to be read in sequence. However, passengers understand the horizontal sign on the right as pointing to the hall (rather than the next sign!). Sign reading seems to be detached from the context of other signs (the information space).

hallway – rather than to the next sign – and passengers indicated that they would run *into* the hallway in case of an emergency. This would create an unfortunate *counter stream* in such a circumstance, because passengers coming from the hallway would be trying to get up the stairs. The system of signs constitutes an *information space* (Chapter 7), but passengers interpret the signs as individual pointers to the *physical space*. They should look for the *next sign* rather than a particular architectural object in the physical environment.

During a real emergency this misinterpretation would in most cases be corrected by instructions from the crew, at least for the majority of passengers moving in large crowds. Some passengers will, however, be moving around on their own looking for relatives, and they would be more likely to be subject to wayfinding mistakes. The problem of passengers looking for relatives ("group binding") has been analyzed and estimated elsewhere (May, 2001a).

Another misinterpretation of the arrow and muster sign appeared in relation to the *ambiguity of horizontal arrows* in the context of staircases (Figure 10.7). In this case some passengers were not sure whether they were supposed to go up or down when following the sign. If the sign was read in sequence, as supposed in its design, the horizontal arrow in Figure 10.7 would be disambiguated by an up-arrow on the opposite wall beside the staircase, but this next sign in the sequence is not visible for passengers approaching the hallway from the right (an example of the problem of *visual access*).

Ambiguity also enters into the semantics of assembly signs in the form of a *choice of route*. In corridor areas (see Figure 10.10) assembly signs are sometimes seen with an adjoining double arrow (Figure 10.8), indicating a free choice of route. This reflects an important safety aspect of the design of ships, i.e. that there are many alternative escape routes, but in an emergency this choice might be fatal for

Figure 10.7 Ambiguity in the use of horizontal arrows.

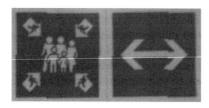

Figure 10.8 Ambiguity of choice. Passengers are left to decide, in a corridor, which exit route to follow for reaching the assembly stations.

passengers, either because one of the routes might actually be unsafe (in case of fire for instance) or because the series of choices (the next sign might also present a double arrow!) might confuse passengers on the run.

A free choice of escape route indicated by a *static* sign might lead passengers in the direction of a fire. In these cases it is obvious that some kind of *dynamic* sign used in an *active wayfinding system* would be safer in selecting only valid routes for directing passengers. In a fire, unsafe routes could be *deselected* from the active wayfinding system and passengers could even be *redirected* during an evacuation if necessary. Active wayfinding systems were recommended by the IMO (International Maritime Organization) in the SOLAS convention (1995).

Another cause of confusion was caused by the *proximity* of muster signs to objects or by the *similarity* of symbols used to label different areas. On one of the ferries taking part in the questionnaire and interview survey (May, 2000), one of the assembly stations with lifejackets was located down in the ship near a large restaurant area, while the rest of the passengers would assemble directly on the open deck (two decks above). This assembly station was labelled "A", but so was a staircase located in the same area (Figure 10.9). Staircase "A" went to the car deck, which is not supposed to be accessed during an emergency. This, however, is not generally known by passengers, and some understood the co-reference of assembly station

Figure 10.9 Passengers can be confused by the use of similar symbols to denote different things: the "A" in the background refers to assembly station A whereas the "A" in the foreground refers to the collocated staircase A leading to the car deck!

and staircase to "A" as meaning that they should assemble on the car deck. Some passenger would – if they were left to their own choice – attempt to go to the car deck, because that is how they entered the ship. This is in accordance with the observation that occupants in buildings will tend to use a *familiar* route over the *designed* escape routes.

In the same area passengers could be confused by misleading "gestalt effects": the proximity of the assembly sign "A" to the elevator (Figure 10.9) does *not* indicate the elevator as an escape route. A few passengers actually interpreted this proximity to indicate that elevators could be used during an emergency to get to the upper deck fast. In fact, elevators should be out of service during an evacuation, but passengers do not generally know this.

The design of assembly signs and their location in the ship environment must take into account not only the individual system of signs, such as the sequence of arrows, but also other system of signs (for staircases, shops, restaurants, cabins etc.) as well as adverts and the whole context of the built environment. Well-known gestalt effects such as *closeness in space* being understood as *closeness of meaning* (arrow and hallway in Figure 10.6; assembly sign/label and elevator in Figure 10.9) should not come as a surprise for designers.

10.4 Cognitive Aspects of Wayfinding on Ships

How do people actually find their way in unfamiliar or slightly familiar settings? As mentioned earlier, maps are not a very good support for the wayfinding of passengers on ships. In everyday non-professional wayfinding (by people who are not trained as navigators), human beings use *landmarks* to identify meaningful and functionally distinctive *places* (habitats) with different perceived *affordances* (different use contexts, different opportunities for action) rather than the *abstract space* of detailed map representations.

There is a safety "trap" here with regard to the design of accommodation space for passengers, because ship architects and interior decorators might consider the use context for the accommodation space on all passenger decks with cabins to be exactly the same for all decks and all corridors. This could support the aesthetic (and inexpensive) design solution of having all cabin decks and corridors designed in exactly the same way. Although consistency is usually a good design strategy it is problematic in this case, because there will be no landmarks to anchor the orientation of passengers relative to the ship's direction of sailing and with regard to left and right relative to the longitudinal axis of the ship (port and starboard). Furthermore there will be no architectural differentiation of areas to help identify different decks (i.e. on which vertical level of the ship the passenger is currently situated). The visual experience of a passenger on such a ship can be illustrated as in (Figure 10.10). When standing at a node in the corridor structure on a passenger deck and looking in three different directions (90° turns), every corridor section will look the same or almost the same.

Some corridors are longer than others, but which one is the "side" corridor (the transverse corridor connecting port and starboard longitudinal corridors)? And is

Figure 10.10 In the cabin area. Looking in three different directions (90° turns) does not give you any clue about where you are or which direction you are going in.

the observer standing to port or starboard? The doors also look the same, so although exit doors are marked, the passenger might easily overlook an exit door. Following a corridor to the end, the passenger would simply be guided into another corridor, which again would look exactly like the first one, and looking at the emergency signs would just indicate to the possibility of going either way! (Figure 10.8). A similar set of questions could arise with regard to the vertical dimension. On which deck is the observer presently located? All cabin decks have the same colour and look just the same. The information is available in symbolic form, but only in connection with the stairs. But where are the stairs? Will they be visible if the passenger follows one of the corridors, or are the stairs hidden behind some of the doors? In the cabin there is a diagram of the ship and the local deck arrangement indicating the way to the stairs, but which way does the diagram turn relative to the present location and direction of view of the observer? Notice how easily a passenger could get confused, even though the spatial arrangement is apparently very simple and not complex like a labyrinth. There is however a certain complexity in the circularity of corridors and the identical layout of each deck.

It can be inferred from the literature on architectural wayfinding (Butler *et al.*, 1993; Arthur and Passini, 1992) that it is important to have:

- *Architectural support* for wayfinding in the form of suggestive *landmarks*
- *Architectural differentiation of areas* into meaningful and functional *places* or "habitats" (rest areas, dining areas, upper/lower decks etc.), for instance by colour coding
- *Architectural simplicity* in the layout of decks (avoiding complex arrangements)

Rather than having a single conception of space as the "real" 3D space, we have to differentiate (as discussed in other parts of this book) between several types of *cognitively relevant space*. This necessity of having different conceptions of space was already pointed out by the mathematician Henri Poincaré in the beginning of the 20th century (Poincaré, 1902), where he discussed a distinction between the geometric space as presupposed by theoretical physics and the "representative space" of our experience (*espace représentatif*). In cognitive science we could make distinctions between:

(a) the "visuo-spatial" *functional space* integrating movement and vision (explored in recent "cognitive neuroscience")

(b) the "symbolized" *experiential space* represented in speaking and reasoning about objects in space

(c) the abstract *topological space* of embodied "image schemata", which seem to "glue together" the space of actual movement and vision (a) with the space we speak and reason about (b)

None of these spaces is identical in any simple way to the geometric space of theoretical physics, i.e. they are all versions of the lived *espace représentatif* presupposed by Poincaré. From a cognitive point of view, spatial knowledge of an environment will be remembered by passengers in the form of *landmarks* and *schematic paths* through a landscape, and only very vaguely in terms of exact locations and routes. The concept of "route knowledge" seems to imply that passengers will remember long descriptions of route decisions, which is quite improbable. What is "picked up" from the environment of the ship by ordinary passengers will generally not be spatial models such as the "general arrangement" conveyed by maps and structural diagrams, but more fragmentary pieces of information, some of which will be *image-like* (the visual landmarks noticed by passengers: a nice shopping mall, an impressive staircase etc.) and some of which will be highly *schematic cognitive structures* of the type described by cognitive semantics ("idealized cognitive models" and "image schemata") (Johnson, 1987).

It is an important assumption in cognitive semantics (sometimes called the "localist hypothesis"), that these *schematic cognitive structures* constitute a common core of simple meanings across different cognitive domains. Image schemas for abstract spatial relations like containment, path-connectedness, and the asymmetries of front–back, left–right and up–down (cf. the schematic and embodied dimensions of orientation in Figure 10.11), are discovered as central to

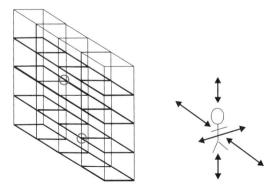

Figure 10.11 Simplified drawing of the structure of corridors on the cabin decks of a passenger ship. Without architectural support passengers cannot use their local visual experience to locate themselves in the global structure relative to their schematic and embodied dimensions of orientation (up–down, left–right and front–back). The circles indicate locations that would look exactly the same for the observer (somewhat like the example given in Figure 10.10).

natural language understanding, but they are also central to the understanding of visual scenes and – in the present context – to the organization of wayfinding tasks. They roughly correspond to what Stephen Kosslyn called *categorial spatial relations* – as opposed to *coordinate spatial relations* (Kosslyn, 1996). What is easy for us to grasp and to remember is not the *global spatial layout* of the environment in terms of its exact *geometry* – that is indeed why professionals need maps for special tasks, such as navigation! – but rather the *local features* we notice (the landmarks) and the *topology* of selected places that have become meaningful to us.

Topology is what the schematic structures are focusing on: *connectedness* between places, for instance (O'Neil, 1999), rather than their exact geometry. Connectedness seems a very abstract property of space, but is in fact a very practical concern in the sense that it expresses the "travelability" between places, the path between one place and another place. Place here is not abstract space, but parts of space that function as a *habitat* in the sense that they *contain and support different meaningful activities*: the resting place defined by some soft chairs and a television set, a particular dining area or the particular cabin occupied by a passenger. In the terminology inspired by Gibson's theory of ecological perception, each place or habitat has its own *affordances* according to the *perceived possibilities* for action and the *activities objectively supported* by each particular place.

In geography, researchers have suggested that the abstract spatial models provided by Geographical Information Systems (GIS), should be extended to include "affordance based models of place" (Jordan *et al.*, 1998). A similar line of thinking would be very important for a deeper understanding of wayfinding (Mark, 1993; Raubal and Egenhofer, 1998); one case study on the use of image schemata for wayfinding looked at wayfinding in airports (Raubal *et al.*, 1997).

Even before the advent of cognitive semantics, early studies in "naïve geography" demonstrated how the discourse of navigation and wayfinding in natural and built environments is mediated by metaphorical structures superimposed on geometric space. In the 1950s, Einar Haugen described how traditional wayfinding in Iceland without a compass would refer to East–West–North–South as practically determined sections of Icelandic coastline: "going East" would mean going to the Eastern part of Iceland even if locally you might be going due North or South (Downs and Stea, 1977). Similar findings were described by Richard Howell for the discourse of orientation on Staten Island in New York: "up-island" and "down-island" did not refer to compass directions (as "up" and "down" on a map), but rather to a non-homogenous mixture of locally determined features such as the direction of main roads and global features of topology such as the connectedness of the upper Eastern and upper Western parts of Staten Island with the rest of New York via important bridges (Downs and Stea, 1977). The importance of this is that wayfinding tasks are mediated conceptually by language at the level of metaphorical structures as well as at a deeper level of semantics (image schemata). We should design for support of wayfinding in ways compatible with findings on human spatial cognition (i.e. how people actually find they way), as well as findings on the cognitive semantics of navigation and wayfinding (i.e. how people talk and reason about wayfinding).

Figure 10.12 An example of a (green on black) photoluminiscent "pictographic" (static graphic symbolic) sign indicating an emergency exit door.

One important suggestion would be that we ought to find ways of giving *local directional support* for wayfinding in emergencies that would be more efficient and natural (i.e. less dependent on arbitrary interpretation) than the present use of systems of symbolic pictographic signs. This is what we try to obtain today by having crew members with different rôles assigned to different positions on the ship during an assembly and subsequent evacuation. Crew members cannot, however, be omnipresent and they have to assemble among themselves first upon receiving orders from the captain. As suggested by Deborah Withington, Judy Edworthy and other Human Factors experts in warning and alarm design, *locally sounding alarms* would be an important "ecological" tool in providing affordances for fast orientation towards valid emergency exits in buildings or on ships.

In the maritime domain however the main alternative to the traditional "pictographic" (static graphic symbolic) signs has been the introduction of *photoluminiscent signs* (Figure 10.12) as well as *dynamic graphic signs* for emergencies. An example of dynamic graphic signs is the "animated network" of arrows that light up in the floor of an aircraft in case of evacuation (they have also been introduced on cruise ships).

In an experimental study at TNO it was found (surprisingly) that animating a system of signs (arrows) did *not* lead to a convincing improvement in the efficiency of wayfinding in corridors. Also it would not constitute an improvement in conditions of smoke and fire, since it would suffer from the same problems of visibility in smoke. It was found that dynamic graphical displays, in the form of LED light strips with an *apparent motion*, did not improve wayfinding in a significant way (Boer, 1998) compared with *static PL-LLL* (Photo-Luminescent Low Location Lighting). The incidence of wayfinding errors was on average 27% with dynamic LED light strips and 25% with static PL-LLL. Static PL-LLL was slightly better in daylight and dynamic LED light strips were slightly better in the dark. Under conditions of daylight as well as ship list the suggested active wayfinding system (dynamic LED light strips) in fact reduced the effectiveness of the simulated assembly by increasing assembly time. The study indicated that more time was needed by passengers to interpret the apparent movement of the LED displays compared with traditional static signs used in PL-LLL along the corridors close to the floor.

In fires there is the added problem of smoke reducing general visibility and visual access to emergency signs. The present way of taking this into account is to use PL-

LLL located close to the floor, since passengers would have to crawl along the corridors if trapped in smoke. PL-LLL is used as a cost-effective way of meeting the requirements of IMO (IMO Resolution A.752(18)) requiring a minimum of one hour emergency lighting (in situations with power failure) at low locations on ships carrying more than 36 passengers. The fluorescent tape used today does, however, not include *direction marks*, which could be a problem when only a fragment of the tape is seen in a part of the corridor at a distance from the directional signs (Arnskov, 1999). The need for orientation support is especially critical in the *initial route selection* by passengers emerging from cabins, because of the uncertainty in the first phase of an evacuation (Boer, 1998).

In a series of experimental evacuation exercises carried out by the Norwegian Fire Research Laboratory SINTEF after the fire disaster on the *Scandinavian Star* in 1990, it was concluded that traditional static graphical exit signs were not effective in evacuating people from fires. In the test trials the subjects followed an evacuation route through corridors in the test facility. A number of doors and exits with steps were set into the corridors. Many types of signs and lighting systems were then tested on 200 experimental subjects who were asked to pass through the smoke-filled evacuation route: "The first test was of traditional signs with lighting that showed the emergency exit. Visibility was poor because of the thick smoke. Just under 40% made different types of mistakes, and could not find the emergency exit. They either passed it, or tried to get out through the wrong door, and some turned round on the way out.... A surprisingly large number of people made serious mistakes. Traditional signs give us little support when we are in motion. They just tell us something about the direction to take, but nothing about walls, floors, corners or steps. These are all very important when we are trying to make our way in poor visibility" (Bjørken, 1993).

In the *Scandinavian Star* tragedy many passengers were found dead very close to emergency exits. They had died from asphyxia in the heavy smoke. The SINTEF study concludes that better emergency lightening and graphic signs will *not* be enough: "we do know that emergency lighting and marking signs do not help to distribute people among the evacuation routes available. People try to get out the same way as they came in, and this can easily cause crowding. Our suspicion that signs do not live up to expectations has been reinforced by a major study that showed that only 8% of the people noticed signs when they were fleeing from a fire" (Bjørken 1993).

Smoke disrupts the channel for verbal communication (because of choking) as well as the channel for graphic-visual communication, and the symbolic use of acoustic signs to carry information in the form of auditory alarms (the evacuation alarm for instance) is problematic. The symbolic coding of the message into a particular sequence of repetitive sounds can hardly be expected to be known and understood by passengers, and even if they do understand its meaning many passengers will prefer to believe that it is probably just a test of the system or an exercise for the crew. The primary problem with passenger behaviour in ferry accidents is generally not panic reactions but the *delayed reaction* to alarms and *denying* that anything is wrong (May, 2000; Harbst and Madsen, 1992; Poole and Springett, 1998).

10.5 Virtual Acoustic Displays

Dynamic and *directional* sound alarms would be an important improvement in supporting wayfinding of passengers during emergencies. We are familiar with the use of sound in *verbal warnings* and *auditory alarms*, but we should be aware that sound as a media channel (a channel of communication) could also be used with other pragmatic functions than *alarming*. On ships the public address system (loudspeakers) would be used by the captain for *informing* the passengers about an accident, but there are other *types of signs* that could be expressed effectively in sound besides arbitrary symbols (sound alarms) and natural language (verbal warnings and situation updates) giving support for other pragmatic functions.

The pragmatic functions supported in ("afforded by") the graphic media channel by *maps* and *networks* are functions such as locating objects relative to a reference object (a typical pragmatic function of a *map* sign) or indicating the direction of a flow through a connected set of locations or objects (a typical pragmatic function of a *network* sign), but with some limitations these pragmatic functions could also be realized through sound maps and sound networks. We have to think of maps and networks as abstract sign types with a core meaning independent of specific media of expression. This way we can systematically explore alternative ways of representing (by selecting sign types: images, maps, graphs, diagrams, symbols and language) and communicating (by selecting media channels: graphic, acoustic or haptic) (May and Andersen, 2001; Andersen and May, 2001; May, 2001b,c).

In order to understand how sound alarms for directing passengers towards safe exits should be designed, we need to *know how directional information can be expressed in sound*. *Acoustic maps* are possible, but due to the transitory nature of sound it would not be feasible to use *global maps of an escape route* expressed in sound, because each part of the map would fade away as a sound representation and disappear from the echoic short-term memory of passengers, while the next part of the route would have to be presented. The global map would have to be reconstructed in the mind from these serialized parts and this would require a considerable mental effort from passengers in distress; it would in fact be even more difficult than listening to a long verbal route description in natural language ("first turn right, follow the corridor, then go up the stairs, then turn left, then ..."). Acoustic maps have been used to assist professional navigators in cockpits for instance, but only in the form of very schematic maps. An example is the *sound maps* (sometimes called "sound images", but as signs they are in fact maps) used to indicate the direction to enemy targets for fighter pilots (King and Oldfield, 1997).

A much better choice is to construct a *network diagram* in sound, but in the form of a *virtual* network covering the whole ship, and in a form where *local access to simple directions* to the next point in the network would be enough to direct passengers to safe exits from anywhere on the ship. Such an acoustic network diagram would constitute a *virtual acoustic display* superimposed on the spatial layout of the ship, augmenting it with directional information. As a virtual acoustic display the network would be *reconfigurable* in the sense that passengers could be redirected if fire or flooding made some pathways of escape unsafe during an accident.

This acoustic dynamic network diagram would correspond to the system of arrows in use today, which is also a virtual three-dimensional network diagram (but static and realized in the graphic channel of communication). The main reason why virtual networks are more efficient than global maps is that passengers do not have to construct and remember the whole route, but can rely on *local procedural information* about what to do next, i.e. *information that directly affords action* without the need to construct, inspect and manipulate a mental map or some other mental model of the ship. This is an important affordance for the inhabitants of this syntagmatic habitat (Chapter 9).

How could an acoustic network representation be constructed to be efficient for passengers? The first step to consider is that sound propagation gives us the opportunity to *let each node in the network* – corresponding to a staircase or an emergency exit on the escape route – *indicate a direction to itself* from any location and orientation of passengers in the vicinity of the node. If each important node in the network is collocated with a sound source, we could in principle obtain this very simple solution, because sound perception does not require *directed attention* like vision (i.e. a graphic sign is overlooked if the passenger does not look in the direction of the sign). This solution does, however, require that passengers can determine the direction to a sound source. The next question therefore is: *how do humans localize sound sources?*

The first plausible theory of the *acoustic cues* used in sound localization was the "duplex theory" proposed by Strutt (Lord Rayleigh) in the end of the 19th century. According to this theory, the distance to a sound source (off to one side relative to the head of the listener) can be evaluated on the basis of differences in the time of arrival of the sound to each of the ears: it will arrive sooner at the ear closer to the source (Figure 10.13). This cue to sound localization is called the *interaural time difference* (ITD). A second cue to localization is the *interaural intensity difference* (IID) resulting from the "shadow effect" of the head for the ear turning away from the sound source (the sound will be louder at the ear closer to the source). In the original theory it was proposed that the intensity difference was primarily used to localize high-frequency sounds, whereas the time difference was thought to be relevant only for low-frequency sounds (with higher frequencies time differences would be

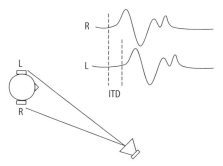

Figure 10.13 The sound from a sound source off the median plane between the ears will reach one ear before the other (in this case the right ear R) causing a small interaural time difference (ITD) that is a perceptual cue for sound localization. Redrawn after Wenzel (1992).

difficult to evaluate because of phase ambiguities). This assumption was, however, an artefact of the single-frequency (sine wave) sounds used in the experiments at the time: time differences can be evaluated with high-frequency sound as well if there is enough bandwith to produce slow modulation of the sound (Wenzel, 1992).

Another problem is that the duplex theory cannot account for our ability to localize sounds in the vertical median plane, where interaural cues will be minimal. In more recent research it has been shown that there is a third factor in localization which is based on *direction- and frequency-dependent filtering* of incoming sound shaped by the individual structure of the outer ear. This "shaping" (filtering) of the sound by the outer ears is described as *head-related transfer functions* (HRTFs). These HRTFs are used to disambiguate the interaural cues. Besides the difficulty of determining the vertical location of a sound source, a phenomenon known as *front–back reversal* can occur (where a sound source near the median plane in front of the listener is heard as if it came from behind). Head movement greatly enhances the ability to disambiguate front–back locations by involving the ear specific HRTFs and by creating variation in time and intensity differences. This variation imposed by head movement is necessary because of the geometry and physics of hearing. If sound localization was based only on ITDs and IIDs for static single-frequency sound (pure tones), we would not be able to disambiguate the cues. This is due to the fact that for any given frequency there will be numerous spatial locations that would generate identical differences in timing as well as intensity. The geometry of these identical ITDs and IIDs would form a surface (an iso-ITD/IID contour) and have the shape of a cone from the outer ear (Figure 10.14).

With no other cues to localization besides ITD and IID, we would not be able to distinguish front–back or up–down for static sound sources in 3D space. The cones are therefore also called the "cones of confusion". Head movement and ear-specific filtering (the HRTFs) will, however, disambiguate locations in most cases, but pure tones are almost impossible to localize.

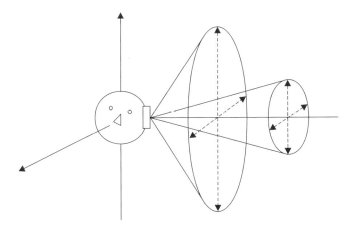

Figure 10.14 "Cones of confusion" for single-frequency sound: all sound sources lying on a cone surface would produce the same ITD and the same IID. ITD and IID are larger for the small cone and smaller for the large cone. Redrawn after Wenzel (1992).

Another problem of localization is associated with sound sources in enclosed spaces. Reflected sound may disturb the cues for localization, but here a phenomenon known as *precedence* or the "law of the first wavefront" helps the listener: the perceived location of a sound source will be dominated by the first wavefront, which takes precedence over later reflected sound. If the delay of the reflected sound is large enough (echoes), it will, however, be perceived as a new sound source. Reverberation and echo effects can disturb localization, but they are important for the perceptual judgement of *distance* to sound sources (Shinn-Cunningham, 2001) and information about direction as well as distance should be included in active wayfinding systems.

The next step is to use the psychoacoustic features of human sound localization to determine the properties of sound beacons to be used in active wayfinding systems. First of all we can infer that we should never use pure tones for sound beacons. Even with the mixed frequency signals previously used by sirens on emergency vehicles, it was found that a frequency range of 500 Hz to 1.8 kHz was far too narrow to establish easy localization. This difficulty accounts for a large number of accidents involving emergency vehicles where other drivers were unable to determine from which direction the emergency vehicle was approaching (Withington, 2000). This was also confirmed in a driving simulator, where for 56% of the time subjects were unable to determine whether the emergency vehicle siren was directly behind or in front of them (Withington, 2001a). In experimental studies with virtual acoustic displays at Leeds University (Rutherford and Withington, 2001) the optimum signal for navigation beacons for emergency egress was found to be *pulsating signals of broadband noise* ("white noise") (Withington, 2000). Using a very large spectrum of frequencies makes the maximum number of cues for localization available for the brain to process. Using sound beacons for *directional sound signals* in addition to graphic wayfinding systems and auditory warnings would improve safety of egress and evacuation from buildings (Rutherford and Withington 2001), from aircraft (Withington, 2001a) and from ships (Withington, 2001b) and even in other situations like escape from tunnels and mine shafts (Brenkley *et al.*, 1999). Full three-dimensional localization with disambiguation of the up–down and front–back asymmetries has been shown to require broadband sound of at least 0–13 kHz or 0–16 kHz for the high-resolution virtual acoustic displays used in the cockpits of fighter aircraft (King and Oldfield, 1997).

Directional sound signals can be used to carry iconic information as well as schematic information about orientation (front–back, up–down, left–right). In fact, the pulsating broadband noise can be shaped by frequency modulation to produce a natural iconic mapping – "natural" according to our embodied image schemata (Johnson, 1987; Raubal *et al.*, 1997) – of rising frequency noise indicating an "up" orientation and a falling frequency noise indicating a "down" orientation, thus directing passengers up or down local stairs to escape smoke-filled corridors.

10.6 Conclusion

In designing for safety, *virtual acoustic displays* that could function as *maps* or *networks* would be an important improvement in *directing* passengers locally to the nearest safe corridors, exit doors and stairs in a way that can be adapted to a changing emergency situation (locally sounding alarms could redirect the flow of passengers if an emergency exit becomes blocked by fire or flooding) and in a way that can be perceived by passengers even in smoke-filled corridors.

In designing for crowd safety in emergency situations on board passenger ships, it will, however, also be necessary to take knowledge about individual and crowd behaviour into account. Design for safe evacuation is not only design of *technical* assistance to wayfinding and design of rescue equipment, but it is also the design of operational procedures. Designers need to know under what conditions panics can be avoided or under what conditions passengers will comply with instructions from the crew (Poole and Springett, 1998; May, 2000; May, 2001a; Jørgensen and May, 2002).

As stated at the beginning, traditional graphic signs are already a form of *augmented reality*, a way of *drawing and writing directly on the reality of the environment*. Static graphic signs are, however, not as safe and efficient as electronic computer-supported augmented reality. This is what we obtain by using *directional sound* to enhance the augmented reality of the ship, thereby creating a *virtual acoustic display* superimposed on the built environment.

This superimposition of a virtual acoustic display on the physical space of the ship creates a *dual space* as discussed in Chapter 9, i.e. an *informational space* and a *spatio-temporal space*. This dual space is *partitioned* in different *habitats* with different action possibilities provided for their "inhabitants" – in this case the passengers moving around on the ship during an emergency.

References

Andersen, P. B. and May, M. (2001) Tearing up interfaces. In Liu, P., Clarke, R. J., Andersen, P. B. and Stamper, R. K. (eds.) *Information, Organization and Technology. Studies in Organizational Semiotics*. Dordrecht: Kluwer.

Arnskov, M. M. (1999) Wayfinding systems. A proposal for new wayfinding systems for passenger ferries. *Report for WP1a of BriteEuram project 97-4229 MEPdesign*. Lyngby: DMI.

Arthur, P. and Passini, R. (1992) *Wayfinding. People, Signs, and Architecture*. Toronto: McGraw-Hill.

Best, G. (1970) Direction-finding in large buildings. In Canter, D. (ed.) *Architectural Psychology*. London: RIBA Publications.

Boer, L. C. (1998) Improved signposting for the evacuation of passenger ships. *Report for WP2a of BriteEuram project 97-4229 MEPdesign*. Soesterberg: TNO.

Bjørken, A. B. (1993) Emergency exits hard to find. *Gemini Magazine*, December. Available at http://www.oslo.sintef.no/.

Brenkly, D., Bennett, S. C. and Jones, B. (1999) Enhancing mine emergency response. *28th International Conference on Safety in Mines*, Sinaia, Romania.

Butler, D. L., Acquino, A. L., Hissong, A. A. and Scott, P. A. (1993) Wayfinding by newcomers in a complex building. *Human Factors*, 35(1), 159–173.

Downs, R. M. and Stea, D. (1977) *Maps in Minds. Reflections on Cognitive Mapping*. New York: Harper & Row.

Harbst, J. and Madsen, F. (1992) *The Behaviour of Passengers in a Critical Situation on Board a Passenger Vessel or Ferry*. Prize Dissertation, Copenhagen.

International Maritime Organization (1993): Guidelines for the evaluation, testing and application of low-location lighting on passenger ships. *IMO Resolution A.752(18)*.

Johnson, M. (1987) *The Body in the Mind. The Bodily Basis of Meaning, Imagination and Reason*. Chicago, IL: University of Chicago Press.

Jordan, T., Raubal, M., Gartrell, G. and Egenhofer, M. (1998) An affordance-based model of place in GIS. In Poiker, T. and Chrisman, N. (eds.), *8th Int. Symposium on Spatial Data Handling, SDH'98*, pp. 98–109. Vancouver, Canada.

Jørgensen, H. D. and May, M. (2002) Human factors management of passenger ship evacuation. *Proceedings of the Conference on Human Factors in Ship Design & Operation II*, 2–3 October, Royal Institute of Naval Architects (RINA), London. Draft available at http://www.maritime-hfe.com/.

King, R. B. and Oldfield, S. R. (1997) The impact of signal bandwidth on auditory localization: Implications for the design of three-dimensional audio displays. *Human Factors*, 39(2), 287–295.

Kosslyn, S. M. (1996) *Image and Brain*. Cambridge, MA: MIT Press.

Mark, D. M. (1993) Human spatial cognition. In Medyckyj-Scott, D. and Hearnshaw, H. M. (eds.) *Human Factors in Geographical Information Systems*. London: Belhaven Press.

May, M. (2000) Group binding. Emergency behaviour of ferry passengers. *Report for WP2c of BriteEuram project 97-4229 MEPdesign*. Lyngby: DMI.

May, M. (2001a) Emergency behaviour of ferry passengers. *8th World conference on Emergency Mangement (TIEMS 2001)*, Oslo, 19–22 June. Available at http://www.maritime-hfe.com/.

May, M. (2001b) Instrument semiotics. *Knowledge-Based Systems*, 14, 431–435. Draft available at http://www.hci-components.com/.

May, M. (2001c) Semantics for instrument components. In Lind, M. (ed.) *Proceedings of the EAM 2001. 20th European Annual Conference on Decision Making and Manual Control*. Technical University of Denmark, Lyngby, 25–27 June. Available at http://www.hci-components.com/.

May, M. (2002) Wayfinding, passenger behaviour and maritime emergency signs. In Ward, D. (ed.) *Proceedings of the European Chapter of the Human Factors and Ergonomics Society Annual Conference 2001*, Turin, 7–9 November. Draft available at http://www.maritime-hfe.com/.

May, M. and Andersen, P. B. (2001) Instrument semiotics. In Liu, P., Clarke, R. J., Andersen, P. B. and Stamper, R. K. (eds.) *Information, Organization and Technology. Studies in Organizational Semiotics*. Dordrecht: Kluwer.

National Transport Safety Board (2001) Fire on board the Liberian Passenger Ship Ecstasy, Miami, Florida, July 20, 1998. *Marine Accident Report, NTSB/MAR-01/01. NTSB*, Washington DC. Available at http://www.ntsb.gov/Publictn/2001/MAR0101.htm/.

O'Neil, M. J. (1999) Theory and research in design of "You Are Here" maps. In Zwanga, H. J. G., Boerseman, T. and Hoonhout, C. M. (eds.) *Visual information for everyday use. Design and research perspectives*. London: Taylor & Francis.

Poincaré H. (1902) *La Science et L'Hypothèse*. Paris: Flammarion (1968).

Poole, T. and Springett, P. (1998) *Understanding Human Behaviour in Emergencies. A Manual for the Cruise and Ferry Sector*. Odyssey Training.

Raubal, M. and Egenhofer, M. J. (1998) Comparing the complexity of wayfinding tasks in built environments. *Environment & Planning* B, 25(6), 895–913.

Raubal, M., Egenhofer, M. J., Pfoser, D. and Tryfona, N. (1997) Structuring space with image schemata: wayfinding in airports as a case study. In Hirtle, S. and Frank, A. (eds.) *Spatial Information Theory – A Theoretical Basis for GIS. International Conference COSIT'97*. Lecture Notes in Computer Science 1329, pp. 85–102. Berlin: Springer-Verlag.

Rutherford, P. and Withington, D. (2001) The application of virtual acoustic techniques for the development of an auditory navigation beacon used in building emergency egress. *Proceedings of the 2001 International Conference on Auditory Displays*, Espoo, Finland, 29 July–1 August.

Shinn-Cunningham, B. G. (2001) Creating three dimensions in virtual auditory displays. In Smith, M. J., Salvendy, G., Harris, D. and Koubek, R. J. (eds.) *Usability Evaluation and Interface Design: Cognitive Engineering, Intelligent Agents and Virtual Reality* (Proceedings of HCI International 2001, New Orleans, 5–10 August). Hillsdale, NJ: Lawrence Erlbaum, pp. 604–608.

Wenzel, E. M. (1992) Localization in virtual acoustic displays. *Presence*, 1(1), 80–97. NASA Ames Research Centre, MS 262-2. Available at http://human-factors.arc.nasa.gov/ihh/spatial/personnel/wenzel.html.

Wickens, C. D. (1992) *Engineering Psychology and Human Performance*. New York: HarperCollins.

Withington, D. (1999) Localisable alarms. In Stanton, N. A. and Edworthy, J. (eds.) *Human Factors in Auditory Warnings*. Aldershot: Ashgate.

Withington, D. (2000) The use of directional sound to improve the safety of auditory warnings. *14th Triennial Congress of the International Ergonomics Association and 44th Annual Meeting of the Human Factors and Ergonomics Society*, San Diego, CA, August.

Withington, D. (2001a) The use of directional sound to aid aircraft evacuation. *The Third Triennial Fire and Cabin Safety Research Conference*, 22–25 October, Atlantic City, NJ. Available at `http://www.fire.tc.faa.gov/conference.html`.

Withington, D. (2001b) Use of directional sound for ship evacuation. *8th World Conference on Emergency Mangement (TIEMS 2001)*, Oslo, 19–21 June.

11

Conceptual Abstraction in Modelling With Physical and Informational Material

Bent Bruun Kristensen, Daniel Chien-Meng May, Palle Nowack

11.1 Abstraction and Tangible Objects

In the vision of ubiquitous (Weiser, 1991) and pervasive (Various, 1999) computing, informational and physical materials are converging to create new types of artefact. These artefacts exist like the physical artefacts that we are used to, but also comprise an additional dimension, one where they can store and compute information. We refer to these objects as *tangible objects*, for we believe that these artefacts will **become** more real, richer and satisfying in our interaction with them – more tangible, as it were. The understanding and discussion of tangible objects forms the subject of our research project, TangO (May *et al.*, 2001a,b; Andersen and Nowack, 2002; Hallenborg and Kristensen, 2002). In Chapter 7, "Habitats for the Digitally Pervasive World", we discussed the TangO project and some underlying background and motivation. That chapter also discusses the notion of habitats, the construct we use for characterizing the environments and spaces in which tangible objects are located. This chapter takes a perspective on tangible objects themselves.

11.1.1 Abstraction and Dimensions

The purpose of this chapter is to discuss the possibilities and limitations of abstraction in relation to our understanding of tangible objects. A central assumption that we make about tangible objects is that they exist across three distinct dimensions: physical, informational and conceptual. Because of this, we need to clarify our understanding of conceptual abstraction in relation to these dimensions.

By abstraction, we mean *conceptual abstraction* – that is, how concepts are formed and related to observed phenomena. The formation and relating of concepts and phenomena takes place in the conceptual dimension; the phenomena that we observe or create exist in physical and informational dimensions. We discuss abstraction by means of material from each of the physical and informational dimensions. Later we focus on abstraction by means of integrated material from both dimensions.

11.1.2 Abstraction: Conceptual Modelling

Our view of conceptual modelling comprises three distinct systems (Jacobsen, 2000); see Figure 11.1. The *target system* represents the part of the world under scrutiny or the problem to be solved. Once we start examining the target system, we start forming ideas about it, fitting it into conceptual frameworks that we have, analyzing and abstracting it in various ways. This takes place in the *referent system*, our conceptual world, so to speak. The referent system is part of a modeller's mind: private and restricted to the individual modeller. The referent system is made explicit by creating a model or representation of it – the *model system* – and is thus shareable. The referent system is an abstraction: we capture and focus on certain details of the target system for our interest and purpose.

Thus, when we create a model system based on a target system, it is never value- or context-free. Implicitly or explicitly, the model system will focus on certain perspectives of the phenomena in the target system as a consequence of the referent system that we create when forming concepts of the target system.

Figure 11.2 uses the zoo as an example. We imagine children who have just come home from the zoo. Some of them draw pictures of the animals on paper and some of them construct animal figures with Lego bricks, while others might mould

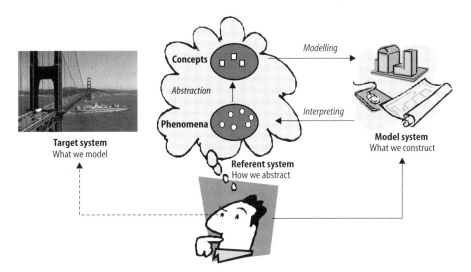

Figure 11.1 Conceptual modelling: we model a target system by abstracting the referent system and constructing the model system.

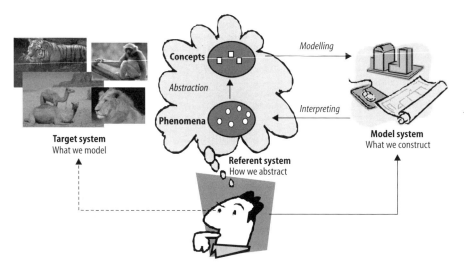

Figure 11.2 Modelling animals with the zoo as the target system.

animal figures out of clay. These models are examples of model systems, demonstrating how representations can vary. If we look more closely at the representations, we would probably find that the children have focused on different aspects of the individual animals they were attracted to. Some children might have tried to accurately model the morphology of the animals, the colour or individual attributes of the animals (such as the giraffe's neck, the elephant's trunk, or the camel's humps). The different foci illustrate the different referent systems used by the various children.

11.1.3 Conceptual Abstraction

We distinguish between abstraction in physical and informational dimensions. Abstraction in the physical dimension is exemplified by *traditional Lego*®, where we only have bricks and other similar basic blocks to create physical structures. For example, structures that we build from Lego bricks exist in the physical dimension, whereas our understanding of these structures is in the conceptual dimension. Abstraction in the informational dimension is exemplified by object-oriented modelling, where we can build informational models of precisely the phenomena that we choose. For example, in a computer game we may play with an informational model that is distinct from physical phenomena. Of course, an informational model may correspond to physical phenomena – our discussion will include informational models of Lego bricks, manipulated by software – but we underline the fact that such informational models are distinct and separate from physical Lego structures.

We will discuss the understanding and the potential of abstraction in the physical dimension from the perspective of conceptual modelling. We will also show that, for the informational dimension, object-oriented modelling supports conceptual

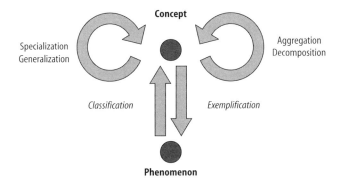

Figure 11.3 Conceptual abstraction by the so-called ovary model.

modelling to a large extent. In conceptual modelling we find different forms of abstraction[1] in terms of concepts and phenomena, namely:

- *Classification* and *exemplification*: a concept classifies a number of phenomena, which themselves exemplfy the concept.
- *Specialization* and *generalization*: a more general concept generalizes a more specific concept, which itself specializes the general concept.
- *Aggregation* and *decomposition*: a whole concept describes the aggregated phenomenon of several part phenomena of part concepts, which themselves can be decomposed from the phenomenon of the whole concept.

Figure 11.3 illustrates the different forms of abstraction and how they relate to the notion of concept and phenomenon. We refer to this model of conceptual abstraction (Kristensen and Østerbye, 1994) as the *ovary* model.

11.1.4 Properties and Their Relations in Specialization and Aggregation

We discuss the relation between properties in relation to specialization and aggregation (Kristensen and Østerbye, 1994); see Figure 11.4.

Specialization: Assume that some *special* concept is specialized from some other *general* concept. Relations between a property of the special concept and a property of the general concept are characterized as *inherited*, *modified* and *additional*:

---

1   Association is usually also seen as an important relation between concepts and phenomena. In general, there are no relations between properties of associated phenomena. If we introduce "objectified associations", where the association itself introduces properties of its associated phenomena, the association describes the actual relation between the properties of the associated phenomena. The association may utilize the properties of the phenomena by prescribing actions to take between the phenomena by involving the properties of the phenomena – the objectified association specifies the relation between the properties of the association.

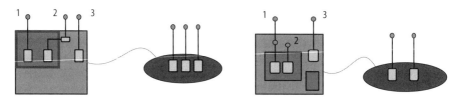

Figure 11.4. Illustration of properties in specialization (left) with (1) *inherited*, (2) *modified* and (3) *additional* properties and in aggregation (right) with (1) *hereditary*, (2) *concealed* and (3) *emerging* properties.

- *Inherited property*: A property of the special concept is an inherited property if it possesses some of the properties of the more general concept. Assume that a Model T-A car chassis is a specialization of a Model T chassis and that Colour is a property of a Model T chassis. As an example of an inherited property, we consider the Colour of a Model T-A chassis to be the Colour of a Model T chassis.
- *Modified property*: A property of the special concept is a modified property if it is seen as a refinement of some of the properties of the more general concept. Assume that Wheel is a property of Vehicle and that Tractor is a specialization of Vehicle. As an example of a modified property we consider the properties Front-wheel and Rear-wheel of Tractor to be refinements of the Wheel of the Vehicle.
- *Additional property*: A property of the special concept is an additional property if it is some property added in the description the special concept. Assume that Cab is a specialization of Car. As an example of an additional property we consider the On/Off Sign on the Cab to be an additional property that ordinary Cars do not have.

Aggregation: Assume that some *whole* concept is aggregated from other *part* concepts. Relations between a property of the whole concept and a property of one of the part concepts are characterized as *emerging*, *hereditary* and *concealed*:

- *Emerging property*: A property of the whole concept is an emerging property if it is not any of the properties of some of the part concepts. We consider the Run ability of a Car to be an example of an emerging property that cannot be attributed to any single part of Car (not the Motor, not the Wheels).
- *Hereditary property*: A property of the whole concept is a hereditary property if it is exactly one of the properties of one of the part concepts. As an example of a hereditary property we consider the Colour of a Car to be the Colour of the Body of the Car – and no other part of the Car.
- *Concealed property*: A property of one of the part concepts is a concealed property if it is not also a property of the whole concept. As an example of a concealed property, we do not consider the Weight of the Bricks of a Wall to be the Weight of the Wall. Neither do we consider the Weight of the Bricks to be a property of the Wall.

11.2 Modelling With Physical Material

Figure 11.5 shows the conceptual model for Lego.

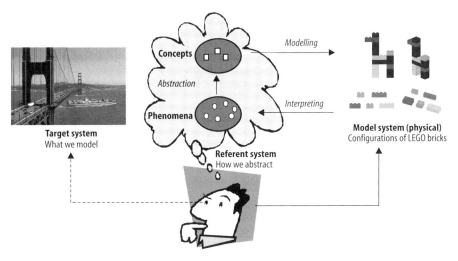

Figure 11.5 We can observe and manipulate Lego bricks and Lego structures in the physical dimension, understanding these as phenomena in the conceptual dimension.

11.2.1 Conceptual Understanding of Lego Bricks as Physical Material

In traditional Lego, we have a brick with 2×2 dots on top. We shall denote this type of brick as 2×2, which describes the concept covering this type of brick. In a box of Lego bricks, we may have a number of such 2×2 bricks – these are all phenomena covered by the concept 2×2. The 2×2 bricks in our box may have different colours. That is possibly the only way we see variations between the 2×2 bricks. Still, each 2×2 brick has its own identity – even two bricks that share the same attributes and properties are still distinct bricks. We may also have bricks with 2×4, 2×3 and 2×1 dots (denoted respectively as 2×4, 2×3, 2×1). Figure 11.6 illustrates Lego bricks (seen as phenomena) of the types 2×1, 2×2, 3×2 and 4×2 (seen as concepts). The concepts 2×1, 2×2, 2×3, 2×4 are elements in an implicit generalization hierarchy with a concept, *Brick*, as the more general (and abstract) concept. Each type of *Brick* has a number of properties in common: they all have a colour property and they have a number of dots. But the values of the properties vary; one *Brick* is red with 2×1 dots whereas another *Brick* is green with 2×2 dots. Other types of *Brick* may exist, for example the *Wheel*. We might also choose to have one most general concept, *Lego Thing*, covering all categories of elements in a Lego box.[2]

---

2   The figures in this chapter illustrate possible Lego structures that can be made. We are also familiar with the construction manuals found in Lego boxes. Such figures and construction manuals are themselves constructs in the informational dimension, but we will not focus on this aspect of the informational dimension in this chapter.

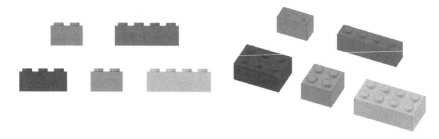

Figure 11.6 Examples of $2 \times 1, 2 \times 2, 2 \times 3$ and 2×4 bricks.

Figure 11.7 Different kinds of Lego brick: so-called *Mini Figures*.

11.2.2 Abstraction Processes (With Physical Material)

We identify the following examples of abstraction in relation to Lego bricks.

- *Classification and exemplification*: 2×2 is a classification of the bricks in our box with 2×2 dots on top. We may exemplify 2×2 by any of these bricks. Similarly, we could choose to classify anything in the box as a *Lego Thing*.
- *Specialization and generalization*: *Brick* is seen as a generalization of $1 \times 2, 2 \times 2, 3 \times 2$ and 4×2, and each of these is seen as a specialization of *Brick*.
- *Decomposition and aggregation*: From a number of $1 \times 2, 2 \times 2, 3 \times 2$ and 4×2 bricks, we may construct a Lego structure that we conceive as a *Wall*. We aggregate the wall phenomenon from a given selection of bricks, and we may decompose the wall into this selection of bricks.

Figure 11.7 illustrates Lego creations of type *Mini Figure*. The illustration shows from which (phenomena of the concepts) specialized kinds of *Brick*s and other *Lego Things* the structures are aggregated.

11.2.3 Properties of Physical Materials

A 2×2 brick has *measurable* properties (Nygaard, 1986) only. We can measure the colour by viewing it, but the brick cannot typically change its colour through some internal mechanism (outside intervention is required, such as someone painting it). Neither can we ask the *2 × 2* brick to move from one position to another. A *2 × 2* brick does not have *transformational* properties.

A *Motor* (a type of brick with some kind of motor in it) has other kinds of properties. You can make the motor start, run, stop, accelerate etc. The behaviour of the motor will change when we use the properties of the motor. However, we are still in the physical dimension with the possibilities and restrictions of physical laws. We can build a *Car* and use a motor to make it run, but we cannot "move" the properties from the motor to the aggregate, the car. The car can run, stop etc., but only if we use the properties of the motor. And the properties of the motor are affected by the construction of the car – if the motor sits in a large car, the motor will probably find itself under greater strain when accelerating than if it were to sit inside a smaller car.

The weight of a brick does not disappear when we build a *Wall* comprising bricks. A *Brick* still has the weight property. However, the user is not able to measure the weight of the individual bricks in the wall. The user can only measure the weight of the wall. So in this sense, even in the physical dimension, in the case where we model aggregation by building creations of Lego bricks, the parts may have *concealed* properties.

The wall has a load-bearing capacity which specifies what load it can withstand before it breaks apart. The load-bearing capacity is an example of an *emergent* property; it emerges as a function of the wall constructed and does not exist as the sum of individual bricks. This load-bearing capacity is not present in a collection of disaggregated bricks: it derives from the bricks built together as a wall.

We can build a bird from bricks and call it – classify it – a *Bird*; we can also do the same for a *Dog*. We can see common characteristics in our conceptual models of these animals: indeed, we have implicitly classified them together by calling them *Animals*. But this relationship does not automatically hold in the physical dimension, for a Lego bird is markedly different from a Lego dog. Figure 11.8 illustrates *Bird* and/or *Dog* phenomena. We have selected a Lego construction and claimed that "this is a Dog" or "this is a Bird". In this way we have introduced a concept, albeit in an informal fashion. And although the construction may look very basic and in no way resemble a dog or a bird, this concept can associate the Lego construction with our predefined understanding of a dog or bird and the properties we attach to dogs and birds in other contexts. You, as the reader, may or may not conceive these creations as birds and dogs, but we claim they are ☺. And when we

Figure 11.8 The differences between *Dog* and *Bird*.

communicate to the reader that we see these creations as birds and dogs, you may form your own conceptual model of these in which they are both seen as (specialized versions of) animals.

11.2.4 Conceptual Models of Lego Bricks – an Example of Physical Material

A person playing with Lego forms conceptual models in his or her mind during play. These conceptual models exist in the conceptual dimension – they capture aspects of the construction in the physical dimension. Some of the conceptual models that are created during play remain stable, while others change as the various bricks are encountered. At least two kinds of change are possible:

1. The properties of a concept covering a certain type of brick may change – some properties may be added, removed or modified from various concepts. For example, during play, we may have been particularly focused on the Colour property of 2×2 bricks, but as we develop the concept of what we are building, we realize that weight is an important factor in our construction and we start incorporating the Weight property into our mental model of 2×2 bricks.
2. The structure of concepts may change, including the relations between the structures. We may experience that certain types of brick, which have so far been unrelated in our mental model, actually have properties in common and therefore could be related in a generalization hierarchy.

For the most part, our conceptual models are implicit and individual – they exist in our minds. A concrete Wall construction is formed from physical bricks. This construction is not classified formally or explicitly by our constructing the Wall out of physical material – only we can do this in the conceptual dimension, and only implicitly and informally. But we can communicate our conception of the Wall through the physical representation of the Wall.

Some of the properties of the bricks in the wall are hidden as a natural consequence of how Lego bricks allow construction (Figure 11.9) – if brick B is placed on top of brick A, then we cannot use the locking properties of brick A for further construction (the physical properties are utilized in the construction). Some properties are preserved during the construction – the locking properties of the top- and bottommost bricks are still available. These properties can be seen as properties of the whole, the Wall, although we have no way of stating whether this should be the case or not – physically they are properties of the Wall.

The colour property of a brick is to some extent also preserved (some surfaces of bricks may be covered by other bricks) and it contributes to the colour of the whole, the Wall. But it is not clear what the colour of the Wall is if 80% of the bricks used are red and the rest of the bricks have various other colours. This is our choice, and forms part of our mental model. Through communication and practice, we might achieve consensus that, for example, if a majority of the bricks in some construction have the same colour then the construction as such has that specific colour.

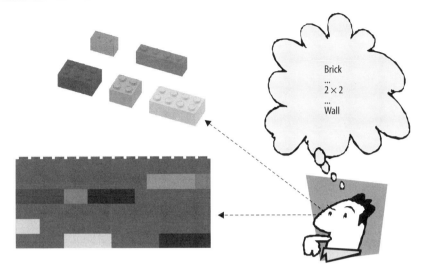

Figure 11.9 Bricks and Wall.

11.3 Modelling With Informational Material

Most of the observations, examples and conclusions in this section are well known. The intention is to go through only enough of it to contrast the preceding section. We point out that in the informational dimension (especially when we choose object-oriented modelling and programming to match conceptual abstraction) we have enormous freedom compared with the physical dimension. In return for this freedom, we need to be explicit and formal about everything. Because the modelling takes place only in the informational dimension, we must explicitly utilize representations in order to depict these informational models – using some hand-drawn notation, language or visualization. By contrast, much of the everyday physical dimension that we encounter is present to our senses, and it is to this that we add our concepts and imagination.

We may see object-oriented modelling as an explicit form of conceptual modelling. We see an object as a model of a phenomenon and a class as a model of a concept. We can discuss to which extent the abstraction mechanisms of object-oriented modelling (e.g. in a notation like UML (Booch *et al.*, 1998) or languages like Beta (Madsen *et al.*, 1993) and Java (Arnold and Gosling 1997)) support the abstraction forms of conceptual modelling, including classification, generalization and aggregation. In our present context, we won't focus on the extent to which these languages support abstraction, but on understanding the possibilities and limitations of abstraction in the informational dimension isolated from the physical dimension. Figure 11.10 illustrates a person who observes and manipulates some objects and classes in a Java program (description and execution) that models elements from the Lego universe. While the person works in the informational dimension, the person's mind creates a model in terms of phenomena and concepts in the conceptual dimension.

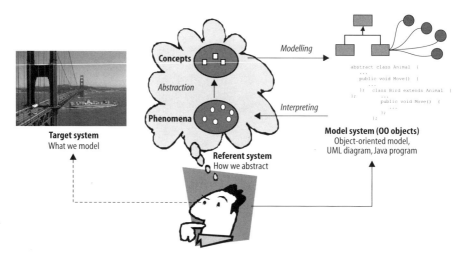

Figure 11.10 We can observe and manipulate some classes and objects (description and execution) in a Java program that models elements from the Lego universe, while thinking about corresponding phenomena (and concepts) in the conceptual dimension.

11.3.1 UML or Java Model as Informational Material

The essential observation is that in this kind of modelling we have much more freedom. We can model whatever universe we choose – in this particular case we model the Lego universe (we build an object-oriented model of Lego bricks in UML or in some object-oriented programming language like Java, where we have classes and objects representing an understanding of this universe). We model the Lego universe – the various forms of bricks etc. form the Lego box – in the usual object-oriented manner. We apply a perspective, through which we choose which properties are relevant for our model, and we create concepts (formally and explicitly as classes) to represent our understanding of the elements of the Lego universe. We relate these concepts in various generalization and aggregation hierarchies. We also create phenomena (formally and explicitly by instantiating objects from the classes) from the concepts to represent and model individual bricks. Few limitations are given by object-oriented modelling. We can add whatever properties we like to the concepts (*Brick, Wall* and other creations). We could choose to make a certain model construction able to talk by including a suitable property in the model construction. Our model makes it possible for us to prescribe constructions – we explicitly define the universe of possible constructions and the properties of the phenomena in this universe. Figure 11.11 illustrates some extracts from UML diagrams and extracts form a Java program. The extracts are descriptions (representations) of classes[3] in the informational dimension which model some *Brick*s and a *Wall*.

---

3 Only classes, not objects, are illustrated in the figure.

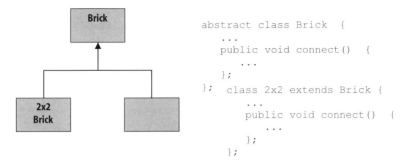

```
abstract class Brick  {
    ...
    public void connect()  {
        ...
    };
};   class 2x2 extends Brick {
        ...
        public void connect()  {
            ...
        };
    };
```

Figure 11.11 UML diagrams and extracts from a Java program: descriptions of some *Bricks* and a *Wall*.

11.3.2 Modelling by Programming – an Example of Informational Material

In the informational dimension, we come close to complete freedom – we can prescribe whatever we can imagine and describe. We can model by programming. Programming seems to be much more complicated than putting bricks on top of each other, so we lose the simplicity and power that derives from physically interacting with bricks. Furthermore, the two worlds do not seem to match in this respect – one is limited by physical laws, while the other gives full freedom and is only limited by our ability to describe the informational model (i.e. our programming language).

In object-oriented modelling and programming, the description is explicit and formal. This implies that all interfaces must be defined. And this further implies that when objects are combined (aggregation hierarchies where part objects forming whole objects) or when concepts are generalized/specialized (classification hierarchies where classes inherit from classes) we must be very specific and concrete about how to combine the interfaces (representing the properties). Fiddling with interfaces is complicated and it is done as a part of relating interfaces/ properties of classes. This problem is not so apparent in the physical dimension because we have "default" interfaces in the physical material around us that we interpret through our senses.

11.3.3 Properties of the Informational Dimension

Thus concepts are explicit in informational models: they can be shared and they are objective. The possibilities ands limitations of working in the informational dimension depend on the language and notation we employ. Using ordinary English language to describe a conceptual model leaves much room for interpretation and imprecision, whilst a programming language yields much more precision, but is much more rigid and requires more formality. Programming languages have reasonable support for conceptual abstraction, except for:

- *Aggregation*: there is no explicit distinction between static and dynamic aggregation, and there is no explicit support for hereditary properties.
- *Specialization*: Overriding methods is problematic.
- *Multiple classification*: Multiple inheritance is problematic.
- *Object evolution*: Poor support for class change, rôles etc.

11.4 Modelling With Tangible Objects

Now we consider the combination of physical and informational materials. As discussed above, we consider the conceptual dimension to be implicitly present whenever we engage in conceptual abstraction in relation to either the physical or informational dimension (Figure 11.12). In the TangO project (May *et al.*, 2001a,b and Chapter 7) we see tangible objects, habitats and associations possessing existing in all the three dimensions – the notions of tangible object, habitat and association are seen as integrated from these dimensions.

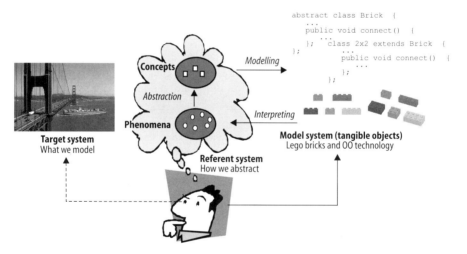

Figure 11.12 Illustration of a person who observes some part of the real world, who thinks about corresponding concepts and phenomena in the conceptual dimension, and who manipulates some material in the form of integrated brick and computer to model his or her observations and thoughts.

11.4.1 Scenario: Library Book as Tangible Object

In a traditional library system, we usually see a combination of the various dimensions. In the physical dimension, we have the books, the borrowers and the book loans. In the informational dimension, we have records in a database system to register the existing books and information about their status and the borrowers. Typically, the aspects of the informational dimension are a model of the aspects of the physical and conceptual dimensions – library database systems try to duplicate a subset of the real world, in order to keep track of what is really happening in the real world. Whenever a relevant event happens in the physical dimension, we try to register information about this event in the information dimension – for example, when a person borrows a book, this fact is recorded via bar code scanner and database update. Whenever certain conditions are observed in the informational model, the system can trigger certain events in the physical dimension. For example, when a book becomes overdue, a late notice is generated on the printer and a librarian places it in an envelope and posts it. The rules, regulations and policies governing the library's operation derive from the conceptual dimension.

The above description represents the traditional view of information systems, which is implicit in their modelling, design and implementation: they capture some aspect of real-world phenomena and execute an informational model of it in another universe. This view is marked by a sharp demarcation between these worlds, with the informational dimension traditionally subordinate to the physical dimension (for the informational is derived from the physical, and constantly tries to reflect the physical). Ubiquitous and pervasive computing alters this relationship by designating a convergence of physical and informational dimensions.

An alternative scenario suggests a tight coupling between a phenomenon in the physical dimension (the book at the library) and the object representing it in the informational dimension (the record/object in the database). We might imagine that such an object is integrated with the physical phenomenon (a chip is put into the back of the book and communicates wirelessly). The activities of the library change, in that maintenance of the informational model is diminished. For example, to check which books are currently shelved and *where*, a request is broadcast through the library and the books can report their status and location. Currently, books in a library may be hidden, stolen or destroyed without the knowledge of staff, resulting in an inaccurate informational model. If we consider books as tangible objects, then we can see that physical actions and activities in the physical world directly result in actions and activities in the informational model.

11.4.2 A Lego Brick With a Computer Inside

We can imagine building tangible objects from the ground up, using Lego bricks as a prototypical example. Let us assume that Lego bricks can have a computer inside them (Figure 11.13). A Lego brick has the usual physical properties, such as size,

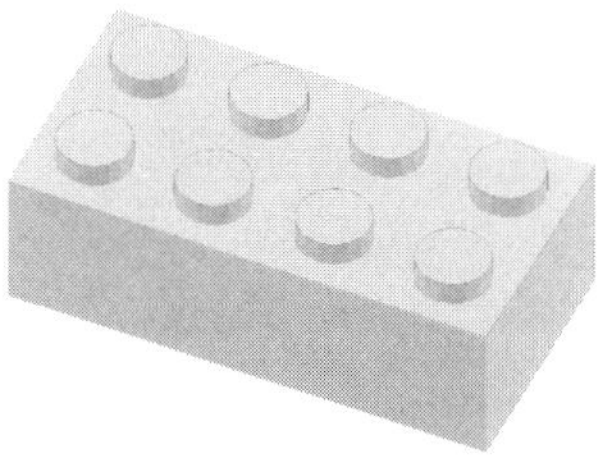

```
abstract class 4x2  {
    ...
    abstract public void Identity();
    abstract public void Size();
    ...
};
            class 4x2' extends 4x2  {
                ...
            };
```

Figure 11.13 A Lego brick with a computer inside as an example of a tangible object where physical and informational materials are combined.

weight and colour. Similarly, a Lego brick with a motor can still run, stop, accelerate etc. All our observations about abstraction with physical material still hold. Now, in addition, we can extend the bricks with informational material. For example, a brick may have informational properties such as an identity and its date of creation. The brick may also be equipped with various built-in properties to communicate with other bricks. These are examples of properties which are part of abstraction with informational material as discussed above.

Now, such abstractions are coupled to the Lego brick, and the informational properties of the brick are combined physically and explicitly with the physical brick. The properties in the informational dimension are additional to the properties in the physical dimension – they do not extend or modify the physical properties as such. This means that all our observations about abstraction in the informational dimension are also still valid. We still need to distinguish between physical and informational properties and we need to discuss how to relate these kinds of properties.[4]

4.3 Combining Physical and Informational Material

When we combine physical and informational material, such as with the Lego brick, additional considerations emerge. We distinguish between the *properties* and *interface* of a physical or informational object. The interface is the means by which we access or modify a given property. In the appendix to this chapter, we discuss not only various forms of interface for both physical and informational material, but also how these interfaces may be connected for the combined material to form a single entity with mixed properties. With respect to interfaces, our discussion is restricted to mechanical sensors and actuators in the physical dimension and Java programming language interfaces in the informational dimension. The appendix discusses the nature of these interfaces and how they might be combined. Such details are not critical here, but we can make the following observations about the physical and informational materials as separate things:

● The brick's physical properties remain unchanged.
● The physical interfaces on the brick can also possess physical properties
● All the modelling capabilities of the informational material are available as a dynamic software object system, i.e. the whole model for a brick is available within the informational material.

As the materials are combined (Figure 11.14), we make the following observations:
● We should only have one classification for the physical brick and its software object system, i.e. the physical brick and the software object system are one.
● We may support physical properties by an informational interface.
● We may support informational properties by a physical interface.

---

4   An obvious question is how to handle "inconsistencies" between properties in physical and informational dimensions. For example, a brick painted red (a property in the physical world) may have an informational property stating that the colour of the brick is yellow.

Figure 11.14 Physical and informational components combined. Left: a Lego brick with sensors on the top and corresponding actuators on the bottom, illustrating physical interfaces. Right: a Java object with its interface, with both serving and notifying possibilities, illustrating informational interfaces. These components are combined to form a tangible object.

11.4.4 Aggregation: Assembling Constructs From Combined Material

In considering how constructs can be assembled from such combined material, we focus on two aspects, namely:

1. How to combine properties of two bricks when these are being assembled as part of a construct-in-progress.
2. How to associate properties with structures that we consider to be assembled constructs (which could still be used in the further assembly of other structures).

Combination of properties can take place through the physical connection of physical interfaces. For example, we derive the weight of a wall through the assembly of bricks. In the aggregation process, when bricks are assembled to form various structures, the physical interfaces connect together and various properties are aggregated by means of construction. In the simple case, we have an actuator from one brick connected to another brick's sensor. This corresponds to an invocation on the Java object. By simple physical construction, the physical interfaces of the bricks are connected – and thus informational interfaces are also connected – so we program by physical construction. We do not program in the traditional sense, capturing some aspects of the physical world in an informational model, but rather, we combine properties of the bricks in both physical and informational dimensions.

When two bricks are assembled physically and the connectors of the brick are connected, then the informational properties of the bricks are also combined simultaneously. Alternatively – or in addition – the combining of informational properties can occur through wireless communication between the two bricks of an assembly (Figure 11.15). We imagine that a brick (with no physical devices to support the connection of properties through the assembly) can know its identity and position (and therefore if/how it is assembled) such that the actual connection of the informational properties is carried out through wireless communication between the bricks. We assume that we can choose the form of connection from schemas in which the actual connection possibilities between the bricks are predefined.

With respect to the association of properties to assembled constructs, we make several observations. Firstly, we can choose certain physical interfaces of selected bricks to represent properties of the aggregated whole. If we consider a wall of bricks, the connectors of the bricks at the very top of the wall are seen to represent

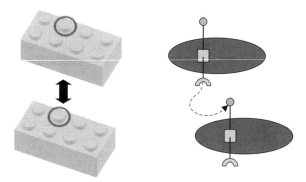

Figure 11.15 Connecting physical and informational interfaces by physical contact or wireless communication. Left: two bricks connect to each other by their physical interfaces. Right: the software objects between two bricks communicate with each other through physical or wireless connection.

the connectors of the wall itself. This seems to be opposite to the Façade pattern (Gamma *et al.*, 1994), often used in object-oriented modelling. In the Façade pattern, concepts are encapsulated by a larger concept that accumulates the interface to the enclosed concepts.

Secondly, the informational properties of bricks can behave as in the discussion on conceptual modelling for informational material. In an assembled construct, we can make a property of the part with a concealed property through the aggregation process if we want to (aggregation in the informational dimension may support all kinds of property relations). But in the physical dimension, we cannot conceal the basic physical properties of the whole.

Finally, we can introduce additional physical interfaces – sensors and actuators – to physical properties, and we can utilize these new interfaces in the physical construction phase. Consider a brick that has a motor integrated into it. When bricks are assembled around it, they will be able to access the properties of the motor-brick. Similarly, the motor-brick is able to access the properties of the bricks around it. Thus, tangible Lego bricks can develop new physical interfaces in the same way as traditional Lego allows physical interfaces to develop for physical properties.

11.4.5 Summary: Tangible Object

The Lego brick with integrated computational capacity is a very general and generic example of a tangible object. Such a combination of physical and informational material implies that we can work all at the same time in the physical, informational and conceptual dimensions – this means that abstraction in terms of tangible objects is a reality. We can also see that the characteristics of physical materials and informational materials that we are commonly accustomed to can continue being useful, for these characteristics are still very much applicable. We cannot really abstract away from the physical parts of the whole, even though we perceive Lego constructs as whole entities. The individual physical components will remain individual components. Physical and informational properties are different in nature and ought to be treated as such, although they can be combined in novel and interesting ways.

11.5 Summary

We have tried to characterize the different dimensions in which we model and design artefacts. These dimensions interact so that we can observe the world, create our own conceptual versions of the worlds, and then represent these concepts in some model system. Traditionally, these dimensions have been disparate and separate as a consequence of the technology available to us. Recent developments in ubiquitous and pervasive computing have focused us on a convergence of these dimensions in such a way that their interplay should be considered.

We have discussed the nature of conceptual abstraction and how we use it to construct and refine the mental models of the world that we create. We then compared how conceptual abstraction takes place in physical dimensions, using Lego bricks to exemplify our discussion. We also looked at how conceptual abstraction takes place in the informational dimension, using object-oriented modelling and programming as a prototypical example. We then looked at how conceptual abstraction takes place with tangible objects, which combine physical and informational material.

11.5.1 Lego Mindstorms: Characterization and Comparison

We have discussed the integration of Lego bricks and computer technology, specifically object-oriented technology. Against this background, we discuss an existing approach to this, Lego Mindstorms, and compare these approaches briefly. With respect to Mindstorms we claim that a Mindstorms construction is characterized as one single aggregated object with properties arising as a consequence of how the bricks have been assembled in the given way. Various identified sensors and actuators are also built into the construction, in such a way that the user can associate behaviour with the actuators and sensors through the RCX computer, which coordinates the construction to behave as a whole.

In other words, a Lego Mindstorms construction is seen as one object of physical material (with sensors and actuators) with which advanced behaviour can be associated as one object of informational material (by measuring its sensors and controlling its actuators) (Figure 11.16). It is a useful starting point for departing from traditional Lego and coupling to the informational dimension, but lacks the flexibility that comes with finer granularity.

11.5.2 Relation to Embedded Systems

We can make some observations from this chapter in relation to embedded systems. An embedded system is one where hardware and software are combined in order to perform a specific function (e.g. guidance control for a missile, steering control for a car). In both embedded systems and tangible Lego bricks,

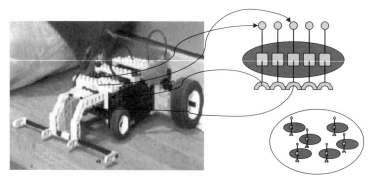

Figure 11.16 A Lego Mindstorms construct is seen as one object of physical material to which (a Façade object for dynamic object modelling of) the model on the RCX (the informational material) is connected.

informational material is integrated with the physical material of the object. Additionally, embedded systems can be seen as aggregates of smaller components, similar to Lego constructs. The prime difference with embedded systems is their dedication to a specific purpose – Lego bricks, as a prototypical tangible object, are designed for general-purpose construction and interaction. Thus the designer of an embedded system plays a similar rôle to someone building with tangible Lego bricks.

11.5.3 Concluding Remarks

This chapter has focused on the nature of conceptual abstraction in modelling physical and informational material. It has provided a particular perspective on the conceptual modelling process, and discusses how we apply this perspective to the physical and informational worlds around us. From this basis, we explored how conceptual abstraction could be applied to physical and informational material that is combined, namely to tangible objects, discussing possibilities and observations from this. The informational material focused on was object-oriented models and programming languages.

There are limitations to the material covered in this chapter. We have focused on conceptual abstraction directed at the most basic level of tangible objects: their base components and constructs created from these components. However, the interaction of tangible objects, constructed at varying degrees of granularity, is likely to be more interesting and relevant to everyday activities. Also not covered is the relation of tangible objects to habitats and associations, other key elements of the TangO ontology. These latter concepts focus on the dimensions that tangible objects find themselves in and the relationships/interactions that tangible objects have. We have also focused on basic physical materials and used the tangible Lego brick as an illustrative example; more exotic materials such as piezoelectric materials or shape memory alloys were not discussed. These may have some impact on the ways in which physical and informational materials may be combined and the interaction that is possible.

A fundamental open question lies at the heart of combining physical and informational material. That is, how do we resolve the tension between the advantages and possibilities inherent in physical and informational material, respectively? Physical material is bounded by physical laws, yet such imposed limits confer a certain advantage: physical material is much more limited in its degrees of freedom for use; it is more obvious to explore what one can do with physical material. Traditional Lego exemplifies this. Informational material is almost unbounded, limited mostly by the representation we choose and of what we can conceive. We often see it as advantageous to design in the informational dimension, for we can create artefacts of far greater depth and complexity than would be possible with physical material. Yet the complexity that we can create with informational material often works against us; models become unwieldy, impenetrable and flawed (and maintaining/improving them becomes arduous because of that complexity).

The tangible Lego brick embodies the tension between these two poles – of the effective simplicity of physical material, and the powerful complexity of informational material. One can imagine the physical brick and its possibilities for combination with other bricks being significantly augmented by an informational component. But the informational brick is tethered by the physical limitations of the brick; connectivity is restricted to connecting or nearby bricks, and computational power is limited to what the brick is capable of physically bearing. Perhaps if we were to create a physical material that were more malleable, akin to the informational properties, we would enjoy greater capabilities for design – then we would have a more complex physical construct, more difficult to understand and to design with, obviating the simplicity and effectiveness exemplified by the Lego brick.

This issue is analogous to the "solution" posed by information appliances (Norman, 1999): the model of designing for a general-purpose computing machine renders artefacts as unwieldy and too complex; it is better to design individual devices with focused purposes – information appliances. For all their usability, information appliances have a self-imposed limit on their flexibility to ensure their effectiveness. For tangible objects, this same issue comes into play. What limits can we expect on our tangible objects and what limits *should we impose*? Our software objects are no longer free to expand in complexity without recourse to the physical world that impinges on their design. This is something that needs to be accounted for, as it would be disappointing for tangible objects to create more complexity in an already informationally complex world. If anything, we hope that tangible objects will simplify and liberate us somewhat, and make the world more real.

Appendix: Properties and Interfaces

Interfaces in the Physical Dimension

Interfaces in the physical dimension correspond to our usual senses, namely, sight, sound, smell, touch and feel. Usually, we consider such properties to be static in the sense that their value (output) does not change over time. The colour and weight of the brick are considered constant.

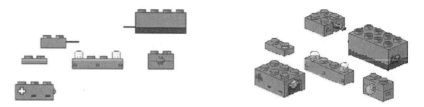

Figure 11.17 Bricks with various kinds of sensors and actuators.

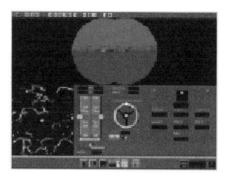

Figure 11.18 Soft instruments.

In the physical dimension, we distinguish between sensors (which detect the state of the environment) and actuators (which cause a change in the environment) (Figure 11.17). Thus a sensor may detect light, movement or temperature; an actuator might be a mechanical arm or a light that illuminates an area.

Usually we consider sensors and actuators in the physical world to have certain properties. They are *stationary*: they remain at the same position, at least locally to the device to which it belongs. They have a *fixed configuration*: they do not come and go, and their number and identity are constant. They *are mono-functional*: they have the same functionality throughout their lifetime.

But in so-called *soft instruments* (Figure 11.18) we have many examples of the opposite, i.e. actuators and sensors which move around, which may appear and disappear, and which may modify their supported functionality according to your needs and the ongoing activity.

In the physical world we also have a *connection* – a physical relation between an actuator and a sensor. An actuator of one device may be connected to a sensor of another device, and an impulse of the actuator may invoke the sensor.

Interfaces in the Informational Dimension

Interfaces in the informational dimension include, among others, *Java-like interfaces, messages and events*, or *serving and notifying facilities* (Kristensen and May, 1996) (Figure 11.19).

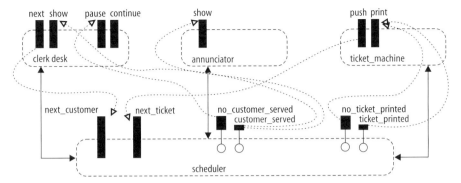

Figure 11.19 Java-like interfaces: a *scheduler* is aggregated from *clerk_desk*, *annunciator* and *ticket_machine* by combining the interfaces with very simple connections in this example from (Kristensen and May, 1996).

In object-oriented modelling and programming, the description of an interface is explicit and formal. This implies that all interfaces must be defined. When objects are combined (aggregation hierarchies where part objects are forming whole objects) or when concepts are generalized/specialized (classification hierarchies where classes inherit from classes), we must be specific about how to combine the interfaces (representing the properties). Fiddling with interfaces is complicated as a part of relating interfaces/properties of classes.

Combining Properties and Interfaces

We see the tangible Lego brick – combining the brick as physical material and the dynamic object system as informational material – as constituting one phenomenon with physical properties and informational properties. We wish to classify this one phenomenon as one concept, so therefore: (a) we choose to see the external features on physical material to serve as a façade through which properties of the material may be accessed (cf. the Façade pattern (Gamma *et al.*, 1994; Figure 11.20), and (b) we choose to organize the informational material represented by the

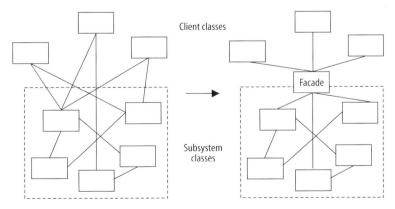

Figure 11.20 The Façade design pattern (Gamma *et al.*, 1994): the classes of the subsystem are capture by the Façade object, which accumulates the interface towards the client classes.

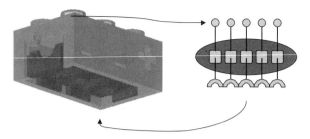

Figure 11.21 Connections between physical and informational façade objects.

dynamic object system by means of the Façade design pattern. In this way the overall façade, comprising physical and informational façades, forms a single phenomenon that can be classified as such.

In the support of physical properties by informational interfaces, we cannot change or exchange the physical properties as such. We can add informational properties to match relevant physical properties (given the chosen perspective for our abstraction). Through the informational façade, we can ask the brick its colour and we can ask the motor to run. The brick becomes like an object with an informational interface to give access to the physical properties of the physical material of the combined Lego brick.

In the support of informational properties by physical interfaces, we can hardwire existing physical interfaces to informational. One possibility is that the coupling of informational properties to the physical features can be configured through physical switches on the brick (in order to configure the brick physically to cooperate with other bricks appropriately when assembled with these bricks in a given way). Alternatively, we can imagine that for each brick, a number of *virtual* informational properties are available and that these are connected to some part of the physical interface (sensors and actuators) on the bricks. We can assume that standard implementations are available for the virtual informational properties; perhaps in the simplest form they simply connect sensors and actuators.

We can program or *load* (perhaps more accurately) a brick with particular informational properties and specify how these properties should match the physical interface (Figure 11.21). This resembles black box substitution in framework technology (Fayad and Schmidt, 1999). This can be done during as Lego constructs are being built. Actually, this could be seen as some kind of specialization of the individual brick among a predefined set of possibilities – in this type of specialization, we choose informational properties and how they relate to physical ones.

References

Andersen, P. B. and Nowack, P. (2002) Tangible objects: connecting informational and physical space. In Qvortrup, L. (ed.) *Virtual Space: The Spatiality of Virtual Inhabited 3D Worlds*. London: Springer-Verlag.

Arnold, K. and Gosling, J. (1997) *The Java Programming Language*. Reading, MA: Addison-Wesley.

Booch, G., Rumbaugh, J. and Jacobson, I. (1998) *The Unified Modeling Language User Guide*. Reading, MA: Addison-Wesley.

Fayad, M. and Schmidt, D. C. (eds.) (1999) *Building Application Frameworks: Object-Oriented Foundations of Framework Design*. New York: John Wiley & Sons.

Gamma, E., Helm, R. and Vlissides, J. (1994) *Design Patterns: Elements of Reusable Object-Oriented Software*. Reading, MA: Addison-Wesley.

Hallenborg, K. and Kristensen, B. B. (2002) Pervasive computing: mapping the TangO model onto Jini technology. *6th World Multiconference on Systemics, Cybernetics and Informatics*, Orlando, FL.

Jacobsen, E. E. (2000) Concepts and language mechanisms in software modelling. *PhD Thesis*, University of Southern Denmark.

Kristensen, B. B. and May, D. C. (1996) Component composition and interaction. *International Conference on Technology of Object-Oriented Languages and Systems*, Melbourne, Australia.

Kristensen, B. B. and Østerbye, K. (1994) Conceptual modeling and programming languages. *Sigplan Notices*, 29(9), 81–90.

Madsen, O. L., Møller-Pedersen, B. and Nygaard, K. (1993) *Object-Oriented Programming in the Beta Programming Language*. Reading, MA: Addison Wesley.

May, D. C., Kristensen, B. B. and Nowack, P. (2001a) *Tangible Objects – Modeling in Style*. Aalborg University.

May, D. C., Kristensen, B. B. and Nowack, P. (2001b) TangO: modeling in style. *Proceedings of Second International Conference on Generative Systems in the Electronic Arts (Second Iteration – Emergence)*, Melbourne, Australia.

Norman, D. (1999) *The Invisible Computer: Why Good Products can Fail, the Personal Computer Is so Complex, and Information Appliances Are the Solution*. Cambridge, MA: MIT Press.

Nygaard, K. (1986) Basic concepts in object oriented programming. *Sigplan Notices*, 21(10), 128–132.

Various (1999) Pervasive computing. *IBM Systems Journal*, 38(4).

Weiser, M. (1991) The computer for the twenty-first century. *Scientific American*, 265 (September), 94–104.

Author Index